AF079016

HAMMER GUNS

in theory and practice

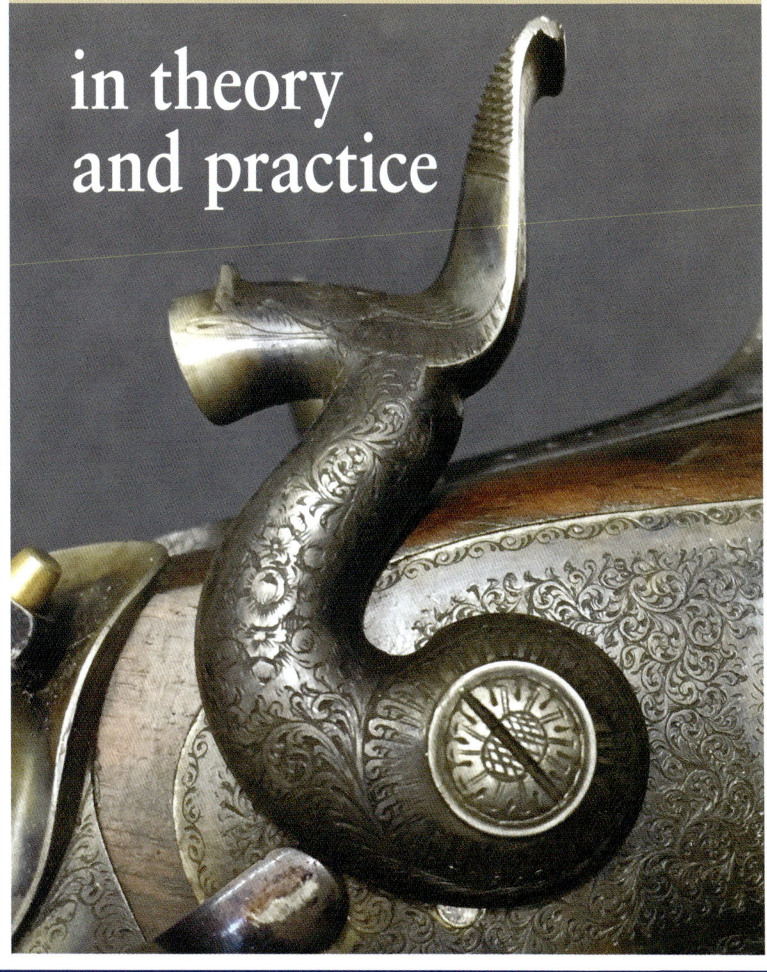

I dedicate this book to gunmaker David Mitchell for his willingness to help a 'civilian' learn from his experience and knowledge, after a chance meeting at a London auction almost two decades ago.

HAMMER GUNS

in theory and practice

Diggory Hadoke

MERLIN UNWIN BOOKS

First published in Great Britain by Merlin Unwin Books Ltd, 2016

Merlin Unwin Books Ltd
Palmers House
7 Corve Street, Ludlow
Shropshire SY8 1DB, UK
www.merlinunwin.co.uk

British Library Cataloguing-in-Publication Data:
A catalogue record for this book is available from the British Library

ISBN 978-1-910723-25-8

Designed in Minion by Merlin Unwin

Printed by 1010 Printing International Ltd

Contents

Also by the same author

Vintage Guns for the Modern Shot

The British Boxlock Gun & Rifle

Contents

Also by the same author

Vintage Guns for the Modern Shot

The British Boxlock Gun & Rifle

Acknowledgements

I am fortunate to have a long line of enthusiastic and expert providers of information and analysis from within the British gun trade, and from my wide client base of collectors and enthusiasts. Without their input and generous assistance I would be incapable of penning a work on this subject with all the detail now contained within these pages. I have relied on others for some of my content and, as in my previous books, feel indebted to my legion of collaborators.

Much of my task as a writer is to record the wise words, and to articulate on paper, the recounted experiences and expertise of men whose skills lie in working on, and making, the remarkable sporting guns which are my subject, rather than merely writing about them. I take some satisfaction in the thought that my work helps to record for posterity a small part of these remarkable lives and the valuable information that would otherwise be lost in a decade or two.

In no particular order, I extend my warmest thanks to: David Mitchell, David Sinnerton, Kirk Merrington, Gavin Gardiner. Patrick Hawes, of Bonham's, Nicholas Holt, Andrew Orr, Chris Beaumont, and Nick Bongers de Rath, of Holt's. Mike Yardley, Cyril Adams, Robin Knowles. Anthony Alborough-Tregear and Simon Clode, of Westley Richards. Graham Greener, Richard Tandy, Bill and Jim Blacker, David Dryhurst, Paul Hodgins, Stephane Dupille, Stephen Grist, Mark Crudgington, Jean-Pierre Daeschler, Kiri Kythreotis, Martin Smith, Mark Newton, Mark Sullivan, Sam Faraway, Capt. Michael Joseph, Bill Pink, John Farrugia of the Cheshire Gun Room, John Hargreaves, Paul Roberts, Tony Murray, Bill McPhail, Brian Bateman, Pete Woodgate, Andy Lloyd, The Birmingham Proof House, Vic Venters, John Gibbs, Robin Brown of A.A. Brown, my editors over the years: James Marchington, Daniel Cote, Colin Fallon, Karen Unwin and Dom Holtam.

Photographic Acknowledgements

All photographs were taken by the author and are his copyright, except the following pages:

Andrew Orr (Holt's): 13, 84, 104, 125, 159, front cover

Gavin Gardiner: 118, 120, 121

Michael Yardley: 196

Ashleigh Cadet: 166, jacket flap, back cover

Ghislain Geenen: 174

Bill McPhail: 80, 81,82,83

Robert Hodges: 78

Teague Engineering: 196

Historical photographs, advertisements, wood-cuts, patent illustrations and line drawings are gathered from various documents and publications, long out of copyright and too numerous to list accurately.

Preface

This is my third book. The first, *Vintage Guns for the Modern Shot,* was an attempt to put forward a reasoned case for the superiority of old English guns. When compared to any modern gun, on an equal cost basis, my argument was, and is, that a vintage British gun is better for a modern game shooter than any of its rivals; better in quality, better in performance, better as an investment.

My second offering, *The British Boxlock Gun & Rifle*, addressed an anomaly in the market as I saw it. The Anson & Deeley gun and its derivatives were misunderstood and undervalued; largely due to widespread ignorance. I sought to remedy the misunderstandings that I commonly encountered and made an attempt to uncover the true history and resurrect the reputation of these fabulous sporting guns.

Now, a little more experienced as a writer and a shooter, and with free reign to produce a treatise on my favourite subject, I can address the enduring love of my shooting life: the hammer gun. The decision to write about them specifically may seem obvious but it required a good number of requests from friends, readers and clients before I was convinced that there was a demand for me to put on paper what I have long advocated verbally and in practice.

Any professed expert or exponent, whatever his chosen field, will be faced at some time with the demand to 'practise what you preach'. This book is me preaching what I practise, expressed to the best of my ability. For, though faced with a bewildering and wonderful array of guns from which to choose, either from stock, from my personal collection, stored by clients or in need of post-refurbishment testing, I genuinely forgo the coveted Purdey over & under 20-bore, the Holland & Holland 'Royals', the Westley Richards 'drop-locks' and the Greener 'G-guns'. What I invariably pick up and take shooting is an 1870s under-lever hammer 12-bore.

Why? Well, the reasons are legion and this book is intended to provide a comprehensive answer as to why I believe that nothing made in the twentieth century compares favourably with the best hammer guns made by the real artisans of the British gun trade: made in the days before celebrity engravers signed their work or CNC machinery standardised every part.

This book is the sum of my personal journey with classic firearms and it brings the reader to where it has left me: holding a relatively primitive, totally hand-built, unique, supremely elegant and satisfying work of art; and feeling that I have a genuine advantage over all those users of expensive modern guns, when addressing my quarry.

Hammer guns are not an affectation, they are the best guns ever made and they are still better to use than anything else available, if you apply yourself to their use and ownership in the right way. This is my way.

Shooting pigeons over African sunflower crops with an 1870s hammer gun.

THE PAST

Hammer Guns Appreciated in Literature and History

'Spaniels without ears' was the well-known phrase attributed to Lord Ripon on the subject of the latest 'hammerless' guns that began appearing in solid numbers on the game shoots of late Victorian England. Ripon doggedly stuck to his back-action island-lock Purdey hammer guns, until dropping dead in the heather at the end of a grouse drive in 1923, still unconvinced by the new-fangled 'improvements' offered by the best gunmakers of the day. King George V shared his preference, as did Lord Walsingham and a few other notables in the Prince of Wales's shooting set.

Most sportsmen of the early twentieth century clamoured for the latest edge that technology could provide and the wealthiest and most discerning were, by then, well acquainted with the 1880 Purdey/Beesley self-opening side-lock ejector, which in my opinion, is the finest, most complete game gun ever built. It is the very acme of everything one could wish a game gun to be and does everything to perfection. The simpler Holland & Holland 'Royal' vied with the Purdey as a representation of all that was right with the British model of sporting shotgun. Whatever your preference, it is hard to argue with the assertion that by WWI there was nothing worthwhile to do, other than make quality guns cheaper to produce in quantity.

With the deaths of the Victorian aristocratic shooting superstars and the decline in social prominence of driven shooting after the First World War, the hammer gun generally fell out of favour. Guns of fabulous quality and pedigree were handed to game keepers, then to gardeners, as the gentleman of the house upgraded to a smooth-profiled, side-lock ejector.

W.W. Greener, writing as early as 1888, comments on the situation then facing the average gun dealer with a shop full of used hammer guns: '...the (hammer gun) stock gets older and mustier, and as its value decreases his denunciation [of hammerless guns] becomes more fierce and worthless and this is how it comes that old diatribes are reiterated year after year, when the value of the invention itself [the hammerless gun] has long been proved beyond all question.' Certain notable traditionalists may have failed to take up the hammerless models of inventive gunmakers like Greener, but the general trend towards hammerless guns was undeniable.

From 1900, big Birmingham factories supplied the world with cheap, reliable Anson & Deeley action guns and London firms like Boss and Purdey delivered graceful, reliable and beautifully made side-lock ejectors that were the turn-of-the-century gun making equivalent of the Bentley motor car.

The twenties were all about being 'modern', the new swept out the old and the Victorian hammer gun looked out of place in polite company. After WWI Robert Churchill was cutting a swath through tradi-

tion with his XXV concept of fast, short, snap-shooting hammerless guns, once again making the finest guns of the previous generation appear obsolete.

To the post-war shooting establishment, 30" damascus barrels and guns with external hammers were passé in the extreme. Their time had passed and they languished in gun rooms, cupboards, under beds and in the back of gun shops; unloved and unwanted. Many were butchered as clumsy attempts were made to 'modernise' them by cutting the barrels down and blacking the damascus. We should not be surprised by this today, as they were, at the time, seen as being valueless and perfectly acceptable as subjects for experimentation. Fashion is cyclical and when something drops out of fashion, it is generally reviled for a few years before being re-evaluated as a classic. Think of disco and flared trousers!

The years between World War Two and the Swinging Sixties may have been wilderness years for hammer guns but voices of dissent could be heard if one listened (or read) carefully. Richard Arnold espoused the beauty and the performance of older guns in his *Shooter's Handbook* of 1955. Richard Akehurst reminded readers in 1969, in *Game Guns & Rifles*, of the exploits of the old guns and their sporting owners. A decade later, Crudgington & Baker brought their truly impressive cataloguing endeavours to public attention in *The British Shotgun Vol.1*, which was the first in-depth attempt to classify and exemplify the plethora of gun patents taken out in Britain between 1850 and 1870.

During the 1980s, Geoffrey Boothroyd, columnist for the British weekly magazine *Shooting Times*, compiled his articles into three volumes, shedding yet more light on the legacy of the obsolete sporting shotguns left to the British public by their grandfathers and great-grandfathers.

Yet, still, hammer guns were mere curiosities to most. It took an American to show us all what should have been staring us in the face. Cyril Adams, a Texan gun dealer and formidable live pigeon shot, took the subject by the scruff of the neck and announced 'God shoots with a Stephen Grant side-lever hammer gun', in *Lock Stock & Barrel*. Cyril started selling hammer guns to shooters, rather than collectors, because he knew they were better than anything else available, not because they were cheap, or quaint, or amusing.

Like many a good gun salesman before him, Adams could sell guns because he could shoot them better than most. When people saw him winning competitions with British hammer guns, the queues started to form.

Cyril was not known for his tact: "What are you shooting that piece of crap for? Get yourself a proper English gun", was apparently a typical sales pitch. He started a revolution in certain circles in the US and a rebirth of appreciation was well underway there before I tried to articulate my own enthusiasm for British classics in 2007 with *Vintage Guns for the Modern Shot*.

Above, the author and Ian Andrews of William & Son, wih Cyril Adams, the man responsible for switching American shooters on to the qualities of British hammer guns. Facing page, European champion Martin Crix and Bill Pink of Historic Guns & Militaria, showing their prowess at driven pheasants with muzzle-loading percussion guns.

The Hammer Gun Era – shorter than you thought

One could be forgiven for thinking that there are millions of old hammer guns around. There seemed a time, not long ago, when every sale room and gun shop had a pile of them looking for new homes. Recent observations would give a better indication of the truth. The emergence of the pin-fire breech-loader as a viable replacement for the old muzzle-loaders began in earnest in the late 1850s. In 1858 John Dickson & Son built one breech-loader (their first) and 59 muzzle-loaders. By 1863 they were building 76 breech-loaders for 28 muzzle-loaders.

If we consider the 'hammerless era' to have started in 1871 with Murcott's so-called, 'Mousetrap', but perhaps look to the 1875 Anson & Deeley patent as the first real game-changer in the mass market, we have a period of 142 years in which hammerless guns have been the norm. Now consider, in particular, the hammerless centre-fire era: it technically began in 1856, if we count Lancaster's base-fire, but a more reliable date would be 1861, with Daw launching his patent centre-fire breech-loader. This is a modern gun, which can shoot modern ammunition and functions in a manner with which modern shooters would find easy to relate.

The pin-fire, however, clung on in certain quarters for some time. John Dickson, the Edinburgh gunmaker, for example, records the first centre-fire gun as being made in 1865 and the number of centre-fires overtaking the number of pin-fires made by the late 1860s. Dickson made their last pin-fire in 1877, well into what we would consider the centre-fire era.

We could argue that the period of true hammer centre-fire dominance lasted only from 1861 until 1875, considering the landmark events noted above. However, hammer gun numbers continued to rival, or better, hammerless guns for most of the second half of the nineteenth century. Purdey records show hammerless guns overtaking hammer guns in production numbers as late as 1886, for example. By 1900, the hammerless gun had finally won the argument and eased ahead comfortably as the new century gathered pace. That being the case, I believe what we should consider to be the 'hammer gun era' for our purposes can be identified as 1861-1900, since this period is the one from which we will find most of the guns of interest to us.

The hammer gun was not perfected as a centre-fire breech-loader and fully developed until around 1867, when rebounding locks, effective bolting mechanisms and a few years of trial and error had tidied up all the minor imperfections in early designs. So, if we narrow our focus and define the period 1867-1900 as the key years of fully developed hammer guns, we have just thirty-three years of manufacture from which to gather all our hammer guns for use in the field today. Thirty-three years of hammer guns against a century and a half of hammerless guns. They are, therefore, less common than one would imagine.

The pool of very good hammer guns in very good condition is small. Time has been unkind to many but there is still a fascinating array of old guns with interesting mechanisms for us rediscover and enjoy.

Examination of the records of some of Britain's leading gunmakers provides illuminating evidence of the relative rarity of quality hammer guns. Purdey made their last hammer gun in 1935 (discounting the modern era hammer guns made after 2005) with the total number of Purdey hammer guns made since 1867 being only 1,625.

Holland & Holland made their last hammer gun around 1900 with total production unknown. Dickson made only 843 hammer breech-loading centre-fires and the last one was delivered in 1922.

Of the 1,004 hammer guns made by Boss, 14 were ejectors and the final order left the factory in 1902. Although Greener made thousands of hammer guns in all grades, the line finished in 1914.

Once British made hammer guns disappeared from catalogues, the very lowest end of the market was picked up by Belgian imports and these hammer guns, often folding .410 side-levers with central hammers, continued as farmers' tools until the Second World War.

The table below illustrates some key developments in locking mechanisms during the hammer gun period

1840 This Lancaster muzzle-loader required no locking system, as the barrels are solid; the permanent breech ends screwed-in tightly.	**1852** The Lefaucheux illustrated on this pin-fire was the first mass produced sporting breech-loader to make inroads in Britain.	In **1856**, Lancaster offered a strong slide-and-tilt action, worked by an under-lever. Slower than snap actions, it was much faster than muzzle loading.	**1859** The Jones 'double grip', an under-lever operated, inert mechanism which persisted into the 20th century.
1860 J.D. Dougall's 'Lockfast' achieved the desired strength that sportsmen sought. Its two-stage opening mechanism was slow to operate.	**1861** Daw's adoption of the Schneider action patent in Britain provided both reliable centre-fire ammunition and a sound under-lever snap-action to house it.	**1863** Early guns with Purdey bolts were operated by snap under-levers which formed part of the trigger guard. It was quick and secure.	**1864** The first Westley Richards top-lever operated a single bolt at the top of the action, which fitted into a slotted doll's head.
William Powell's **1864** lift-up top lever and single bite snap action saw limited use well into the hammerless era.	**1865** The advent of the Scott spindle allowed Purdey bolted guns to utilise a top-lever. Purdey's patent remains in force for another twelve years.	**1870** James Lang's treble-grip sliding-bolt and screw-grip action, patent 687, is essentially an improved, snap-action version of the Jones screw-grip.	**1871** J. Thomas patent 3091 top-lever with rectangular wedge-bolt locking system was put to use by several makers.
1871 Hodges patent 251 treble-grip snap action is the basis for the famous Stephen Grant sidelever guns, also adopted by John Dickson and Henry Egg.	**1873** Greener's 'Treble Wedge Fast' with cross bolt was one of many third bites used by gunmakers to add extra strength.	**1877** Tolley's 'Giant Grip' looks convoluted and unnecessary in comparison with other guns of the period. Generally, guns are looking sleeker and more uniform.	**1878** The patent protection for the Purdey bolt expires, making it free to use and become generally adopted, while most other systems fell into disuse.

The Breech-Loader makes an entrance

Muzzle-loading had been the accepted method for loading sporting guns since barrels and gunpowder were first combined in hand-held 'fowling pieces. The diaries of Col. Peter Hawker provide us with an amusing and enlightening account of the forays of a sportsman equipped with the traditional shooting accoutrements of the early 19th century.

Hawker was born in 1786 and died in 1853. He began his sporting career with flintlocks and lived to see the pin-fire breech-loader introduced to the London crowds at the Great Exhibition of 1851, where he also exhibited his wild-fowling equipment, punt guns and some of his own inventions.

The inventive and enthusiastic gentleman sportsman of the early Victorian period, represented by Hawker at the newly-built Crystal Palace, was unknowingly witnessing the beginning of a furious period of innovation in British gun-making.

The Crystal Palace hosted the Great Exhibition from 1 May to 15 October 1851.

Joseph Lang

The spark that was to set off this powder keg of activity was the embodiment of a continental idea, one which Hawker had previously called 'a horrid ancient invention, revived by foreign makers, that is dangerous in the extreme.'

Exhibit 1301 at the Great Exhibition, which took place in London from 1st March to 15th October 1851, was a breech-loading gun with self-contained ammunition. The patent was that of Casimir Lefaucheux and it attracted the attention of a London gunmaker, also exhibiting his wares.

Joseph Lang, son-in-law to James Purdey, is largely credited with taking the 'French Crutch Gun', as it was disparagingly referred to in certain quarters, and introducing his version of the Lefaucheux to the British public.

David Baker and Don Masters suggest the actual conduit was the Crystal Palace gunmaker Edwin Charles Hodges, who made a copy and sold it to Lang. Whatever the truth, Lang was quickly advertising that he had a breech-loader 'on an entirely new principle, the simplest and quickest ever offered to the public'. Lang also claimed his gun 'combines strength and durability'. Unfortunately, he was over-stating this, as the forward-facing, single screw-grip, under-lever gun which he sold from 1853 suffered from the Lefaucheux weakness of the bolt being rather too close to the hinge and being prone to shoot loose quickly. Sir Ralph Payne-Gallway called Lang's breech-loader 'a crude forerunner of the modern breech-loader'. Examination of these early pin-fires also indicates they were built too light and on frames that were flimsy when compared to later guns, which generally have stronger bars, deeper fences and barrels thicker at the breech end. Despite its shortcomings, Lang's gun represented a relatively fast-loading, nice handling and lightweight game gun.

The 1850s saw pin-fire gain in popularity as new patents vied with one another to provide the perfect combination of strength, reliability and speed of loading.

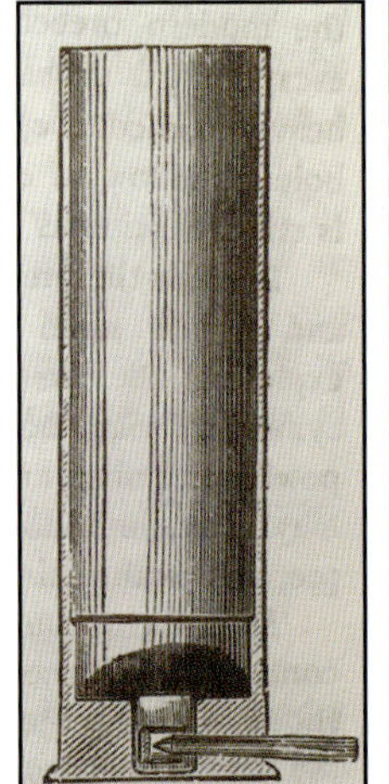

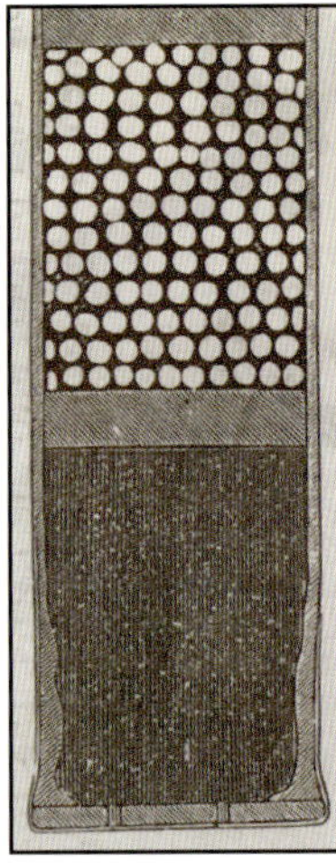

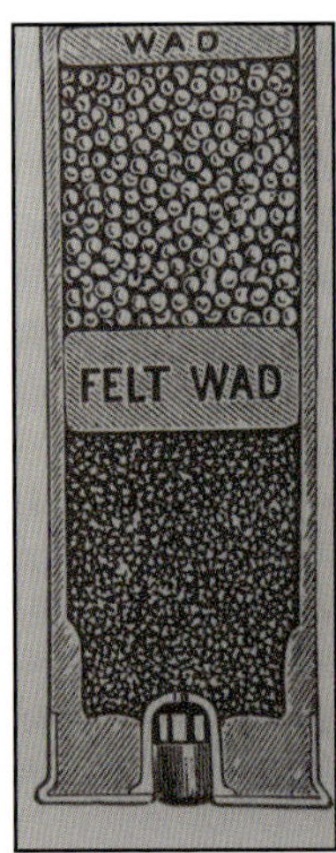

Pin-fire, base-fire and centre-fire cartridges.

Pin-fire catches on

As mechanisms improved, pin-fire cemented its place in the market. Initially, successful patents cured the action of weakness, with inert 'slide and drop' mechanisms like Dougall's and Lancaster's working better than most. Later, loading speed was improved with the introduction of snap-action guns.

By 1860 pin-fires were safe and dependable. The problem was the ammunition. Having to deal with the small protrusions from the side of the cartridge was not convenient, either for carriage or loading; and detonation was not yet failsafe.

The cartridge incorporated the old percussion system into a single unit, making copper caps obsolete.

The False Dawn of Base-fire

Charles Lancaster introduced another idea to the British public around 1856. His slide and drop action was excellent and his ammunition, called 'base-fire' was promising. However, his attempt to hold a monopoly over manufacture and distribution of ammunition contributed to its failure to catch the wider imagination. The majority of breech-loaders continued to be made on the pin-fire system.

Pin-fire was a much faster system than percussion and pin-fire guns cemented the breech-loader's reputation.

Most Victorian sportsmen were used to loading their guns from the muzzle.

The pin-fire was exhibited by Lefaucheux at Crystal Palace where British gunmakers took note of its possibilities.

The holes in the barrels accommodate the 'pins' and the flat nose of the hammer drives the pin into the ignition compound inside.

A 4-bore pin-fire of classic Lefaucheux profile with metal forward-facing lever integral with the forend.

The Arrival of Centre-fire

MR DAW

George Daw is often given credit for introducing the centre-fire shotgun to the British public. Sometimes he is even described as the inventor of centre-fire. However, Daw actually bought his patent from a Frenchman, François Eugene Schneider, who lodged it in Britain in 1861. The purchase marked a watershed in the development of the sporting gun in the United Kingdom, for it heralded the beginning of the modern shotgun in its recognisable form.

Daw, a gunmaker based in London's Threadneedle Street, should be respected for his recognition of the qualities of Schneider's patent, 1487 of 1861, and for sowing the seeds of centre-fire breech loading in the mind of the British sportsman. Schneider's gun was a centre-fire non-ejector, with a snap under-lever action.

Note the rounded bar bolting system and the concave seating in the bar for the barrels. Daw's 1861 central-fire gun looks very similar to later back-action hammer guns in profile and functions very efficiently.

The snap-underlever became known throughout the gun trade as the 'Daw lever' and was later used with other bolting systems, like the Purdey bolt.

Importantly, it was accompanied by reliable ammunition, based on Pottet's 1855 patent and improved by Schneider. In Britain, Daw tried unsuccessfully to protect the patent for his improvements (patent 1594 of 1862), just as Charles Lancaster had done earlier with his 1852 'base-fire' gun and cartridges.

Unlike Lancaster, Daw failed when he tried to stop Eley Bros from making the cartridges for general sale, with the threat of legal action. In 1865, Eley called his bluff and started selling the ammunition. Daw went to court and ultimately lost because the Eley cartridges had two anvils as opposed to Daw's single anvil. This proved to be unlucky for Daw but good for the rest of the gun trade, which eagerly set about building centre-fire guns and improving on the locking mechanism.

With readily available commercial ammunition, the public warmed to the new idea and the death of pin-fire was settled, though, as with most developments, the old systems died slowly rather than abruptly and pin-fire guns of later manufacture prove this. Catalogues of the 1930s, still advertising pin-fire cartridges, indicate just how long they were in use.

When teamed with another universally available action; the Jones under-lever of 1859, the centre-fire gun envisaged by Daw reached a form which would continue in production until 1900 or beyond. However, we are getting slightly ahead of ourselves. An examination of the Daw gun would be a useful exercise before we consign it to history and move on.

The photos show a 12-bore: it has nice quality back-action, non-rebound, hammer locks, with a snap under-lever and Schneider-type locking mechanism of rounded bars locking under the two barrels.

Hammer gun users of today will recognise the form and feel comfortable with the handling of the gun. It really did get things right quickly and it is no surprise that the sporting public reacted well, having earlier, weakly bolted pin-fire guns to compare it with, like the early Lefaucheux, the Adams or the Lang forward facing under-lever.

Daw's gun feels eminently shootable. The operating system is an easy snap action, it feels tight and stable and the proportion and balance are as good as most quality hammer breech-loaders. It feels neither heavy, flimsy nor ungainly. In its year of introduction, one can imagine that the proud owner of a new Daw gun would think he had the best, most modern and convenient sporting gun yet made.

The period beginning with Daw's launch of the centre-fire in 1861 to the perfection of the hammer gun in what we may consider its final development was a short, fraught period of invention, which saw sporting breech-loaders develop at a rapid pace.

The outward form of the gun and its handling qualities were well recognised. In fact, the perfected percussion muzzle-loader was lacking in nothing, once loaded. The problem for the makers of breech-loaders was firstly to make them secure and secondly to make them faster to operate, and both of these aims had to be achieved without compromising the well-made muzzle-loader's exquisite balance and handling.

Daw's adoption of Schneider's patent was very influential and his ammunition was a useful development of the earlier Lancaster base-fire. Eley's robust assertion that the centre-fire concept was not defensible under patent law proved key in its wider adoption.

The Lefaucheux action (above) which was the introduction of pinfire breech-loaders to Britain, in 1851, gave way to stronger inert actions, like the Henry Jones screw-grip during the pinfire era (below). These in turn were surpassed by faster, snap-action patents during a frenzy of patent activity during the last half of the 19th century, as pinfire gave way to centre-fire.

Locking mechanisms develop through the pin-fire era and into the centre-fire era

In the following pages, we shall examine some of the successful, and less successful, attempts made by gunmakers to gain an advantage over their rivals. When considering the swath of inventions presented to the trade and, by extension, to the public, we must note that gunmakers were not only trying to make a better system, but one that would relieve them of having to pay a royalty to the patentee of an existing one.

The gunmakers of London, Birmingham and the provinces feature in the guns we will encounter in this section of the book. From the Islington workshops of E.C. Hodges, to Pape's North of England Gun Works, to the back streets of Edinburgh and the very heart of the Gun Quarter in Birmingham, invention was the business of the day. We are fortunate today that most of these guns were so well made that when we encounter them, with a little bit of care and attention, we can even go and shoot them.

CHARLES LANCASTER AND HIS SLIDE AND TILT MECHANISM

While his classic 'base-fire' action is well-known and many examples survive, Lancaster actually bought the rights to an 1853 patent from Frenchman L.J. Gastinne, in 1856 (Donald Dallas notes that patent agent Auguste Bellford registered patent 2778 in November 1853 and assigned it to Lancaster in November 1856). Guns made by Lancaster, and others under licence, like John Dickson, have engraved on the bar of each gun; 'Charles Lancaster's Patent', thereby claiming credit in a manner that many gunmakers continued to follow in later years with other patents. Like the later Dougall 'Lockfast', the Lancaster barrels are pushed forwards off the breech face by a camming action, before they locate the hinge pin and drop down to open.

The Lancaster mechanism is operated by a 'lever under guard' superficially like the later, and more common, Jones under-lever. When the barrels are locked closed, the operation of the lever slides them back on the horizontal plane and a lug mates with the breech face. It is very strong. When open, the action feels loose but this is a feature of it, not a fault. When closed, it is very tight.

The Lancaster slide-and-tilt action is most commonly encountered in tandem with the 'base-fire' cartridge that Lancaster attempted to popularise and monopolise. The guns are beautifully made with remarkable quality and precision. Base-fire guns of this

Base-fire strikers and the cam clearly visible here.

Operated by an inert underlever, the Lancaster action is beautifully engineered and secure.

An early Lockfast. Note the short, set-back lever.

A later model with downward operating lever.

Note the gap at the breech as the barrels cam forward.

Locking bosses, onto which the breech ends of the barrels cam make a very strong action.

type were made into the late 1850s, by which time Pottet had patented what was really the first true centre-fire cartridge; one using a percussion cap with anvil. Some base-fire guns were converted to centre-fire and the slide-and-tilt action continued to be made into the mid 1860s as a true centre-fire gun.

The example on page 14 (S.N 3016) was made by Lancaster in 1857 and is a base-fire version, marked 'Patent Breech loader'. Note the recessed breech face to house the bosses on the barrels and the conical base-fire type strikers. The closed gun is graceful and balanced. One can certainly see that it was a development ahead of its time and infinitely more likeable than some of the clumsy operating systems that bridged the gap between this and the general utilisation of Jones type or Purdey bolt locking breech-loaders of the late 1870s.

DOUGALL AND HIS 'LOCKFAST'

The principles of the Lefaucheux system were flawed and, despite efforts to improve it, it could not withstand repeated firing without shaking loose. Other gunmakers were working on the same challenges and applying different solutions. With reliable centre-fire ammunition after 1861, demand came for ever more powerful charges and guns that could cope with them. The old pin-fire lock-ups were generally not good enough. Of those that spanned the change-over, J.D. Dougall provided a fairly well-used patent that can still be found on working centre-fire guns and it copes well with the demands of intensive shooting.

Dougall was a gunmaker, established in Glasgow in 1818, who patented this, his best-known action, in May 1860, a year before Daw brought the centre-fire cartridge to the attention of the British gun trade. The patent number is 1128 and it was originally an upward-operating sidelever, but latterly a downward-operating one. Moving the side-lever down activates a cam and slides the barrels forward a little way, then drops them down on the hinge-pin to sit in the conventional 'open' position. These action types are commonly known as 'slide-and-tilt'. The face of the action has protruding bosses, into which the barrels fit when they slide closed in the final 'lock-fast' movement.

This arrangement produces a very strong mechanical bond between barrels and breech and it continued in service for some time into the breech-loading era. Dougall had met one of the key challenges faced by early breech-loader design, in that his patent action delivered strength in abundance. However, the two-stage movement would not compare for convenience with later one-stage operating systems, many of which lacked the sheer strength of the over-engineered 'Lock-fast' but proved sufficient for practical purposes and offered the benefits of swifter operation.

HENRY JONES AND THE ROTARY SCREW-GRIP UNDER-LEVER

The under-lever with screw-grip was generally referred to in gunmakers' records as an 'under-lever' or a 'lever-over-guard' while Greener called it the 'double grip'. Today, most commentators credit the mechanism as the 'Jones under-lever', largely thanks to the efforts of Crudgington & Baker and Geoffrey Boothroyd.

The Jones (patent 2040 of 1859) works by means of a lever under (or over, depending on your point of view!) the trigger guard, which has a protrusion to enable it to be gripped by forefinger and thumb. Lateral movement to the right opens the gun by releasing a coarse screw thread, which bears on cut-out bites in the lumps and hold the barrels tight on the action.

This Purdey incorporates an early version of the 'island' lock and the screw-grip.

Rather than simply filling a bite with a sliding bolt, or block, to prevent the barrels from dropping open, the Jones screw-grip actually tightens the barrels hard onto the action flats. It is very strong, a quality shared with the Dougall and Lancaster guns, but having no camming action, it is a one-stage operation, rather than two-stage, and is, therefore, faster.

Having no spring to work the lever, the entire operation is inert, requiring the user to move the lever to open the gun and again, in the opposite direction, to close it. It is the cart horse of breech-loading systems. Not super-fast, but immensely robust, long-lived and reliable in service. Even the generally grudging W.W. Greener had to allow 'The double grip is considered by all practical gunmakers to be the strongest and most durable arrangement ....Nothing can be more simple or do the work better', when he discussed the then-available actions, in *Modern Breech-loaders 1871.*

Some early screw-grip guns were occasionally made with Lefaucheux type levers under the forend rather than a lever over guard, indeed, some early trade records list guns as 'Lefaucheux', when they were in fact made with Jones patent screw grips.

Webley attempted to convert the inert Jones mechanism into a snap-action in 1866 with patent No. 3022 of that year. This was adopted by some makers, who presumably wanted the secure locking of the Jones original with the speed of the snap-actions that were, by then, becoming universal. Purdey made a number of double rifles on the Webley patent. I have handled several in .303 calibre. However, if not operated carefully, the lever snaps back on the shooter's fingers,

Another early 1860s gun by Reilly, with slim, pin-fire type fences and Jones screw-grip.

in a scissor-like motion, which is potentially painful and dangerous, especially on a double rifle. I have seen a small number of shotguns with the Webley variation but the original Jones is far more common.

The Jones later gave way to snap-actions, which were faster to operate, rather than stronger. However, its use was continued well into the 20th century for guns where strength and reliability were valued over speed and convenience. I have in my possession the penultimate hammer gun made by Boss; a 1902 12-bore pigeon gun with steel barrels and Jones under-lever. The gun is plain but of superb quality and was clearly ordered by a wealthy and particular competition shooter who knew exactly what his priorities were. Makers of large bore guns for wild fowling also found the Jones system the most useful, as strength and simplicity outweighed speed as merits on the foreshore.

WESTLEY RICHARDS INTRODUCE THE TOP-LEVER AND BOLTED DOLL'S HEAD

While the Jones system was strong and low maintenance, it was not all that the market desired. The need for speed increased with the rising popularity of driven pheasant shooting and snap-action systems were the answer. Another Birmingham gunmaker, albeit one far more wealthy and influential than Henry Jones, made an early and very successful attempt at producing a fast, convenient mechanism of this type.

Patent 2623 of 1864 was Westley Richards' final incarnation of a plan that had started with his 1858 patent for a bolted doll's-head rib extension. When teamed with a top-lever, operated by pushing to the right with the thumb, thereby sliding back the locking bolt, it proved to be secure as well as easy to operate. As the bolt was operated by a return spring, opening required simple manipulation of the top-lever and closing required only moving the barrels up into the 'closed' position. Unlike previously described systems, this 'snap-action' type requires no manual operation of a lever to secure the gun, once the barrels are in the 'closed' position.

Westley Richards: his firm was hugely influential in the 19th century and quick to enter the breech-loading frenzy of invention.

1860s Westley Richards 'crab joint' breech-loaders in pin-fire and centre-fire were early benchmarks for quality and security.

Under examination, the Westley Richards appears deceptively flimsy; a simple sliding bolt locating with the doll's head, which has a slot machined in it to receive it. It provides no impediment to the barrels moving forward under pressure, other than the hook in the single lump being firmly in contact with the hinge pin. The bolting arrangement simply prevents the barrels from pivoting downwards.

When compared with the inert Dougall and Jones systems, the Westley Richards offers improved speed, while the former two boast greater strength. To find the the perfect operating system, the gun trade had to devise the ideal compromise between these two basic requirements: strength and speed.

A Westley Richards pin-fire converted to centre-fire. The bolted doll's head spanned both eras.

THREE MANIFESTATIONS OF THE WESTLEY RICHARDS BOLTED DOLL'S HEAD AND TOP-LEVER

This early Westley Richards pin-fire has a sliding bolt.

Rather than operating by a turning lever, it pulls back.

The second version of the patent features a bolting top lever.

In both early versions, the bolted 'doll's head' is the sole closure. It is surprisingly effective.

The third version of the 'doll's head' sees it teamed with Purdey's patent bolt of 1863.

This is the most secure version. It has been in service from the early centre-fire era to the present day.

JAMES PURDEY INTRODUCES HIS UNDER-BOLT

May 2nd is my birthday, it is also the day in 1863 on which James Purdey, probably the best-known and most revered gunmaker of his day, secured patent protection for perhaps the single most popular means by which a breech-loader has since been secured. Patent 1104 recorded the 'Purdey double bolt'.

Originally it operated by a 'thumbhole lever', which, when pushed forward, instigated a backward movement to the bolt. When released, a return spring snapped the lever forward again and the bolt with it. The sliding bolt in the bar locked into square bites in the lumps and held the breech closed very securely (which is why it is sometimes referred to as an 'under-bolt'). Purdey used two versions of his thumb lever, referred to as 'First Patent' (May 1863) and 'Second variant'. The second was somewhat neater than the first, in which the lever runs under the bar for an inch and a half.

The Purdey bolt was further applied to guns operated by means of a side-lever or a lever running over the trigger guard and pushed forward by means of its projecting extremity. The latter is sometimes called a 'Daw lever', as it outwardly resembles the style which that maker used on his first centre-fire gun. The preferred and most common application of the Purdey bolt is a later type, operated by a top-lever with either Scott or Greener patent linkages, which began to appear in the mid-to-late 1860s.

Purdey kept the patent in force for the maximum allowable fourteen years. It seems likely that the use of many of the other mechanisms described in this book owe their existence to this financially astute move by the patentee. Anyone wanting to use the bolt before 1878 had to pay Purdey a £2 royalty on each gun made. To contextualise this cost, Greener offered a 'Superior Keeper's Gun' in their 1879 catalogue, with Jones under-lever for 10 guineas. So, £2 represented close to 20% on top of the cost of a cheap gun, had the Purdey bolt been used instead. The going rate for a best gun in the 1870s was 35-40 guineas, so the extra £2 was less of a barrier in the top tier market.

Above: The original mechanism for the Purdey bolt: the 'first pattern' thumb lever. Note the lever extending along the bar. Below, the neater 'second variant'.

Purdey's bolt was a simple concept but it serves its purpose perfectly and made him a fortune.

Early guns feature this extractor system, operated by a cam which slots into the bar either side of the lump.

A later version, with more conventional looking lumps and extractors. Note the bites for the sliding bolt.

The bar of the earlier gun. Note the cut-outs for the extractor cam and the absence of a cross bar.

The later gun, showing cross bar and through lumps.

SCOTT LINKS THE TOP LEVER WITH THE PURDEY BOLT

The Westley Richards top lever gained popularity because of its convenience. Purdey's bolt was admired for its ergonomics and neatness as well as its strength. It is no surprise that work to use them in conjunction with one another was quickly underway.

The first and best link was the patent of the great Birmingham gunmaker William Middleditch Scott, of W&C Scott. His patent 2752 of 1865 created a top-lever and Purdey-bolt arrangement that differed from the Westley Richards in that it did not include a top-bolt and doll's head. Scott, of Birmingham, and Purdey, of London, cleverly collaborated to combine their patents and split the royalties that would come in abundance from selling it to other gunmakers. Scott got paid when Birmingham gunmakers used it and Purdey when London gunmakers did. The royalty fee, as mentioned earlier, was £2 per gun. To put this fee into further perspective, a carpenter in London earned 6s 6d a week in 1865, making the Scott/Purdey royalty equal to paying a carpenter for a month every time another gunmaker used it to build a gun.

Westley Richards retained their own bolted lever with doll's head and added the spindle and the Purdey bolt to their own guns shortly afterwards. The firm uses it to this day, though the Westley Richards bolted top-lever was never widely adopted by other gunmakers.

Scott's lever work, mated with Purdey's bolt, makes a gun with clean lines and easy operation.

W.W. GREENER APPLIES BELT AND BRACES

William Wellington Greener was a man who courted controversy. He was many things to many people. A man who not only coped with disability (he was almost blind) but appeared to ignore it and built a mighty business notwithstanding. He was an organiser of men, a leader, an innovator and something of a visionary. He was also a gifted marketer of his wares, saw the commercial advantages to be gained from the written word and published several large, important and fascinating books on gun making and shooting.

Greener was always his own man. He stood proudly for the virtues of Birmingham as the heart of the gun trade and championed it as the true home of the innovator, rather than a poor relation to the fashionable names from London.

Scott's spindle. Purdey and Scott did a deal to split royalties when their patents were teamed up.

Greener retained Purdey's bolt and added a third bolt through the rib extension.

Greener's writing, and his guns, have a theme which is often re-visited in print and in wood and metal. The theme is strength. Greener really cemented the reputation of his guns and those of the Birmingham trade, many of which followed his lead, for actions that would shoot countless thousands of rounds without fault or wear. Part of the solution was the use of fine materials and high quality manufacture. The most visible part was the application of a third locking bolt, (or 'third bite') in addition to the Purdey under-bolt.

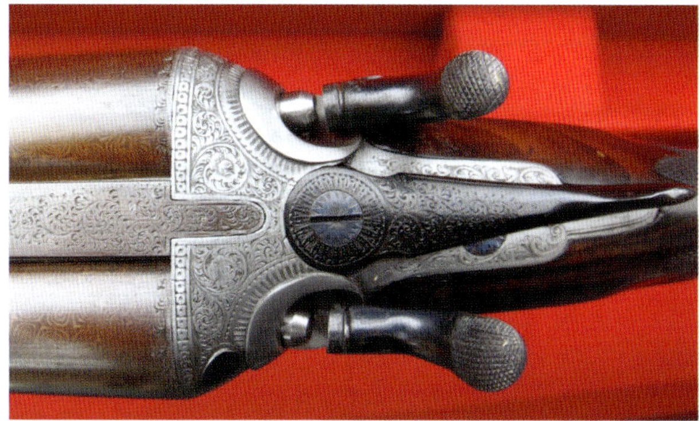

The Greener system was popular in Birmingham and the provinces. This is a Pape probably made by Osborne.

As we have seen, the Purdey bolt appeared in 1863. By 1865 it was mated with a top-lever, either by means of a Scott spindle or Greener's rather clumsier, but cheaper-to-make, lever work. Greener, naturally, preferred his own patent lever work for all grades of gun. The trade at large tended to use the Scott type for higher quality guns and Greener type for lower grade guns.

The London trade is noted for the clean lines of its best guns. After experimenting with third bites, most London makers decided the Purdey bolt was sufficient and that the breech was better looking and easier to load without a protrusion from the rib getting in the way. Exceptions were made for double rifles and pigeon guns.

Greener was rather unimpressed by this and wrote of the need for third bites in some detail when he penned *Modern Shot Guns* in 1888. Here, he outlined the results of his tests with a specially constructed gun using a clamp to hold silver foil between breech and barrel joint, so as to ensure it broke if there was any movement upon firing the gun. When a round, Greener-type cross bolt was used, the foil did not break, without one, it did, once the load was increased sufficiently.

Greener's answer to the lock-up of a breech-loader was to utilise Purdey's bolting system but to add the third bite he considered essential. His best-known and most instantly recognised patent is the 'Treble Wedge Fast' of 1873. It is a round bolt, which slides into a hole drilled into a flat rib extension, which, in turn, slots into a gap in the breech.

Greener argued that his system prevented lateral movement, stopped the barrels from gapping at the top and was an essential companion to the Purdey bolt. He wrote of it:

> *The Greener Treble Wedge Fast gun may be fired hundreds of thousands of times without any repairs being required..... Dr Carver in 1878 fired 130,000 times without any repairs being done or required.*

The Greener round section bolt was copied by many Birmingham makers and can be found on guns by many firms, at all price points. However, as Greener pointed out at the time, unless correctly made and carefully fitted, it was of little use.

Greener proved the theoretical benefits of his third grip for ultimate security but a strongly made action with normal game loads does not need more than a Purdey bolt.

Greener's lever work was an alternative to Scott's spindle and was somewhat cheaper to make. Greener used it on all qualities of gun but it found wider favour in the gun trade for use on mid-to-lower quality guns.

THREE MANIFESTATIONS OF GREENER'S TOP BOLT AND RIB EXTENSION

A mid-weight game gun by Lang & Son.

Greener 10-bore. This split-bolt variant may be unique.

The Boswell Pigeon Gun – pigeon guns benefit from the extra security as they fire heavier charges.

WILLIAM POWELL DOES PUSH-UPS

One of Birmingham's most noted and ultimately long-lived gunmaking firms, William Powell, waded into the fight to improve Lefaucheux's breech-loader in the mid 1860s. This was the pin-fire era, but his system persisted into the modern era. 'Powell's Patent Snap Action' (patent 1163 of 1864) is operated by a thumb lever on the top-strap. The barrels are opened by pushing the lever upwards, thereby withdrawing a bolt which project from a recess in the breech-face and blocks the drop of the barrels by meeting a projection on the lump, which is also fitted into a recess in the standing breech.

The barrels hinge as in the Lefaucheux design, falling with gravity when the bolt is released. Many of these guns incorporated mechanical retraction of the strikers when the lever is pushed up to open the gun.

William Powell described his mechanism, in a letter from his Carr's Lane shop, as *'very safe and not liable to get out of order.... can be more rapidly fired than any of the ordinary breech-loaders.'*

It was certainly met with enough positivity for it to enjoy fairly wide usage and impressive longevity, which spanned the pin-fire, centre-fire hammer gun and hammerless ejector periods.

I have encountered the Powell system on guns by several other makers. It is fairly common on hammer guns but it maintained popularity into the hammerless era and was widely used on boxlocks by various makers. I have also seen at least two mid-20th century sidelock examples. With care and maintenance the mechanism is practical and pleasant. Paul Hueppe, a collector with an extensive array of Powell guns, now exceeding sixty in number, reports years of happy game and clay shooting with his lift-up-lever guns. My own experience of using a hammer gun of this type on a cold, wet driven pheasant shoot involved stiff thumbs and skinned knuckles. The fitting tightened and stuck as the day progressed and the barrels got hot. Paul maintains the importance of keeping the bolt clean and lightly oiled. With this done, his experience is of trouble-free operation. Powell certainly made these guns for other firms in the 1860s and continued to use it themselves into the 1920s, in small numbers.

A bar-in-wood version of Powell's patent action by W.S. Reilly.

The single bite is released by pushing up the lever.

Side view of the bolt.

Bottom view showing the extended rear lump, which seats in the standing breech.

Powell's patent stamp.

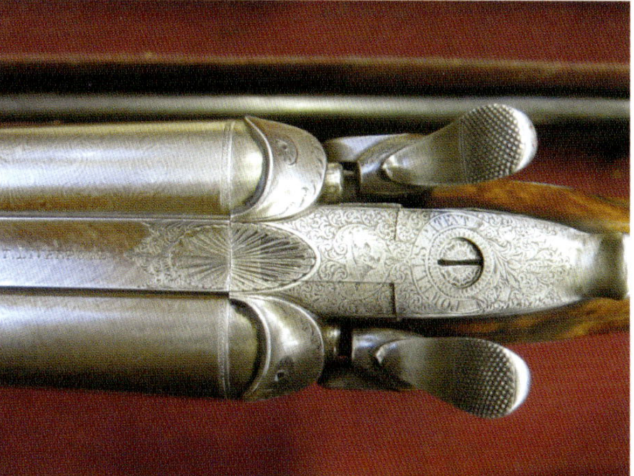
A view of the neat work that is a hallmark of Powell hammer guns.

Pape with patent thumb tab.

The top of the gun is uncluttered.

The tab is relatively unobtrusive.

THUMBS-UP FOR PAPE?

William Rochester Pape was an interesting man. A gunmaker from Newcastle-upon-Tyne, in the north-east of England, he was a 'Geordie' doing rather well in an industry dominated by 'Brummies', as the denizens of Birmingham and the Black Country are known. For some reason, which may be linked to Pape's 1866 patent for choke boring and then Greener's impressive harnessing and marketing of the idea, the two gunmakers appear to have had a long-running feud. Pape's cheating in one of the 'Field Trials' (cylinder vs choke-bored guns) cannot have helped (Pape was found to have used shot-concentrators).

Amongst the short-lived snap-actions the hammer gun buyer will encounter, there is a patent (1504 of 1866) by Pape, which Greener dismissed in 1871 with this rather terse summary:

> *Many of these so-called improvements [to snap-action levers] were simply contemptible, being only studs or thumb-bits, not worthy of the name of levers, requiring only a simple pressure of the thumb to disengage the barrels for loading. When these guns become foul, it is difficult to get them open at all. They also had a very bad habit of flying open at the critical moment of discharge.*

Personal experience does not confirm Greener's negative assessment of Pape's gun. Several have been through my business and I know of a number still in regular use. I have yet to encounter a report of any of the failures Greener alleges.

The thumb tab is a simple and convenient system, which does lack the leverage of a longer top, or side, lever; so Greener's worry about a fouled action being hard to operate may be well-founded. The tab operates a single bolt engaging with the lump, so lock-up should be theoretically the same as any other snap-action bolted under the barrels in this manner, though, perhaps lacking the benefits of the double bite locking provided by Purdey's bolt.

Pape's design was not universally popular and other makers appear not to have adopted it, though some were made for Pape by others, like Wilkinson, and the quality of these guns is invariably very high. As was the natural order of things in gun-making development, the ultimately popular systems were the best and were adopted quickly, while the unpopular sank into disuse, as the market dictated success or failure.

W.M. SCOTT GETS IT UNCHARACTERISTICALLY WRONG

The man who provided the perfect means to link the top lever with the double under-bolt, a system still in general use today, must have had a glass of sherry too many when he allowed his 1874 patent to be unleashed on an unsuspecting public.

One would have imagined his fellow gunmakers of the day might have acted as a sober restraint but some of the best-known firms actually adopted this rather ungainly gun, to a limited extent. The patent in question is No.2052 of 1874 and it is a conventional Scott spindle with Purdey bolt gun with the addition of receptors on either side of the barrels, each of which is engaged by a cylindrical bolt, operated by the top lever and providing additional grips.

Considering that the gun was patented shortly before the Anson & Deeley boxlock, at a time when hammer guns of grace, strength and beauty were the norm, this engineering marvel (or aesthetic abomination, depending on your point of view), appears not of its time.

I have seen two examples, one by Holland & Holland, the other by Scott. Like many actions criticised in print, the gun actually appears beautifully made which, in the hands, belies its clumsy physique. Oddity or not, these guns were constructed by masters with magnificent skills.

I'm inclined to be kinder than most commentators. I'd be happy to own and shoot one of these eccentric pieces, but their rarity and quality puts them beyond my means. I can understand why the design quietly faded from view but I'm happy it exists to illustrate the unfettered imaginations of our greatest gunmakers and their attempted solutions to the problems of the day. The quality of the action filing on the Scott gun in these photographs is outstanding.

William Middleditch Scott made a fortune from his 1865 spindle patent, but I'm not sure he made much from this one.

Scott's extra bolting came as bolsters on either side of the fences.

The round bolts slot into recesses in bolsters set into the breech ends of the barrels.

The top view shows the extra width of the action and the obtrusive bolsters. Beautifuly made, of course.

HENRY TOLLEY GETS A GRIP

Henry Tolley was late to the party with his patent 461 of 1877 because Purdey had long since created the double under-bolt and seen it mated with Scott's spindle or Greener's alternative to effect swift operation via a top-lever.

However, Birmingham still had something of an obsession with strengthening the lock-up. Greener labours the point in *The Gun & its Development* right up to the last edition of 1909. Most Birmingham guns featured doll's head rib extensions, largely based on the Westley Richards original, some being bolted, others not. However, by 1877, rather than rib extensions being the sole means of bolting, they were fitted in addition to the Purdey bolt.

Into this arena stepped Tolley. His gun was conventional in that it had a top-lever and Purdey bolt, but extending forward from the top-lever was a hook. Extending back from the rib was a type of doll's head, with a square-sided 'L' shaped profile, which slotted into the standing breech, with the short base of the 'L' pointing upwards. When closed, the hook projecting from the top lever mated laterally with the 'L' shaped

Top left: Tolley's finest work is neat, finely executed and finished to the highest standard.
Left: The rib extension slots into the top of the standing breech.
Below: The Giant Grip looks rather extreme in the open position.

This example is engraved with the 'Giant Grip' name and may have been a special production.

doll's head and added a third grip. The firm gave it the title 'Giant Grip' and I have seen examples from time-to-time; hammer guns and boxlocks. They have tended to feature on guns of decent but unremarkable quality and have always been a curiosity.

However, I recently uncovered a very fine hammer gun by J&W Tolley, with rounded profile bar, quality damascus barrels, early, straight-drive strikers and 'C' scroll hammers, (later hammer guns have the strikers at an oblique angle, as they are less prone to stick in soft centre-fire cartridge caps that way) and very tasteful full-coverage engraving. It also had the most beautifully filed fences and was certainly the best example of a Tolley 'Giant Grip' I have ever seen. It even had the name 'Giant Grip' engraved in finely-executed script on the rib.

I wonder if it could have been a demonstration piece or a special example, perhaps even the first gun of its kind? It is certainly odd. Why would a maker like Tolley go to the expense of making such a hammer gun in the late 1870s with a near-obsolete action and a new patent bolting mechanism and finish it to such a beautifully high standard? We can only guess. Unsurprisingly, the Giant Grip proved to be something the wider gun trade ignored.

When closed, the jointing is so well executed that it can't be seen when fully home.

The development of the Jones Screw Grip

The best-known version of the screw grip action is the common lever-over-guard type, or 'under-lever'. However, the 1859 patent can be found locking breech loaders shut with other lever styles.

A number of makers used the early variant forward-facing under-lever. This sits under the forend in a similar fashion to the Lefaucheux lever, but employing the stronger Jones screw-grip on the bites in the lumps. This style can be seen in the photos of the Boss on the facing page. It was converted from muzzle-loader using this variation of the Jones lever.

On this page, a Purdey .500 BPE centre-fire double rifle shows another early version of unlocking the screw-grip. The entire trigger guard becomes the lever. It is sprung so that it sits firmly in place, with a small notch and protrusion which hold it secure when closed. While both these early types of lever work quite well, the later style settled on by most makers, exemplified by the Rigby on the facing page, became the preferred option for the trade at large and is universal by the mid-1860s.

This under-lever action saw continued service well into the 20th century. Where simplicity and strength trumped speed and beauty, the Jones ruled.

A view of the 'guard-as-lever' in closed position.

Early versions of the Henry Jones under-lever incorporated the entire trigger guard. This produces huge leverage and was popular for a time on Purdey double rifles, like this .500 BPE.

The screw-grip idea was used on guns with a forward-facing lever in the early days.

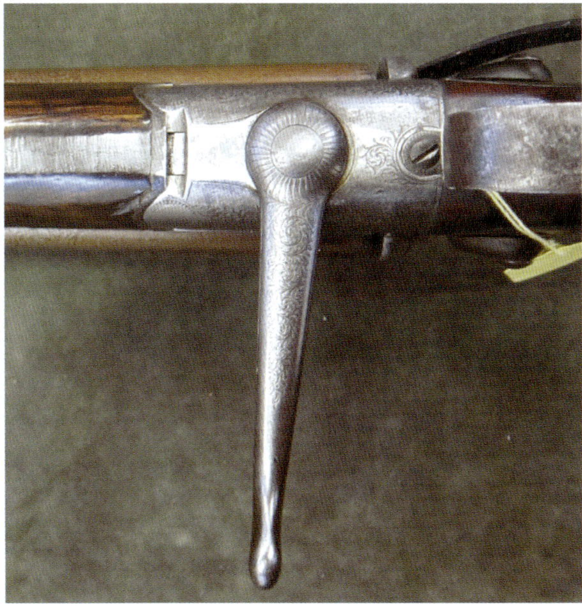

This Boss 12-bore has a forward facing under-lever with screw-grip locking mechanism.

The bites for the screw-grip are inward facing, allowing the grip to bear down, drawing the barrels onto the bar flats.

A classic game gun: John Rigby 12-bore with rebounding bar locks and the Jones under-lever in its most common variant of lever-over guard. Slower than snap actions but excellent sporting guns in every other respect.

G. Jeffries 'side-motion' gun

George Jeffries may not be a household 'London name' in the minds of today's collectors. Indeed, I very much doubt one in a hundred regular shooters has heard of him. Although considered a gunmaker of Norwich, he was probably a brother to the well-known Lincoln Jeffries of Birmingham and it is likely that the manufacture of his guns took place there.

One of the joys of dealing in British hammer guns is the sheer variety of mechanisms that appear for inspection. They are invariably beautifully made and clever in concept. One can often understand from a historical perspective why a gun may not have found wider popularity but these old gems certainly bear evidence to these very clever Victorians working to solve the problems of the day.

The gun illustrated is George Jeffries' second attempt at making a gun which opened sideways rather than downwards. This conforms to his patent No.330 of 1862 and the use number shows us that, at that point, 346 had been made. It looks bizarre to modern eyes but the 'side motion gun', as Jeffries called it, was once seen as a real contender. The gun was exhibited at the 1870 Workman's Exhibition, where it won a gold medal. It was in production for ten years.

Jeffries advertised the gun widely as a pin-fire or centre-fire, claiming it to have *'Five times the resisting surface of any double grip drop guns'*. He added a little dig that it was *'the only sporting breech-loader invented in Great Britain'*. In this, he was referring to the continental origins of the Lefaucheux and the Schneider guns championed by Lang and Daw.

As strength was a big issue, in light of the flaws in the Lefaucheux design, Jeffries' claim that *'Two hard pieces of tempered steel working together in the vital parts never before attained'* would have attracted appreciation. Like the Jones under-lever, the Jeffries under-lever operation is inert and requires the lever to be drawn manually back into the locked position.

With the tide of history moving in the direction of faster snap-action guns, Jeffries' side-motion gun was an heroic attempt at solving the lock-up problem but is now remembered as a dead-end. However, as with many old designs that never survived beyond their childhood, a few quality examples remain to show the modern enthusiast that there are many ways to achieve a functional sporting breech-loader and they offer a working alternative to conventional guns.

The side-motion gun in closed position.

Slim fences hint at the early breech-loader style.

The fit of parts is complex and beautifully jointed.

G. Jeffries Quad-lump action

We have seen evidence of the talents of George Jeffries earlier, in the form of his 1862 'side motion gun'. The gun illustrated here is another by the same man and is another illustration of his elastic approach to engineering problems.

This patent dates from 1874 and the bolting mirrors Purdey's bolt in practice. The bites in the lumps are filled by the bolt sliding forwards under spring pressure to lock the gun tight. Jeffries' guns exist with two bolted bites (in the rearmost lumps) or four.

Split lumps were not novel to Jeffries: there are earlier ones dating back to 1858 and Greener experimented with the concept in some early Facile Princeps guns in the 1880s. However, the benefits were dubious and gunmakers found two lumps in-line with a Purdey double bolt engaging the bites was a system easier to make and more robust. Gunmakers tell me that the re-jointing of these quad-bolt guns is harder than conventional types and that they shoot loose quicker.

The example here is a 12-bore made on an early variant of Jeffries' patent No. 3442 of October 1874. It has extended rear lumps acting on the sliding bolt, via vertical cams in the standing breech. Later guns had a simpler sliding bolt and bite arrangement.

Quad lumps were something of an experiment but proved harder to joint and no more robust than conventional guns with two lumps.

Horsley pull-back top lever

The Horsley gun has something of a cult following. In its classic form it incorporates the Horsley patents for retracting strikers (1867), pull back top-lever and single bite snap action (1863). Thomas Horsley was a York-based gunmaker of note. He was inventive and produced guns of high quality, quite distinctive from most of those his contemporaries were making in the 1860s and 1870s.

The ultimate development of the Horsley lever can be seen in his 1888 patent in which the sliding top-lever operates a Purdey double bolt via a complex arrangement with a leaf spring mounted on the trigger plate.

The gun illustrated here is a classic Horsley with two lumps, bolted in the rear and placed within a wood-bar action. The unusually engraved gun was made for the Duke of Abergavenny and has conventional hammers, while the other gun has Horsley's retracting striker system.

The most representative Horsley gun is based on patent 2410 (probably) taken out by the younger Thomas Horsley in October 1863. David Baker believes around 500 such guns were made and he has something of an attachment to the Horsley way of gun-making, having amassed quite a collection and undertaking the task of producing a comprehensive and self-published book *Thomas Horsley; Gunmaker of York*, which should be required reading for all proud Yorkshire men with an interest in their county's gun-making heritage.

Considering the age of the patent, Horsley's gun of 1863 looks and feels lively and effective in the hands. A well-made example in good condition feels no more out of place in a rough shooting situation, walking the hedges with a couple of spaniels, than any of the later hammer gun models made in the 1880s. The Horsley gun is a beautiful, clever snap-action that fulfils the needs of the sportsman nicely. Unfortunately, finding a really good example today is difficult.

This Horsley has the distinctive engraving of a type unique to guns owned by the Duke of Abergavenny.

The sliding top lever is neat in appearance and Horsley's guns are always well-made.

A more conventionally engraved example, with retracting strikers.

Hodges Patent Side-lever Gun

Of E.C. Hodges's collaborations with Stephen Grant, perhaps the iconic configuration is the side-lever back-action hammer gun built to patent 251 of 1871. There comes point in many a collector's life when he can be heard to utter the words 'I want a Stephen Grant side-lever'.

Examining these guns, one will generally find 'Grant & Hodges Patent' stamped on the action flats and/or 'Grant's Patent' engraved on the top strap, along the bar or on the underside of the bar. Careful examination may also uncover 'ECH' in a trademark triangle stamped on the flats or face and 'ECH' as the barrel maker's mark. Most of these guns were probably made by Hodges in his Islington workshops.

The Hodges patent gun has in-line lumps in the conventional manner of Purdey-bolted guns, with the addition of a projection into the breech-face. However, the sliding bolt, while engaging with a bite in the rear lump, also slides forward, over two horizontal projections in the rear lump, adding further security against the breech gapping upon discharge of the cartridge. Variations abound; some have lateral projections on both lumps.

By far the most common incarnation of Grant & Hodges patent side-lever gun is the back-action form. For every bar-action example, I see perhaps twenty back-actions. Robert Hodges believes that just under 1000 examples of the Hodges patent gun were made for Stephen Grant in the 1870s.

Stephen Grant became famous for the 1871 Hodges gun.

We shall read more about E.C. Hodges later in the book. For now we should just note that in the manner of many patent collaborations, Hodges was the true patent holder and Grant appears to have entered into a business arrangement to have sole use of the design for a number of years.

There is something ergonomically 'right' about a side-lever. It matters little which side it is on. Pairs of guns were often made with the lever on the left, regardless of the shooter's handedness.

The lumps on a Hodges-made gun by Stephen Grant.

Note the cut-outs either side of the lump holes.

Wiggan & Elliott's patent gun

There are many obscure locking mechanisms for breech loaders dating back to the 1860s and the inclusion of this particular gun as a feature on this page rests on the repeated emergence of it in a familiar form during my travels. I have seen it in 12-bore, 28-bore and as a single barrel 20-bore, to name but three manifestations which are easily recalled.

As with so many short-lived patent guns of the 1860s, every example has been of the very best quality. It is interesting to note that guns like this were being built in small numbers and the men working on them did not have decades of familiarity with a particular action to rely on.

They were using their innate skills and judgements, combined with the instructions from the 'gaffer' and the patent drawings, to create beautifully engineered and attractive sporting guns to the best of their considerable abilities. Every gun would have involved new lessons being learned and tiny improvements being made.

Like the Horsley, the Wiggan & Elliott feels like a modern sporting gun when in the hands. Proportion, balance and operation are comfortable and pleasing. Guns like this must have played a large part in convincing the public that breech-loading snap-action hammer guns were the correct road ahead for sporting guns.

These photographs show Henry Elliott's patent No.1782 of 1863. Again, like the Horsley, the Elliott appeared in the pin-fire era and lived to see use as a centre-fire. The action operates as a snap under-lever. The bolt itself is a hook-shaped projection from the breech face, which extends into a hollow section of the rib with a shield-shaped section. In locking design, it is similar to the Westley Richards Doll's head in providing a locking point which is far from the pivot point of the hook on the hinge pin.

Apart from the neat lines and beautiful construction values this demonstrates, we should consider the inevitable accompaniment to the Elliott patent action of the distinctive 'upside down' stock profile. The heel is narrow and the toe wide. The belly is wide and the stock tapers upwards to the comb.

It looks odd but feels comfortable and practical. Quite why Wiggan & Elliott stuck to this shape, which can be seen on a lot of guns of the flintlock era, when no other gunmaker of the breech-loading era thought doing so was a good idea, one can only speculate.

For an early breech-loader, the Wiggan & Elliott is remarkably composed and attractive.

Here the recess in the rib can be seen. This accepts the hook which protrudes from the breech face.

This example shows how the wood-bar style can be practical and robust, long-term.

Left: The Wiggan & Elliott style of butt is a hangover from flintlock guns, where the belly was often fatter than the comb. The shape of the butt plate shows the profile, which carries on through the stock.

Quality of manufacture and finishing on these guns is invariably excellent.

Lang's variation on the Jones Screw Grip

Joseph Lang began our story of the British breech-loader with his Lefaucheux-type guns inspired by the 1851 Great Exhibition. Lang's use of the Lefaucheux action with his forward-facing under lever was quickly surpassed by a number of stronger actions, key among them the Henry Jones screw grip of 1859.

While strong and reliable, the Jones action had in its disfavour the handicap of being an inert action, which requires manual manipulation of the lever to return it to locked position. Snap-action guns of various form overtook the Jones in desirability for many gunmakers, as speed was a key factor in the development of a marketable action.

Joseph's son, James Lang, added a useful contribution to the development of the original Jones pattern by devising a snap-action variation. This is encapsulated in his 1870 patent No.687. He couples the screw-grip with a sliding bolt. The bolt, operated by top-lever and spindle pushes the screw round, via a forward projection. Two transverse levers operated by the bottom of the spindle rotate the screw when the top-lever is turned, thereby unlocking the gun, as the sliding bolt simultaneously retracts.

The result of this rather clever design is a treble-grip gun, consisting of a single Purdey-type bolting of the rear lump and a screw-grip bolting between forward and rear lumps. The whole thing operates seamlessly and feels just like any other top-lever snap-action gun.

The reason it is relatively rarely encountered is probably the issue of over-complicating what had, by the mid-1870s, become a fairly well-understood mechanism in the simpler forms then already available for securing barrels to breech. The extra complication probably did not offer sufficient advantages over simpler ones more universally applied by the trade to overcome the additional work involved in making it.

Like many of the snap-action, top-lever back-lock guns available in the 1870s, the James Lang patent looks 'normal' when closed. By that, I mean the aesthetic silhouette of a game gun had become reasonably standardised and Lang's gun conforms. The tell-tale round disc on the bottom of the bar, declaring 'Lang's Patent' and rotating when the gun is opened or closed, is the sole give-away.

The side view of the Lang is conventional.

Only the rotating screw grip under the bar looks odd.

Needham's Breech-Loader

Needham's business was eventually absorbed into the Greener empire but J.V. Needham was a fairly important and innovative gunmaker in his prime. He was to make his mark for posterity with the first barrel cocking gun and the first effective ejector gun. However, those achievements came over a decade after this, his 1862 patent side lever gun with a cam that lifts the non-rebounding hammers back to half cock.

Although patented in 1862 (No.1544), the gun was evidently still being made in 1871. This was another action which traversed the pin-fire/centre-fire eras. Needham's advertisement in *The Field* in August 1871 claims *'Needham's self half-cocking breech-loader, having now stood the test of six seasons, is acknowledged the safest and most desirable of snap action guns extant'.*

The example shown here is in remarkably good, original condition and functions perfectly. The side lever, bearing 'Needham's Patent' engraving, is depressed to activate a single bolt, which holds down the projection from the rear lump. As this operation takes place, the stud on the rear of the side-lever pushes the hammer to the half-cock position. When the gun is closed, all the levers snap back into place automatically.

The Needham is a pleasant gun to use, being beautifully constructed and well-balanced. The operating system is an easy one with which to become familiar and even today, makes a viable sporting gun for moderate volume shooting.

Needham's gun is attractive and balanced. This example is in excellent original condition.

Open, we can see the extended single bite rear lump.

This projection lifts the hammers to half cock.

Showing the gun closed and at half cock. Below, full cock.

The Solid Self-Locking Vertical Grip

The gun illustrated is by Conway but was probably made for him by either the patent holder or a gun-making factory licensed to do so (Crudgington & Baker suggest Tipping and Lawden).

The gun looks quite conventional when closed, with a top-lever snap-action. However, the locking mechanism is not the Scott spindle operating the Purdey bolt, which, by then, was five years in existence.

The patent is that of John Thomas and dates from 1870 (No.324). I have encountered the gun as a bar-action hammer and as a back-action hammer, by various makers in a range of qualities.

The rear lump has a projection. This slots into a cut-out in the standing breech. A rotating turret, operated by the top lever, slides over the lump projection to hold the barrels down. In closing, it operates as a snap action, with the projection pushing the turret against a v-spring, which snaps it back into place.

Thomas appears to have branded the action his 'Solid Self-locking Vertical Grip', as some guns have this engraved on the lever. While attractive, neat and serviceable, it lacks the two bolting points of the Purdey bolt or the three bolts of alternatives like the Grant & Hodges.

The grips on the Thomas patent. They offer no advantage over a Purdey bolt but differ enough to avoid patent infringement.

The back lump has a projection, the front has a bite for a single bolt.

The Thomas patent gun seems to have been quite widely used but rarely by the top makers of the day.

Robert Adams' Gun

An interesting and beautifully-made mechanism, Robert Adams made this gun as a pin-fire and it was later converted to centre-fire, as were many quality guns that spanned the transition between firing systems during their working lives.

It incorporates the idea of an under-lever, initially reminiscent of the later Daw snap lever. However, this is inert and simple in concept. The lever is held in place by a catch, released by pressing a button at its extremity. The patent is number 285 of 1860.

Once released, forward motion of the lever draws the grip from the semi-circular bearing surfaces on the T-sectioned rear lump. The trajectory of the claw-like gripping surfaces on the forward part of the lever draw the lump tight into the concave surfaces of the bar and hold it secure. The Adams gun is just one of many clever actions that achieved modest popularity before being eclipsed by more practical alternatives.

This illustrates the delicately shaped wood covering the bar and cupping the barrel tubes when the gun is closed.

The beautifully shaped lever with its incorporated button release.

Below: The lump closest to the breech is a rounded 'T' shape. The locking mechanism on the lever engages this and pulls the lump tight down into the bar, where it holds it firm.

Semi-hammerless Guns

As the centre-fire gun developed and then began to face serious competition from hammerless actions, a sideshow was playing in the form of guns which generally housed the firing mechanism inside the action but maintained outward hammers of various types.

The idea of putting the mechanism inside the locks pre-dates Murcott's 'Mousetrap' or Anson & Deeley's boxlock. F.H Grey patented a gun (No.2743) in October 1865, which has the external appearance of a pin-fire. However, the strikers are acted upon by internal hammer noses. The external hammers are linked to the striking hammers. They could be considered to provide the function of large cocking indicators but they also act to cock the gun manually.

Bissell's 1865 patent (No.1461) gun features external 'hammers' which have no noses, since they have no strikers with which to connect. Strikers are set into the breech face, like a conventional hammerless side-lock. They are struck by inner hammers, which fall in tandem with the outer ones. The outer hammers can be used to cock the gun or to relieve the springs when the gun has been cocked.

One might be forgiven for thinking that these early patents would become overtaken by hammerless guns. However, the idea persisted well into what we normally consider the 'hammerless era'.

Bentley's 1884 patent (No.17037) is referred to as 'semi hammerless' and differs from earlier examples in that it has genuine external hammers and the strikers are visible when the gun is closed, like a conventional hammer gun.

However, the hammers are small semi-circular vestiges of normal hammers and are set into the lock plates. They are the closest one can get to the reverse of a normal side-lock. The hammers are the same, just set on the other side of the lock plate.

Considering this was devised four years after the Beesley spring-opener made an entrance at Purdey's and nine years into Anson & Deeley's life, it appears to have been totally obsolete even on the day it was patented. Examples appear on sale with

Facing page: Grey's 1865 patent on a 12-bore by William Morre & Grey, looks like a pin-fire but activates internal centre-fire strikers. The 'hammers' act as cocking levers.

Above: Bissell's 1865 patent gun showing the hammerless-type striker arrangement and the external cocking levers.

Right: D. Bentley's 1884 patent gun has functional hammers set in on the lock-plate with the strikers set into a recess.

surprising regularity, suggesting it was quite well received. Patents for guns with internal strikers and external 'hammers' are more numerous than they should be.

As a collector, finding these oddities is an amusing pastime and they are usually very well-made and functional. I have no experience of using one for any length of time but see no reason why these guns would be anything other than reliable and pleasant to shoot with.

CONCLUSION

This concludes our analysis of the major (and some notably interesting minor) action types which progressed the breech-loader from rickety novelty to the perfection of the centre-fire hammer gun. An observation on the use of hammer guns made in the 1860s, '70s and '80s on these systems is that many have been re-proofed for nitro cartridges. The characteristics of the nitro pressure waves differ from those of the black powders for which many of these guns were designed. Nitro powders give more of a 'kick' at the breech end and burn faster. This puts more pressure on the hook and the locking mechanism than the slower burning black powders. That being so, one could again make a case for the advocacy of the Birmingham gunmakers for an extra locking bolt. Guns made with one may be less liable to shoot loose than those without. However, re-jointing guns with third bites is a trickier job and they offer no advantage unless fitted perfectly.

Gun Editor of *Shooting Times*, Gough Thomas, writing in 1963, reflected on the stresses inflicted on a double shotgun action when fired and his assertion was that the bar flexes, not simply on a horizontal plane, but also in a semi-lateral 'twist' as each barrel is fired. The fit of barrels to action face has to be tight but sufficient gap must be left between action flat and barrel flat to allow for the bar to flex. His assertion is that any third grip will naturally 'bed-in' quickly and that the gape at the breech will occur, third grip or no. They are, therefore, not materially useful in preventing a gun from shooting loose and they do not prevent the flexing of the bar upon discharge. They may be a security against the gun coming open, should the main bolting mechanism fail, but that is so unlikely as to be irrelevant.

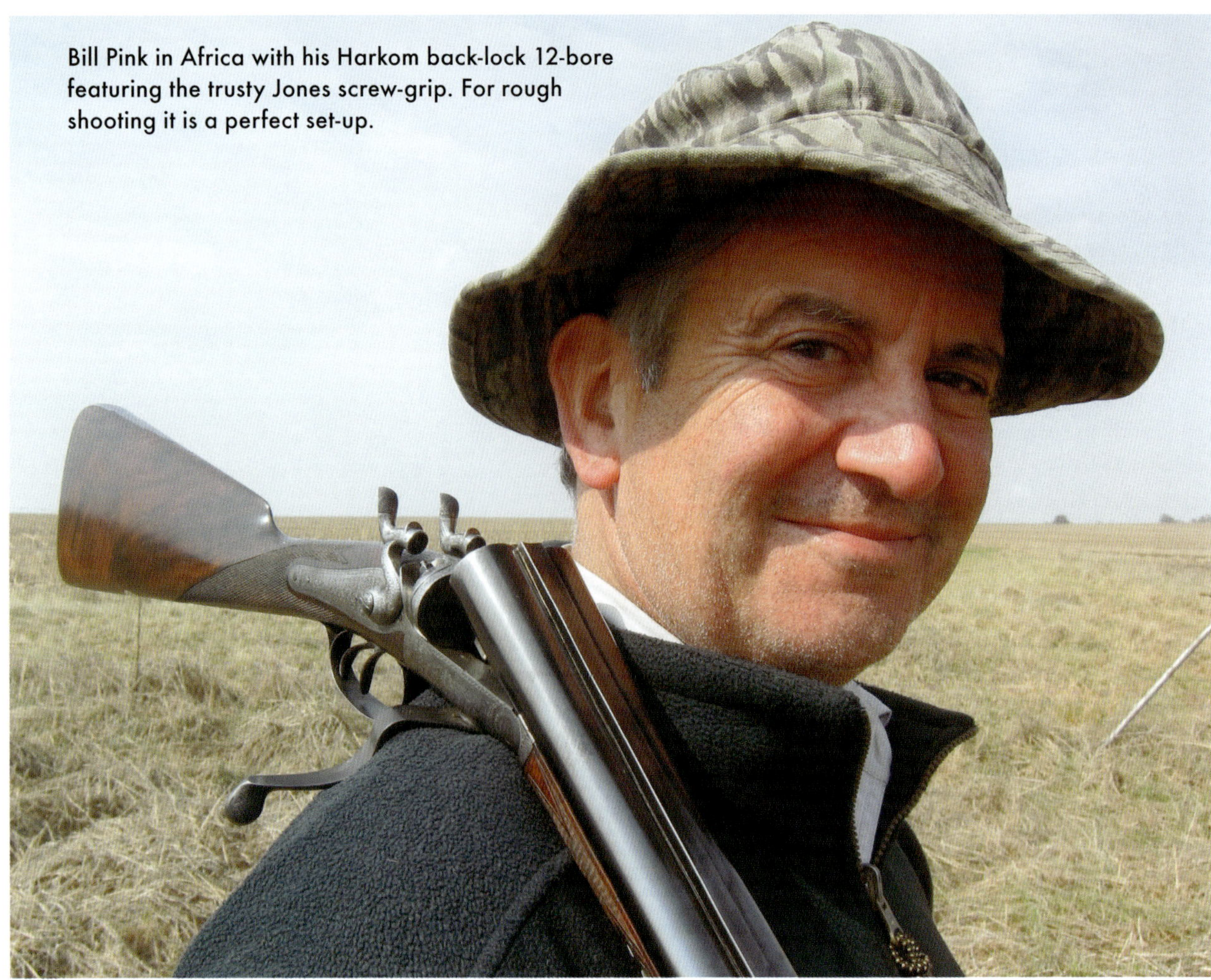

Bill Pink in Africa with his Harkom back-lock 12-bore featuring the trusty Jones screw-grip. For rough shooting it is a perfect set-up.

From early centre-fire breech loader to single trigger over & under	
Date	**Maker & Patent**
1860	Dougal Lockfast. Patent 1128 of 1860.
1862	Daw patent 1594 of 1862.
1862	Needham patent 1544 of 1862.
1863	Purdey patent 1104 of 1863 Second pattern thumbhole & double bite).
1864	Powell patent 1163 of 1864. Lift-up top lever rotating single bolt.
1865	Scott patent top-lever & spindle with Purdey bolt. Scott patent 2752 of 1865.
1866	Fred. Baker patent 1866 rotary under-lever patent 403 of 1866.
1867	Horsley patent self-retracting striker patent 1138 of 1867.
1868	Greener patent 800 of 1868, self-acting strikers.
1870	Thomas patent 324 of 1870 'solid self locking vertical grip, rotating bolt single bite.
1871	E.C. Hodges patent triple bite side-lever, patent 251 of 1871.
1872	Woodward & Emme patent triple bite action No.267 of 1872.
1873	Greener patent 'Treble Wedge Fast' No. 3084 of 1873.
1874	W.M. Scott patent quadruple lump. Patent 2052 of 1874.
1875	Anson & Deeley patent 1756 of 1875.
1876	Charles Lancaster self-cocker. Southgate & Woodward patent 600 of 1876.
1877	Tolley 'Giant Grip' Henry Tolley patent 461 of 1877.
1878	Holland & Holland 'Climax Safety Hammerless' Scott & Baker patent 761 of 1878.
1879	James MacNaughton. Lever cocking hammerless 'The Edinburgh' Gun. MacNaughton patent 2848 of 1879.
1880	Purdey / Beesley patent of 1880.
1881	W.W. Greener patent 2003 of 1881 'self acting ejector'.
1882	Dickson 16-bore three barrel gun. Dickson & Murray patent 873 of 1882.
1883	Holland & Holland 'First model' 'Royal'. Holland & Robertson patent 23 of 1883.
1884	Bonehill 'Belmont Interchangeable'. Patent 1884 'clip lump'.
1885	Jeffries patent 7895 of 1885. Hammer ejector.
1886	Henry Tolley & Co. 'The Times Gun'. Tolley patent 'slide cocking' No. 10303 of 1886.
1887	Holland & Holland Perkes patent 12176 ejectors of 1887.
1888	Boss & Co. Holland & Robertson improved ejectors, patent 16691 of 1888.
1889	W.W. Greener. Harry Greener patent 1567 of 1889 'Unique' ejector. (made 1900).
1902	Last Boss hammer gun.
1905	William Evans 16-bore. Evans & Corrie single-trigger patent 4472 of 1905.
1909	Boss over & under. J. Robertson patents 3307 & 3308 of 1909, and patent single trigger 11278 of 1905.
1935	Last Purdey hammer gun.

The Real 'Golden Age' of Gun-making

The magic era for the cataloguing of British sporting shotguns is 1929-1939. For some reason the 1930s have become known as the non plus ultra; the best decade, the 'Golden Era' in which the guns we all love were produced. A 1930s Purdey is the 'best of the best': easy to sell, highly sought-after.

However, as befits a book about hammer guns, I am about to argue that 'conventional wisdom' has got it wrong. It is the 1870s, rather than the 1930s that I have gravitated towards over the last few years and not, I would argue, without good reason.

While the wares of the 1930s gunmaker offer us sound investments and beautiful shooting companions, they are expensive and not all of us can afford them. However, I do not think we lose out by looking back another half a century for our guns. Indeed, I think we get proportionately more for our investment of time and money.

Before I slur the reputation of the greatest decade of sporting gun production, when the British trade was in its pomp in terms of workmanship and organisation and the technical sophistication of the guns was essentially modern, let us examine further why the 1930s 'Golden Age' is seen as such. In socio-economic terms it is an oddity from the very start.

The Wall Street Crash of October 1929 saw a ten-year slump in worldwide economic activity and it took World War Two to herald the end of the period of financial misery that enveloped the majority of the populations of modern industrial nations. So, what was going on that makes the 1930s the supposed acme of sporting gun production in the minds of modern collectors? Why not the far more prosperous 1920s, when more people had more money?

Comparing the decades is interesting; Purdey made 300 guns in 1928 but only 100 a year from 1931-1934, reflecting the dismal times, when many of their craftsmen were sent home due to lack of work. Holland & Holland reduced their working week to thirty hours in 1932. These were hard times for gunmakers. To be fair, not every modern commentator insists on the 1930s as the key decade. David Baker has 1900 as the central point of his book *Heyday of the Shotgun*, but the market generally perceives the 1930s as the decade from which to buy, if you can afford to.

Here are some considerations which I believe are material in comparing pre-war guns: 1920s guns were likely to get shot quite a lot. Society was busy being social between the wars and shooting parties were in full swing. All the major developments of the modern shotgun were, by then, in place: single triggers, ejectors, bar-action side-locks of conventional 'stocked to the fences' form and enough time had elapsed from the initial developments of the successful patterns of each mechanism and form for them to be perfected and established as a norm. British side-locks have not significantly altered from this norm in the subsequent eighty years. The buyer of a 1995 Purdey would have collected essentially the same gun his grandfather could have walked out of Audley House with in 1925.

In comparison, 1930s guns were often shot much less. While being as technically developed as 1920s guns, they had fewer years of use before their

Sporting opportunities at home and abroad were unlimited and demanding sportsmen needed dependable guns throughout the price range. An Indian tiger hunt like this was typical of the age.

Quality .450 and .500 BPE double hammer rifles were very popular with tiger hunters and saw long service.

owners had to put them away to fight a war. Many owners of 1930s guns never returned and many that did found the austere post-war decades too economically difficult to include much formal shooting. Country houses were being demolished at an alarming rate in the face of post-war dilapidation, dropping agricultural profits, socialist tax policies and death duties breaking-up landed estates, as well as a lack of servants to run them. In many cases, heirs to the estates were in short supply, having become wartime casualties. Empire was shrinking rapidly into Commonwealth and the old days looked to have gone forever. England was past her best and the decline of the old order, its social trappings and conventions appeared to have consigned the sport of driven shooting to the dustbin of history.

Perhaps the 'as new' condition of many 1930s guns has contributed to their modern popularity. A 1936 Purdey, Dickson or Holland & Holland with relatively few rounds through the mechanism and little chance for rough treatment ticks all the boxes for the modern buyer. It will safely last three or four more generations of fair use and, if kept in current condition, will be a safe haven for whatever funds are sunk into the purchase. Anyone looking for a modern sidelock or boxlock would do well to buy a 1930s example. It will invariably encapsulate all the modern features desired and the visual style and quality of the gun will be conventional and impressive. They certainly compare favourably with later output. Put a 1939 Churchill 'Hercules' best boxlock alongside a 1970s version of the same gun and the 1930s gun stands out in every respect.

So what is my point? Well, we have stuck ourselves with the assumption that everyone wants a best London top-lever, sidelock or boxlock ejector. Maybe they do. I don't. I have had them and loved them and shot everything with them. Then I sold them. To explain why, I mentally drift back in time to unveil the work of a slower age, when men in every sizeable town in England worked at their provincial benches by gas light or sunlight and turned out unique guns by their own hand; all different, all the best the man could deliver for the price paid. A time when individuals had their own ideas about what was going to be useful, effective, admired. Specialists existed in the rabbit-warren gun quarter of Birmingham and the surrounding districts, providing components of wonderful quality and hand-made integrity.

Eighteenth and nineteenth century furniture shows the sophisticated appreciation of fine wood and the shaping, bending and finishing of it into chairs, tables and cabinets, that marked the age. These skills and this knowledge permeated through the gun trade. Quality wood was abundant. It was properly aged, selected for form and function and shaped by hand and eye to flow gracefully from the metal, and fit the shooter perfectly in a seemingly effortless balance of shape, weight and proportion.

1870 was the start of an interesting decade. We were five years away from Anson & Deeley showing the world that hammerless guns could be simple, reliable, neat and technically efficient. We were three years into the era of the rebounding lock; Stanton and others having shown the way to dispense with the old need to pull the hammers back manually to release the pressure on the strikers.

Breech-loading was technically in its seventeenth year in Britain (taking the Great Exhibition of 1851 as the introductory date) but had only really been accepted as superior since around 1856. Centre-fire was nine years old, Daw having patented his idea in 1861, but the previous decade had seen pin-fires still very much in demand and competing for space with centre-fire guns (and muzzle-loaders) in the order books, because conservative sportsmen were unsure if the new system would prevail.

Breech-loaders, of course, were, by 1870, the modern norm for the twenty-year-old sportsman contemplating a new gun on reaching his majority, their having been in circulation for eighteen years of his two decades on earth. The Jones under-lever had been reliably screwing actions to barrels for eleven years and sporting guns had become much faster to operate than users of muzzle-loaders could have imagined a quarter of a century earlier.

The craftsmen who built the beautifully perfected muzzle-loaders of the 1850s were still at the bench and applying their skills to blend the handling characteristics of their old masterpieces into the new-style guns. To see the evidence of this, pick up a late muzzle-loader and feel the perfect symmetry it shows and the natural way it mounts and swings. Richard Arnold in *The Shooters Handbook* asserts that nothing modern compares favourably with the old

The author's 1875 Thorn, still in use on driven grouse in 2014.

Internally, the lock work on guns of this vintage shows hidden quality that is breathtaking when revealed after over a century.

muzzle-loaders and he is not wrong. However, breech-loaders are what we require today, so let us move on and consider a late 1860s or early 1870s hammer gun. It will very likely resemble the muzzle-loader in shape, proportion and handling.

Shotguns in 1870 could do everything we need them to do. Shotguns from that decade still do. What is more, they have character. Character matters. At least, it matters to me. Now, of course, in 1870 we did not have a homogenous level of output countrywide. Guns took time to build and many delivered in the early 1870s were built on 1860s patents and mechanisms. We have to remember that lots of patents were being registered every year but adoption of them was not instant, as it is in these days of key-pad communication. It took time. This makes it an interesting decade to consider, as guns made then can be typical of their time, behind the times or anticipating trends that would later dominate.

1870s guns are individual, many are one-offs. Each one has a character. The collector of 1870s guns also has more to choose from because there was never a time when more makers were making centre-fire guns themselves, rather than ordering off-the-shelf guns from Birmingham with their own names added to locks and barrels. An 1870 Pape is distinctively a Pape, a 1900 Pape is largely a product of Birmingham, built on the generic Rodgers' action, or the Anson & Deeley, and indistinguishable from an Army & Navy or William Evans gun of the same period and grade.

1865 saw the combination of the Purdey double under-bolt with the Scott spindle and top-lever. By 1880 this was in general use across the trade. Greener lever work was a variation used on all Greener guns and adopted by the trade for cheaper guns due to its ease of manufacture, being set behind the action body rather than drilled through it. Westley Richards persevered with their own bolted lever-work, again a variant, more complex and less efficient ergonomically than Scott's spindle but something of a trademark.

Less popular operating systems, like the Thomas patent top-lever bolting system and the Jones under-lever, work surprisingly well. The former is theoretically weaker than conventional bolting and the latter is slower, being inert. Does one need to worry about it? Not in my opinion.

The 1870s production model for most makers, most of the time, was the hammer gun. Bar-action, back-action and wood-bar models vied for favour. Top-levers, side-levers and under-levers were options and weight, proportion and balance were established. Damascus tubes from English suppliers and from Belgium were available and quality was high. Gunmakers were established as tradesmen and apprenticeships were the major

In the early 1870s Jones screw-grip back-action guns with rebounding locks were very popular, like this Grant.

A Thomas patent gun by F.T. Baker. Many actions were in use, as the best remained under patent protection.

form of entry. Once trained and productive, the norm was for a gunmaker to continue working at the bench for the rest of his life.

Labour was cheap, time was available and standards were high. No monumental political or international events interfered with production, supply of materials or workforce and demand for guns was good throughout the trade. Business was booming. Birmingham had become rich on the supply of weapons to both sides in what my southern friends call the American War of Northern Aggression and The Empire continued to supply orders for sporting guns of all types.

So, what is the archetype of the British sporting gun in the 1870s? Form will vary from maker to maker but hammers will generally be higher and more elaborate than later guns. Hammer shapes in the 1880s became more generic and less ornate, as components were supplied from Birmingham to set types, individual variations becoming minor. Hammer noses will be more elaborate. Many retain the recessed nose shape from percussion cap days, designed to prevent copper splinters reaching the eyes of the sportsman. Some will have fluted or squared off noses, others are dolphin shaped or serpentine.

Fences also often retain the beautifully carved and recessed striker borders, sometimes known as shell fences, again a hangover from percussion detonation (hence the term 'detonating' used by some firms to describe fences to this day). When one examines the quality, symmetry and flawless nature of this filing and finishing and the crude tools used to perform the work, it is hard not to admire and wonder at the time and skill involved in producing such shapes. Modern sidelocks by comparison look somewhat bland and straightforward, at least to me.

These were pre-choke days; remember choke was patented in England in 1866 by W.R. Pape and did not gain wide acceptance until after W.W. Greener proved its effectiveness in the 1875 trials hosted by J.H. Walsh and his influential magazine, *The Field*. Barrels were bored by experience rather than science. Barrel makers and borers applied their art to good effect at the pattern plate to produce guns throwing extraordinarily even patters of a chosen load at a given distance, despite the handicap of rolled-turnover cartridges. It was a time consuming and skilled business. I like to check the undersides of the tubes on any guns I take in, to find the small stamped impression of the barrel maker which indicates the man responsible with two discreet initials.

Many of these men today are forgotten but those initials stand testament to their work and their contribution as strongly as they did on the day they were struck. Ribs of damascus steel were soldered with flux and tin to the tubes and struck-up flawlessly. I use the rib as a clear indication of original quality when assessing a gun. The best are without deviation, with straight sides and sharp and unblemished smoothness on the surfaces. Gutters are invisibly seamed and the rib blends into the tube faultlessly all along the join.

Engraving on guns of this period is most unlike that favoured today. Small rose and scroll had not yet become firmly established as the norm and high quality guns with minimal border and large scroll engraving vied with others of full coverage scrolls for favour. Clearly some still appreciated the seamless fit

Pheasants were still shot walked-up but the fashion for driven shooting influenced designers to build faster-loading guns.

of metal-to-metal and wood-to-metal and did not need elaborate engraving to add further embellishment. The quality was already clearly apparent to the discerning eye. It still is. Interestingly, game and dog scenes were already emerging on gun locks and they range from the crude, to the comic, to the characterful.

Percussion-type fences remained popular during this period. They are often beautifully filed-up.

From a collecting point of view, the 1868-1880 period offers far more than other periods because each maker produced distinctive breech-loading guns on his own premises and the styles are as recognisable as they are varied. Thomas Horsley of York is a good example of this distinctive style. By 1900 his guns had become generic Webley-produced boxlocks and sidelocks. In the 1870s his hammer guns carried his own stylistic preferences as well as his own patents: high hammers with spurs to activate the self-retracting strikers and his famous sliding top-lever activating the locking bolt, all beautifully shaped and moulded to the distinctively contoured and finished stocks.

Collecting is one consideration and appreciation of workmanship and acknowledgement of design and development is an interesting part of the process. However, these are guns and they are made to be shot. Most of my clients and friends love their guns from both the artistic and aesthetic angles but they also love shooting and want their guns to be up to the job.

I always maintain that a pretty gun is just an object. A pretty gun that shoots beautifully is a treasure to be cherished. The 1870s sportsman was no fool. He understood his guns, had probably shot all his life and knew what he wanted. The 1870s gunsmith had the pedigree to supply just such a thing.

I do not believe fine guns should be left on the wall or locked away to be brought out for admiration from time to time.

On a recent trip to South Africa to shoot spurfowl, geese and guineas I packed my 1870 J. Thompson 12-bore. I am no clay shooter but while there, I managed to win a clay shooting competition against the locals on their own sporting layout. They laughed when I un-slipped the old girl but they weren't laughing when we added up the totals.

What are the practical disadvantages of using a Jones under-lever hammer gun against modern equivalents? I believe there are none. In South Africa we rose at dawn to head out for the long grass. Bird-dog handler Andre du Toit and his German short-haired pointers did a fantastic job of flushing the Swenson's spur fowl, francolin and guinea fowl. The Thompson swung straight, easy and true and down came the birds. An ounce of number 7 and ranges from 20 yards to fifty yards saw birds in the bag almost every time. The even patterns from the improved cylinder muzzles even bagged 21 ducks and geese for 28 shots at one evening flight.

On doves over the sunflower fields, I shot between 90–350 birds a day with a strike rate of close to 85 percent despite the strong winds and fast, wily late

The author's Thompson 12-bore on active service in Africa. The simplicity of the Jones action and lack of ejectors makes it a reliable travelling companion despite its age.

season birds. The gun mounts and swings much faster than my peers' Brownings and I got off my shots with speed and composure regardless of angle and approach. On the day, I had the best tool for the job and dove after dove crashed into the stubble to prove it. True, the inert under-lever action is a little slower to load, not helped by the lack of ejectors but this was no real disadvantage.

On a practical note, 1870s hammer guns need careful appraisal to ensure they are fit for use today. As with all guns, original quality and current condition are the key factors to start your evaluation with. These will be crucial factors in assessing the price to pay. You will pay extra for a well-known name but will not suffer a loss of quality by choosing wisely from less renowned ones. Some of the very finest hammer guns and boxlocks I have seen bear the names of lesser known gunmakers like Thomas Jackson, Thomas Horsley, Frederick Baker, William Ford, W. Thorn, Wilkinson and W.S. Riley.

The reason some of these firms are largely unappreciated today is that they operated for the lifetime of the founder, or perhaps that of his son as well, then, like many businesses, were sold and vanished. We know mostly about the gun-making dynasties like Greener, Purdey, Holland & Holland and firms like Stephen Grant and Henry Atkin or E.J. Churchill, who are still making guns today. I especially like finding exceptional guns by unheralded makers from my favourite period. They can be brilliant value as you are paying nothing for the name, just for the quality and condition.

Once quality is established, it is important to also establish the proof status of the gun. Many guns of the period will have been proofed for black powder only. Measure the bores to match the numbers with the original dimensions stamped on the flats. If they measure within ten thousandths of an inch of these, they are within proof. Next get some chamber gauges inserted and see if they have been elongated as this will render them out of proof unless they have subsequently been re-proofed. I recently bought a neglected old H. Holland hammer gun for £100 to restore and was unsurprised to note the chambers were now 2¾" but the proof marks only for 2½". The gun was therefore illegal to sell until it had been submitted for nitro proof for 70mm chambers, which it now has.

Wall thickness is important, as it will tell you the amount of life left in the gun; not because you are going to shoot the walls thinner (you won't) but because you have less scope for future removal of dents or for lapping out rust.

It would be too obvious to point out that it is better not to dent your barrels or let them go rusty but I have done so now! Damascus barrels could be very thick when originally made. The Baker gun described above arrived with a minimum wall thickness of 50 thou' but they will continue to perform faultlessly even when reduced to the high teens in the last third. Don't pay too much for a thin walled gun but don't be afraid of it either; it could be your way to shooting a classy gun without paying more than you can afford.

Most guns will have undergone some lapping and it is useful to establish where they are thinnest and if the thin spots are going to be a practical issue or just one affecting retail value. At a recent auction, I measured the barrels of two hammer guns on sale to find they were down to 13 thou', despite having recent proof marks. Remember that proof does not include any consideration of wall thickness. Generally speaking, clean barrels thin in the last third will still give good service and can be bought relatively cheaply; but 13 thou' is pushing it a bit far, to say the least.

Black powder express rifles of the period are perhaps the finest guns ever built.

Look for pits and pay special attention to those facing the rib, between seven o'clock and 11 o'clock as you look down from the breech end, as this is a section of wall that cannot be measured. Check that the barrels ring true and the ribs and loop are sound. Finally, don't forget to look into the chamber walls for pitting while you are about it.

If the gun has been re-proofed, check for any changes from original; many will have had chambers extended and bear re-proof marks for longer shells and nitro powders. This makes them more practical, especially when travelling to countries where ammunition availability may be limited.

Don't be afraid of the exotic or unusual. I find these features a particular delight and shooting in company is always fun if your gun is very different in appearance. Self-retracting strikers, grip safety bars on the bottom strap, loaded indicators, lift-up top-levers; all these features are examples of the struggle for perfection being fought by really inventive and creative gunmakers at the height of their powers. Many of the guns were made from paper drawings or from none at all, many are unique and a surprising number of them function and handle as beautifully as any gun you are likely to pick up.

Personally, I like the 1870s hammer guns much better than the hammerless designs which then abounded, in often experimental form, but many of which never saw widespread acceptance.

These clumsy hammerless guns, which followed on from Murcott's 1871 'Mousetrap' make it easy to understand why many sportsmen hung on to the elegant hammer guns, which traced their blood lines through 200 years of percussion gun to have reached their zenith by 1875. At this time, hammerless guns were spotty teenagers by comparison, yet to grow into their looks and shed their puppy fat.

However, as a collector, the era offers some very interesting and unusual guns, which can be bought for relatively little money due to their unlovely appearance. Look closer though: some odd looking hammerless guns can be beautifully made and exhibit gun making skills of the very highest order. Many will have been made in tiny numbers and some will be unique.

This can be a fascinating area to base a collection around, as the closer you look into bizarre designs, the more interesting and attractive they become and the more pleasure you can get from shooting with them, especially as you begin to uncover their history.

Theophilus Murcott's 'Mousetrap' patent gun of 1871.

A Murcott hammer pigeon gun of a similar age.

Bar-action or Back-action?

Breech-loading hammer guns will present themselves to the shooter or collector in one of two basic forms. They will be of either the bar-action lock or the back-action lock variety. The difference can be established by a quick examination of the gun's external form.

The bar-lock has the spring in front of the hammer.

The recess for fitting the bar-lock into the stock and action.

The lock plate on the bar-action gun has a forward facing limb, which engages with a corresponding cut-out in the metal of the bar of the action. The back-action gun's lock plate butts up against the action but the plate itself extends back towards the hand.

Removing the lock and examining the inside, one can see the main-spring location in either lock is indicative of the name. In the bar-lock, the spring is located forward of the hammer, in the bar of the action. In the back-lock, the spring is located behind the hammer, in the pointed end of the lock plate.

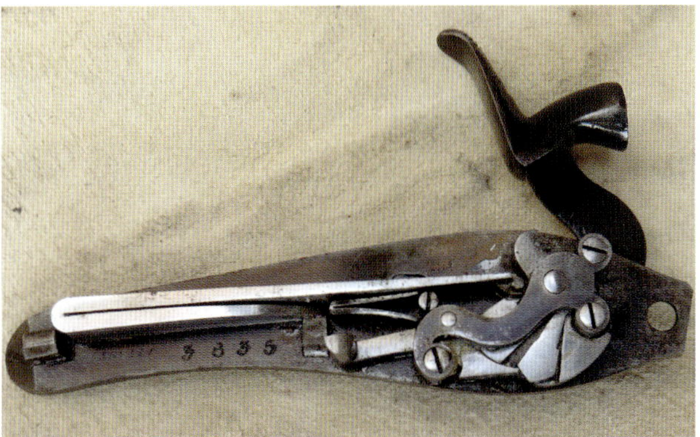

The back-action mainspring sits behind the hammer, along the elongated lock plate.

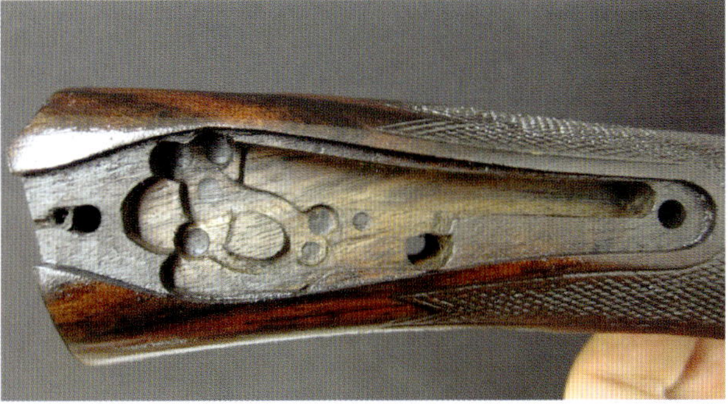

A back-lock removed to show the recess required to house it in the head of the stock.
The action remains solid.

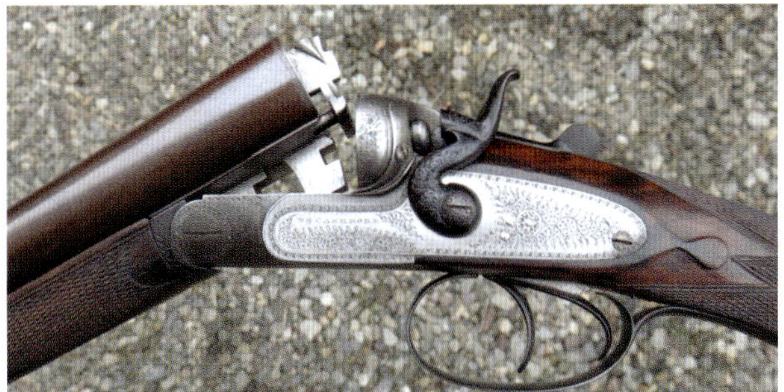

This Cashmore lock is shaped like a bar-lock but is a back-lock. Note the missing pin for the mainspring in the bar section.

Most back-action locks are of the 'peninsular' type. Their foremost edge abuts the metal of the action, where it meets the head of the stock. Some makers (notably, but not exclusively Purdey) made locks which were totally encased in wood and which are known as 'island' locks.

When assessing the merits of the two main lock-types, one should consider:

- Mechanical Efficiency
- Reliability and Durability
- Handling and Shooting Characteristics
- Aesthetics

Any comparison on the points noted above must assume that the two guns under comparison are of equal quality in terms of materials and manufacture. We are not assessing grade of gun here; simply the merits of the systems employed to house the lock work.

Much has been written in times past about the merits of various gun actions. Much of what was written was theoretical, more was reflective of the times when component parts, especially ammunition, were not of the standardised high quality that we take for granted today.

In the transition from flint-lock to percussion and from percussion to breech-loader, issues carried over from one era to the next. Often, they were based on unmerited worries, which have proven in time to be practically inconsequential.

The assessment of the merits of bar-action and back-action lock choice and the guns that carry them, focus on strength and on quickness of lock time. In these days of ubiquitous coil-spring operated over/under game guns, made in Europe, these reified assessments can be dismissed as being over-sensitive.

A Purdey 'island' lock (right) and a more conventional 'peninsular' lock on a William Powell (below).

Wood-Bar actions

Pin-fire and centre-fire guns built in the 1860s and 1870s will often be found to have a veneer of wood covering the metal bar of the action, continuing under the bar as far as the knuckle. From a stocking perspective, this a difficult job, very little opportunity to correct errors exists and the thin areas of wood in some sections are prone to splitting with the grain or chipping at the edges.

Examining wood-bar guns in good, original condition shows that they are more robust than one would imagine, from the evidence of old, worn and damaged guns of this type. The quality and thickness of the wood over the bar and the expert fitting executed by men who were clearly masters of their craft proves guns of this configuration were practical as well as attractive.

Wood-bar (also known as 'bar-in-wood') guns are not uncommon and the popularity of the style and its relative longevity indicates that it was not inherently weak or damage prone. Most hammer guns from the 1880s onwards were made with a solid bar in either back-action or bar-action form, as fashions changed. Aesthetically, one can see the look of the percussion gun in the assembled wood-bar gun, the style becoming pared-down as breech-loaders developed their own conventional identities.

Early Westley Richards 'crab joint' wood-bar guns look very much of their era. Later Purdey wood-bar guns already have a more 'modern' appearance. Generally, as the years progress, the amount of wood cladding decreases. Some gunmakers continued the idea into the hammerless era, with classics like the MacNaughton 'Edinburgh' gun showing the wood-bar style could be developed into the modern age as a viable and beautiful alternative to the 'London pattern' side-lock.

Contemplating ownership of an old wood-bar gun, one should take care to inspect all the potentially weak areas for damage, thinning, oil ingress or gapping. Re-stocking a gun of this type is expensive and even very skilled modern stockers struggle to mirror the elegant shapes and proportions of the old masters, as they are rarely called upon to re-stock wood-bar guns.

This disassembled Horsley wood-bar-action shows the metalwork stripped bare, exposing the long bar and cut-outs to accommodate the wood veneer. Below: a Purdey game gun in excellent condition, showing typical bar-in-wood profile. Both guns date from 1871.

A well made bar-action or back-action hammer gun, with quality leaf springs and sharp, burnished, hard sears and bents is a much finer precision tool than those the majority of modern shooters grow up with.

The theoretical difference in lock time between bar-lock and back-lock is of no practical consequence. Well-made hammer guns of either type will withstand continuous normal use without issue. However, we can discuss the basic points of comparison and any problems that may arise as result of them.

Rather than start with the theory, let us consider what can go wrong. A breech-loader can crack at the radius (the angle between breech face and the flat of the action bar). Other commentators have thought the bar-lock gun more prone to this, citing the removal of metal in the bar of the action, extending back towards the head of the stock, to accommodate the mainspring. For a full examination of these criticisms see *Vintage Guns for the Modern Shot.*

However, consider that most bar-action hammer guns have a square bar, one which is significantly broader and often deeper than a back-action gun. Despite having a more solid appearance, the back-action is unlikely to be stronger as it is typically a smaller, rounded profile object with no more material to provide structure than a bar-action gun.

Personal experience of firing many dozens, perhaps hundreds of hammer guns, is that the felt flexing of the action when in use is more often encountered in light back-action guns than it is in bar-action guns. To put the matter simply, I find that the supposed greater bar strength of a back-lock gun is unreflective of reality when using one.

The back-action gun has been criticised for the removal of wood in the hand further back than is necessary in a bar-action gun; removing wood where the stock is the weakest. This is a fact. I see many back-action guns which have cracked around the hand pin, where it is rather short of material.

However, the cause is usually not this fact alone. It usually accompanies another defect, such as a loose breech-pin or hand-pin, mineral-oil ingress (making the wood degenerate), impact from a blow or pressure stress from someone sitting or leaning on the gun. To observe this point as the weakest point of the stock (every stock has a weakest point) is not to dismiss the design as weak, as it will stand up to decades of normal use without mishap.

Where the back-lock dispenses with a common weak point of the bar-lock is at the head of the stock. On a bar-action, the over and under 'horns' are thin, elongated and prone to cracking, the back-action has a much smaller area of metal removed to accommodate the point at which the forward part of the lock plate abuts the flat back of the action.

Aesthetic qualities are subjective. As a dealer, I have as many clients ask specifically for a back-action gun as for a bar-action gun. Some argue that the elegant taper of the back-lock makes a racier appearance, that the blending of wood and metal is more gradual and attractive. A good number of history's influential sportsmen took this view: The Marquis of Ripon's favourite Purdeys are all back-lock guns, as were the Stephen Grants built (in 1871) as a birthday and Christmas present for the then-Prince of Wales, by his mother, Queen Victoria.

My own preference is a bar-action. I prefer the weight in the action it provides, I like the rigid feel and lack of flex or vibration in a good one and I use them more than any other type of gun these days. I do not advocate the bar-lock type as superior, I just prefer it. The reader will make up his own mind, secure in the knowledge that both alternatives are time-proven and long lived, if cared for.

Bland 4-bore back-lock and a Tolley 4-bore bar-lock.

Three styles of gun in simultaneous production: a bar-lock with wood-bar, a back-lock with solid bar and a bar-lock with solid bar. There is no 'best' option; selection is a matter of personal preference, now as it was in the 1870s.

Non-rebounding and Rebounding Locks

Hammer locks of the breech-loading era had roots firmly in the earlier era of the muzzle-loader. When fired, the hammer of the muzzle-loader came to rest firmly on the nipple with its, now spent, copper cap compressed between the two. When pin-fire followed, the pin-fire hammers came to rest on top of the barrels, where the pins protruded prior to firing. When centre-fire guns first saw commercial success, they, like the previous systems, left the fallen hammer resting where it lay; on the striker, in their case. However, this was an obstacle to rapid loading.

The reason it was an impediment is that the hammer nose, resting hard on the striker, jammed the gun shut. The gun could not be opened easily until the hammer was pulled back, allowing the downward movement of the barrels to then break the link between striker and cartridge primer.

Early hammer guns can still be found with these non-rebounding locks. They are slower to load and fire than later guns, as they require more operations to be performed in the process. After Stanton's patent 367 of 1867, which caused the hammer to rise off the striker after firing and come to rest a little above it, the majority of sportsmen preferred the new locks and ordered them in preference, though The Marquis of Ripon obstinately continued to have his trios of Purdey hammer guns built with non-rebounding locks. He shot with two loaders and had his guns handed to him at full cock. He was the exception!

The non-rebounding system invented by Stanton in 1867 dispenses with the need to pull hammers to 'half-cock'. Greener described the new locks to his readers in 1871 thus:

> *It is accomplished by lengthening the top part of the mainspring and extending it towards the tumbler; the crank of the tumbler is lengthened beyond the swivel and projects over the top part of the mainspring. At half cock the crank of the tumbler rests upon the top part of the mainspring and keeps the hammers from coming into contact with the strikers. This arrangement makes the locks partly self acting; the hammers only require to be raised from half cock to full cock.*

Because the falling hammer has to slightly compress the top part of the mainspring before it can strike the strikers, it does not deliver quite the same strength of blow a non-rebound lock of the same power would. This being the case, some rebound locks were made with stronger springs to compensate. Greener felt the first non-rebound locks not satisfactory with much of the then available ammunition. As the quality of ammunition improved, these concerns died away. Another objection was the escape of gas back through the cap, because the strikers were not held tight to keep it from so doing. Again, better quality ammunition resolved the issue and today modern users of hammer guns can ignore Greener's objections, which may have had some validity at the time of writing.

A non-rebounding bar-lock, best quality.

A rebounding bar-lock, medium quality.

INTERNAL VIEWS OF NON-REBOUND, CONVERTED AND REBOUND LOCKS

Many hammer guns were converted from non-rebound to rebound locks and by the mid-1870s most were made with the later system in preference to the older one. Many modern hammer gun shooters shy away from non-rebounding lock guns but with a little practice they can be operated almost as fast as rebounding ones. You can often buy a non-rebounding lock gun for a significant discount; if you can, I would go ahead. The little extra practice needed to become familiar with them is rewarding and the quality of these early-to-mid 1870s hammer guns can be stunning. I use one for shooting driven grouse.

A non-rebound bar-lock from a Thomas Horsley.

The Horsley 'at cock', exterior view.

An Adams converted to rebound from non-rebound.

The Robert Adams, external view, 'at cock'.

A rebounding bar-lock by John Squires.

The Squires lock 'at cock'.

Well-made locks continue to work for decades. This bar-action gun had not been stripped for a century or more. Once the old dirt and grease were cleaned off, the locks shone like new.

The Classic Lock-makers of the Era

Wolverhampton, then on the outskirts of Birmingham, became established in the 1700s as a well-known centre of gun lock manufacturing. Since the Industrial Revolution, the town had been a centre for artisans working in metal, as the ore, limestone and coal necessary were in abundance and Birmingham's close proximity provided demand for all manner of such goods. The established firms responsible for nineteenth century gun locks bear long-standing family names from the Wolverhampton area.

The lock was always a specialist part of a firearm. In 1820, a best London flintlock cost £45, the cost of the locks was about 10% that of the gun. These locks were produced predominantly by small firms of artisans. As the nineteenth century progressed, this system began to make way for larger firms, incorporating specialists in each detail of lock making.

A lock making firm may have employed men as forgers, filers, makers of pins, and spring makers. While the larger factories operated an 'in-house' system, smaller 'outworker' businesses continued to supply work on contract basis. A lock-maker typically apprenticed for the full term of seven years, graduating at age twenty-one. By the centre-fire breech-loader era, lock making had become a mature and polished manufacturing process, using modern machinery, quality materials and highly skilled workforces. Demand was high and business thriving in the middle years of Victoria's reign. However, decline set in during the early twentieth century as other industries, such as bicycle or motor vehicle manufacture offered more opportunities to the lock-makers.

The heyday of lock making was certainly represented by Victorian Wolverhampton. Stripping a gun of quality from the era, even a filthy one, which may not have been apart for a hundred and fifty years, reveals burnished bright limbs, perfect angles and an inner beauty that continues to perform faultlessly, a true testament to the skills of the men whose work was never seen by the public but carried out to breathtaking quality control standards and functional perfection.

An 1867 lock, from a Purdey. This is a very early rebounding lock, bearing 'Stanton's Patent'.

'Ashes' was Brazier's works. The name stamp is just visible alongside the mainspring.

The lock plate from this Horsley 12-bore bears the maker's name, 'A. Gardner', stamped on the inside of the bar.

Developments in lock-making, as in other areas of gun manufacture, were subject to patents, infringements and business rivalries. A case in point is John Stanton's legal notice printed in the newspapers in 1867, when un-licensed use of his patent rebounding lock was clearly causing annoyance:

> *It having come to the knowledge of the Patentee that certain persons are making and vending John Stanton's "Patent Improved Self-acting Half-cock Safety Gun-lock" without his license or authority, and thereby infringing his patent, Notice is hereby given that all such persons will be proceeded against for such infringement.*
>
> *Purchasers of Gun-locks are hereby cautioned not to buy any Gun-lock made upon John Stanton's patented principle unless the same bears his name. Any persons vending such locks not so marked after this notice will be held responsible, and be proceeded against accordingly.*

Most gun-lock makers were small firms employing just one or two craftsmen. In the larger firms, the 'master' would employ tradesmen, often with specialisation in particular areas of manufacture, like forging, filing, pin-making and spring-making. In the 19th century, there were dozens of tiny workshops in the 'Black Country' inhabited by skilled men working with forging hearths, foot-treadle lathes, chisels and files, most specialist equipment like jigs and dies were made in-house. They contributed the precision working movements of the guns that would later be presented to wealthy sportsmen by famous London, Birmingham or provincial firms.

Names like Brazier, Chilton and Stanton are well known to enthusiasts today but the gunlocks we use today, still functioning perfectly after a century and a half, often neglected and lacking even routine maintenance, were made by the anonymous hands of hundreds of small family firms, journeymen being paid a day-rate for their work and delivering quality that rivals the finest work of the best watch makers of their time. Victorian gun locks are true marvels to behold.

Factories and Artisans

WHO REALLY MADE THIS GUN?

The hammer breech-loading era was one in which the production of sporting guns increased and in which the number of new patents and development created a demand for the latest invention of one gunmaker or another. At this time, many of the new inventions were protected by patent or were so new that few gunmakers were willing or felt able to produce them faithfully.

In such cases, a gunmaker who had a customer for a particular patent action or a gun with features just developed by a larger gunmaker, would order a gun from that maker but request his own name be placed on the locks and rib. This is the reason we encounter guns that very much look like classic examples of one maker's work yet cary another name and address.

The surviving records of some of the larger and longer established firms confirm that this practice was not uncommon. The example opposite illustrates the relationship between maker and retailer nicely.

It is evident from the photographs that the gun

List No. 2 61st Edition

THIS EDITION CANCELS ALL PREVIOUS ISSUES.
1934-1935 Prices.

Catalogue of
SPORTING GUNS, etc.

DEMON

List of CARTRIDGES—On application.
" FISHING TACKLE "

RIFLES
REVOLVERS
IMPLEMENTS

ESTABLISHED 1878.
Bankers: Midland Bank Ltd., Temple Row, Birmingham, Eng.

MIDLAND GUN COMPANY
GUN MAKERS, BATH STREET, BIRMINGHAM(4) ENGLAND
THE SPORTSMAN'S PROVIDER

TELEPHONE: No. 1254 CENTRAL.
TELEGRAMS: "RIFLES, BIRMINGHAM."

CODES: A.B.C. 5th Edition BENTLEYS.

INDEX TO CATALOGUE

	Page.
Adaptor	29
Adjustable Try Gun	13
Aiming Device	57
Air Guns	41, 44, 45, 47
Air Gun Slugs	47
Air Pistols	40
Alarm Guns	58
Aperture Sights	36, 37, 56
Automatic Pistols all bores	42, 43
Automatic Rifles	38, 39
Barrel Preservers	53
Barrel Stoppers	Cover 3
Bell Target	47
Bird Throwers, Hand and Spring	62
Blank Pistols	55
Bolto	58
B.S.A. Repeating Rifle	36
B.S.A. Target and Sporting Rifles	36, 37
Cartridges, etc. (See Special List)	37, 41, 42, 59
Cartridge Bags & Belts	53
Cartridge Magazines	53
Catapults	58
Cattle Killers	59
Clay Bird Guns	15
Clay Bird Traps	62
Clay Pigeons	62
Cleaning Brushes	56
Cleaning Patches	56
Cleaning Outfits	54
Collector's Guns, Single	31, 32
Cordite Rifles	34
Decoy Calls	58
Decoy Ducks	58
Decoy Pigeons	58
Demon Hammerless Gun in Case	11
Double Barrel Guns	1-24, 33
Ejector Guns	10-24
Featherweight Guns	12, 18, 24
Ferreting Tackle	60
Finger Protector	54
Folding Guns, Single and Double	31, 32
Fuse for Rabbits	60
Game Bags	53
Game Carriers	57
Garden Guns	31, 32
Gun Cases	52, 53
Gun Covers	52
Gun Parts	63, 64
Gun Stocks	46
Hand Guards	60
Hammer Guns	8-10, 27, 33
Hammerless Guns	1, 10-24, 27
Implements	50, 51
Knives	48, 60
Knockabout Guns	28, 29, 33

INDEX TO CATALOGUE

	Page
Knuckle Dusters	54
Ladies' and Youth's Guns	27
Life Preservers	60
Mars Oil for Boots	49
Martini .22 bore Rifles	37
Martini Shotguns	35
Measurement Directions	13
Miscellaneous Tools	51
Monograms, etc.	Cover 3
Muzzle Loading Guns	30
Nets	60
Oil, Cleaning	49
Optical Sight	54
Percussion Caps	30
Pigeon Guns, Single	25
Pistols, Automatic	42, 43
Pistol Cartridges	42
Pistols, Smooth Bore	41
Pistols, Starting	55
Proof Marks	Cover 2
Pull-throughs	50, 51
Rabbiting Fuse	60
Rabbit Nets	60
Rabbit Snare Wire	60
Recoil Pads	15, 48
Releasall	62
Repeating Rifles	36-40
Re-rifling	48
Rifles, 22 Bore	36-40
Rifles, Cordite, Double	34
Rifles, Mauser Pattern	35
Second-hand Guns	Cover 3
Shot Sizes	Cover 2
Sights	17, 36, 37, 54-57
Sights (Double)	57
Silencers	40
Single Barrel Guns	25-33
Single Trigger Mechanism	24
Small Bore Rifles	36-40
Snap Caps	58
Sporting Guns	1-33
Swivels	5
Sword Sticks	59
Targets (Air Rifle)	47, 57
Targets, Card	47
Tow	49
Traps of all descriptions	61
Try Gun	13
Walking Stick Guns	41
Wire, Snaring	60

Copyright—Midland Gun Co.

PRINTED IN ENGLAND.

is a William Powell. The fence shape, the lock style and the patent lever work all look 'classic Powell' of the era. Speculation is often heard as to how much work was undertaken by the named gunmaker and how much was done by the provider of the donor action. Factory catalogues show clearly that all the major and minor components for manufacture were readily available from the trade and this enabled provincial and small scale makers to construct their guns, either from rough parts, barrelled actions or guns 'in the white'.

For example, big-bore specialist builders like J&W Tolley would have provided a number of makers with barrelled actions of 4-bore and 8-bore double guns; the retailer would then have these filed and engraved and stocked and finished in their own workshops in the relevant 'house style' before selling the guns as their own.

However, it is evident that many retailers simply took advantage of the production capacity and expertise of the larger makers and had orders filled in the manner that W. Richards did through his relationship with William Powell. This particularly applies to the 1860s, 1870s and early 1880s. Guns from this period can often be recognised as the house style of a particular maker – with a Westley Richards bolted top-lever, or a Hodges patent side-lever snap action, or some other feature that indicates its origins may not be the address on the gun itself.

Edwin Hodges provides a useful study with regard to the matter of third parties involved in the gun making process, other than the 'gunmaker' and the client. Hodges was an action filer by trade. It is widely held that he was the gunmaker responsible for inducing Joseph Lang to build modified Lefaucheux-type guns,

Above: W. Richards 12-bore wood-bar gun made by William Powell, using Powell's patent lift-up lever.

Left: Midland Gun Co. made and sold guns under their own name as well as providing guns to the trade.

An 1866 patent Stephen Grant 12-bore by E.C. Hodges. He made these for several London firms, like Alfred Lancaster but is best known for his work for Grant.

following the Great Exhibition of 1851, which culminated in the Lang forward facing undercover guns of 1856.

As a builder of guns to the trade, Hodges was (along with Thomas Perkes and John Robertson) among the leading men of his day in London. Thomas Boss had Hodges make his first breech-loader in 1858. Hodges had new premises built in Islington, north London, in 1860 and from there he serviced the better quality London gunmakers of the era, until closing down in 1909.

Hodges actioned guns for Henry Atkin, Purdey, Boss, Lang, Alfred Lancaster and certainly others for whom records are no longer accessible, like Henry Egg. He is best known perhaps for his 1866 and 1871 patent hammer guns which are seen today as the classic Stephen Grant side-lever and under-lever guns of the mid 19th century. Occasionally a gun bearing Hodges' own name appears but the vast majority of his work bears the names of better-known gunmakers, who take the credit today, just as they did then. With a bit of experience, one can begin to identify a Hodges actioned hammer gun, regardless of the maker's name in the scroll banner.

Hodges guns share some identifiable features, such as cylindrical lever bosses and the location of the lever-securing pin head for the Jones lever being located

Hodges' trademark tower can be found on the flats, also note the screw retaining the Jones grip is on the bar flats, not the underside of the bar.

on the bar flats rather than the underside, also his guns often had cut-out sections in the bar flats beside the front lump and a circular section to the slot closest to the face. These are all stylistic tell-tales of Hodges' work, which were pointed out to me by Stephen Grist, formerly with John Wilkes of London.

The gun trade has always been one in which those whom Marx called the 'owners of the means of production' took the credit and the workers who made the guns remained in the shadows. Wilkinson made guns for Pape, Thomas Perkes made them for William Evans, William Baker made them for Charles Lancaster and Westley Richards made them for W. Richards of Preston, Williams & Powell and probably others. John Emme, of Soho, made guns for Alfred Lancaster and others. Gunmaker Ian Crudgington drew my attention to Samuel Mills, a Weaman Street, Birmingham gunmaker who, he said, provided high quality hammer guns to provincial and London firms, like F.T. Baker and Charles Boswell. They often feature coil spring top-levers and many of his actions are signed with a stamp on the back.

Sometimes the origin of a gun may be indicated by a particular style, or confirmed by the 'cash books' recording who was paid for what, but more often than not the actual maker will remain a mystery, while the name on the locks and the address on the rib carry the credit but frequently tell only part of the story.

A beautifully made Stephen Grant by E.C Hodges. Cutting these shapes into the bar with such precision is phenomenally difficult.

Gunmaker John Robertson, who made guns for several London firms before taking control of Boss & Co.

Component Parts and the Role of the Trade Supplier

Some collectors and students of gun making stand accused of obsessing about matters of little consequence. It is a danger that, in the meticulous collection of reams of data, one loses perspective and the ability to filter mere fact from relevance.

Cynics are often heard to dismiss a claim of 'best' gun making by the association any firm might have with any other. This is especially the case today. They think that unless a single gunmaker made everything from scratch, in-house, the gun amounts to little more than an assembly of foreign parts.

I have always argued that the source of the material or components is, and always was, of no matter. What mattered was the quality.

This is the second earliest H. Holland gun known to exist. He would have had it built 'in the trade' to his specifications.

Harris Holland; tobacconist, live pigeon shooter and founder of one of Britain's best-known gunmakers.

The gunmaker responsible for putting his name on the finished article, had to have an eye for quality and the discipline to achieve it consistently and apply it to every aspect of the build.

The customer, then, as now, unfortunately cannot always see quality, or appreciate it. Only when the finished article works entirely as intended, looks 'right' and functions reliably for decades, can the job be said to have been finished to the satisfaction of all concerned.

Among these contentious issues we can list the making of entire guns by other firms, then badged by the selling 'gunmaker' as his own work. At the other end of the spectrum, we see guns made entirely in-house but the factory being serviced by suppliers of key component parts and materials.

This is only logical. A gunmaker cannot be expected to grow his own trees or own a steel foundry, just to service his own, relatively small, need for action forgings and wood blanks. By extension, the gunmakers of London, Birmingham and the provinces had a plethora of trades related to their special needs.

To use a prominent example, before they built a London factory of their own (in 1893) Holland & Holland had all their guns built 'in the trade' by leading Birmingham makers, like Scott, and their rook rifles by Ellis Bros. Even afterwards, many of their guns were built by others, the London factory being used exclusively to make 'Royal' hammerless guns and rifles.

Once established as a true manufacturer, however, Holland & Holland still relied on component suppliers in order to build guns at Harrow Road. That they did so, indicates that these suppliers must also have supplied other gunmakers, as none of them would have survived on a client list of one!

The table below shows who supplied what to Holland & Holland (and by extension to the wider gun trade) in the first thirty years of the twentieth century. Some of the big Birmingham factories supplied the wider trade with component parts, as well as barrelled actions, or fully finished guns. Therefore, whoever may have put their name on your Victorian hammer gun, be it a famous London firm, a Birmingham maker or a provincial one, the number of different contributors to its manufacture will be many.

Charles Osborne & Co. exemplify this well in their 1899 'Trade Catalogue', in which they list a large number of components available for smaller gunmakers to purchase. Some examples are listed in the table on page 77.

Osborne would have been supplying gunmakers all over the country with these components. A range of qualities was available, with cheaper parts being used for cheaper guns and best quality parts for best guns.

A 16-bore back-lock hammer gun made by W&C Scott for Holland & Holland in the mid 1880s. Unlike Purdey and Boss, Holland & Holland sold guns across the range from best down to third quality. Scott provided most of these guns to order, although some of the best quality guns are likely to have been made by some of the London outworkers to the trade. Once they opened their own factory, in 1893, the hammerless era was well underway and production was restriced to 'Royal' hammerless guns, although they may have finished some special order, best-quality, late hammer guns in-house.

COMPONENT SUPPLIERS TO HOLLAND & HOLLAND

BARREL TUBES	Vickers, Armstrong, English Steel, Whitworth, BSA, Webley & Scott, Butcher, Smith
MACHINING	Miles, Webley & Scott
CASTINGS (for top-levers etc)	Bartle, Clive, G. Wales & Co, S. Russell & Co
FORGINGS (for actions)	Parfrey, Waldron, Vickers, Edwin Chilton & Son, W. Bennett
STAMPINGS (for trigger guards, etc)	Carpenter & Son, Edwin Chilton & Son, G.N. Green
GOLD	Westwood Ltd
SILVER OVALS	Westwood Ltd
COIL SPRINGS	Salter, Edwin Chilton & Son, Terry & Son, Dart & Co
TOP-LEVER SPRINGS	J. Brazier, Salter, S.B. Mansfield, J. Stanton & Son
EJECTOR & MAINSPRINGS	J. Brazier, F. Chilton & Son, J. Stanton & Son
PINS & SCREWS	Clackett, Webley & Scott
STRIKERS & NIPPLES	Clackett
LOCKS	J. Brazier, W. Baker
LUMPS AND LOOPS	Waldron
RIBS	Woodcock, W. Trueman & Son
FURNITURE	J. Hemming & Son, W. Bennett
HEEL PLATES	F.C. Scott, Tranter Bros

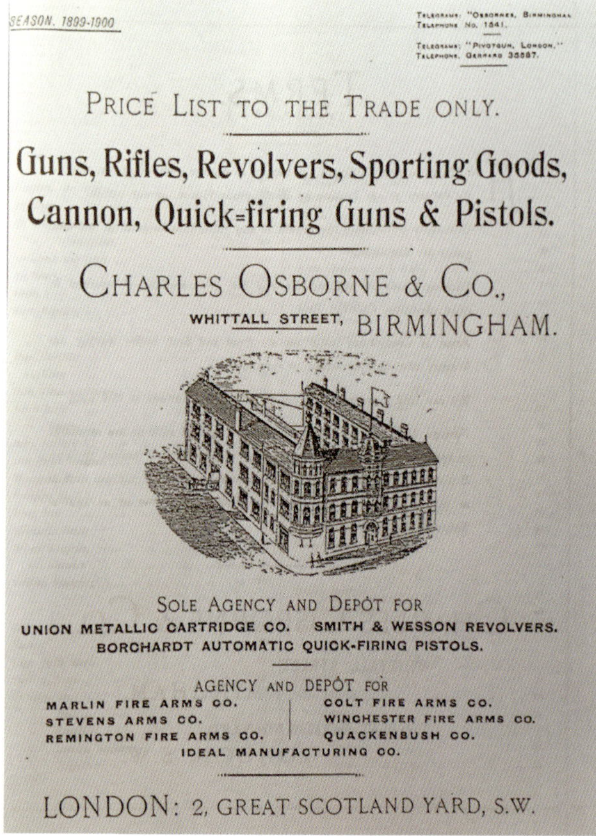

SEASON. 1899-1900

Telegrams: "Osbornes, Birmingham."
Telephone No. 1541.

Telegrams: "Pivotgun, London."
Telephone, Gerrard 35597.

PRICE LIST TO THE TRADE ONLY.

Guns, Rifles, Revolvers, Sporting Goods,
Cannon, Quick-firing Guns & Pistols.

CHARLES OSBORNE & CO.,
WHITTALL STREET, BIRMINGHAM.

SOLE AGENCY AND DEPÔT FOR
UNION METALLIC CARTRIDGE CO. SMITH & WESSON REVOLVERS.
BORCHARDT AUTOMATIC QUICK-FIRING PISTOLS.

AGENCY AND DEPÔT FOR
MARLIN FIRE ARMS CO. | COLT FIRE ARMS CO.
STEVENS ARMS CO. | WINCHESTER FIRE ARMS CO.
REMINGTON FIRE ARMS CO. | QUACKENBUSH CO.
IDEAL MANUFACTURING CO.

LONDON: 2, GREAT SCOTLAND YARD, S.W.

It was common for provincial and London gunmakers to buy part-made guns, as described by the Birmingham firm Bentley & Playfair: *'Actions and barrels with snap forend, rebounding locks and furniture complete'* in their 1911 trade catalogue. Amongst others, Bentley & Playfair provided finished and part-finished guns to Rigby in London and Armstrong in Newcastle.

They also list *'Double grip, lever over guard action, barrels, locks, furniture and snap forend complete'.* A gun delivered like this, 'in the white' and un-stocked would cost the buyer £3/10s/0d for the lowest quality and £19/5s/0d for the best. Bar-action or back-action styles were available at the same cost. Bore sizes available were 12, 14, 16, 20, 24 and 28.

Charles Osborne's trade catalogue (left) and a Pape 12-bore that probably started life in Osborne's factory. Big Birmingham factories supplied smaller makers with complete guns, gunsmiths with component parts and forgings, and other firms with barrelled actions for stocking and finishing. They sold a huge range of guns and components and catered to a full range of quality and price points.

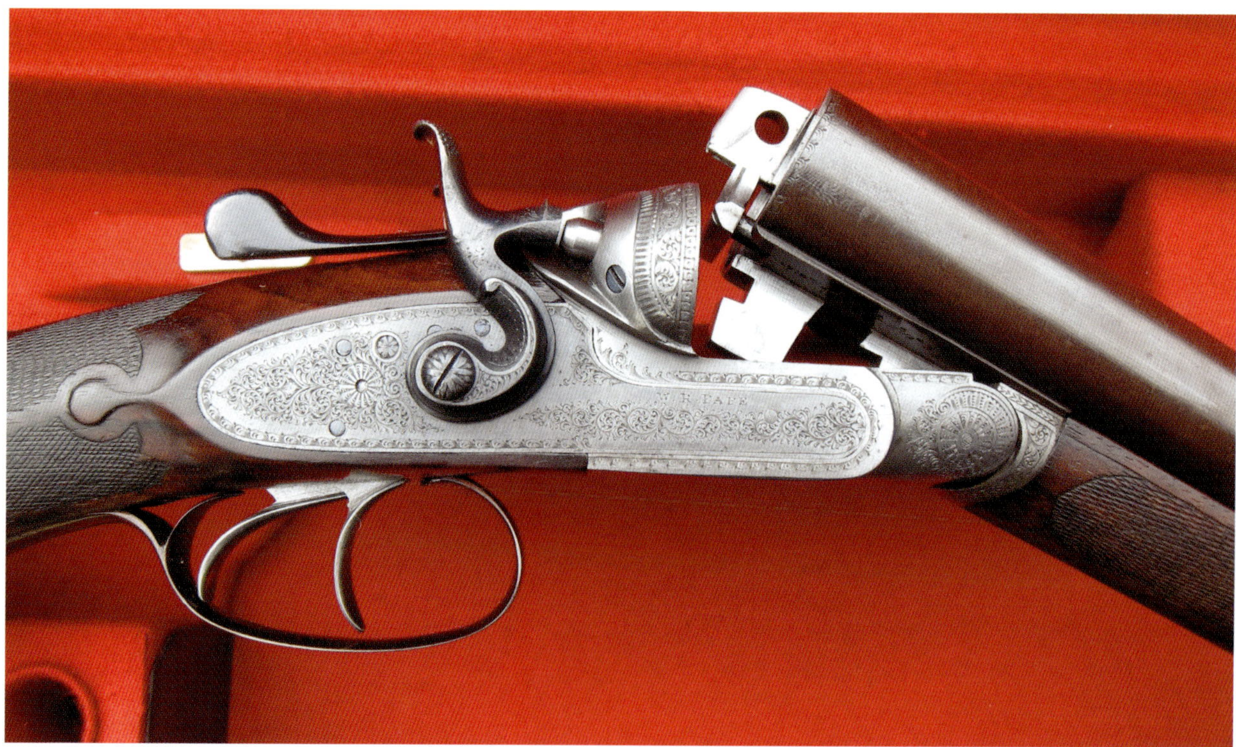

A Manufrance factory scene from their catalogue circa 1900.

Gun shops could also elect to buy a completely finished hammer gun, bearing their own name. This was not a practice limited to provincial ironmongers, as we have seen, because celebrated firms like Holland & Holland, William Evans (from W&C Scott) and W.R. Pape (from Wilkinson) did this too.

Charles Osborne could provide complete hammer guns, for example, what they describe as *'Back-action, three pin, steel, freed rebounding locks, top-lever, double bolt, percussion fence action, damascus or steel barrels, finely bored, left choke, finished well, snap forend, well engraved and freed'* for £11.00.

If a higher grade was required, they describe their 'Bar rebounding steel locks, top lever, double bolt, percussion fence action with cross bolt, fine damascus barrels, finely bored, left choke, fine chequered walnut stock and forend, neatly engraved, well finished and freed, leg-over-sear locks, solid spindle action, best throughout, Anson forend snap'. This cost £17. It is therefore no surprise that a tutored eye can recognise the hammer guns of many 'makers' as having started life in one of the big wholesale factories of Birmingham, regardless of the final finish and name on the gun.

What this also shows us is that these wholesale factories in Birmingham were able to produce hammer guns every bit as fine as the best made in London. A good example would be to look at the wonderful W&C Scott 'Premier' grade hammer guns sold under their own name in the United States and Australia. However, Birmingham guns continue to suffer from misguided prejudice. I remember an American insisting I get him a 'London best' 20-bore hammer gun. He flatly refused to look at any gun bearing the name of a Birmingham maker. However, when shown a third quality, W&C Scott-made back-action hammer gun bearing the name 'Holland & Holland' he was very interested. A classic case of being unable to see quality and being fixated on an idea which the evidence does not support.

TABLE SHOWING COMPONENTS AND PRICES FROM THE CHARLES OSBORNE & CO 1899 TRADE CATALOGUE

Component	Price (£/s/d)
Double Trigger Plate Casting (per dozen)	0/1/2
Trigger (Stamped) (per lb)	0/2/0
Trigger (Forged) (per dozen)	0/5/0
Trigger (Cast) (per lb)	0/1/2
Plain, Drilled Lumps for Double Barrels (per dozen)	0/8/0
Back Action Springs (per dozen) (flat, un-filed)	0/2/0
Breech Pins (Forged) (per dozen)	0/10/0
Back Action Main Springs (best) (per dozen)	0/16/0
Bar Action Main Springs (best) (per dozen)	0/16/0
Guard Screws (best) (per dozen)	0/2/0
Breech Loading Hammers (engraved) (per pair)	0/8/0
Nipples / Strikers / Springs (per dozen sets)	0/8/0
Steel Lock Pins (per dozen)	0/4/0

But surely, the best London makers when producing their best guns must have done it all in-house? What about Boss? Fortunately, the Boss records are well kept and they show accurately what went in to producing one of their justly famed 'best' guns.

The embryonic Boss could have begun life as an action forging from John & James Waldron of St Mary's Row, Birmingham. The furniture, triggers etc were supplied by J. Hemming of Watford. Onto this we have a pair of barrel tubes supplied by W.G. Armstrong Whitworth of Woodstock Street, London and the locks made by J. Stanton & Sons of Wolverhampton. The stock blank came from J.C. Montrieux of Bath Street, Birmingham and may have been given to H.A. Hodges, a London outworker, for stocking.

When time came to engrave the gun, it may well have gone to John Sumner of Bateman Street, Soho, or, if inlay work was required, to A.C. Hayes of Frith Street, Soho. Ribs, for file-cutting went to Phillipson & Nephew in Birmingham and barrels, for blacking, to Richard Collet in nearby Wardour Street.

When finished, the gun would be cased by Robert Bryant of Drury Lane and fitted with cleaning kit and turn-screws by G & J.W. Hawksley of Sheffield, before a Boss label was attached to the inside of the lid. The customer could now come and collect his best London gun from that most famous of makers. Not once would he have questioned its pedigree then, nor should we now, whoever the maker happens to be.

In conclusion, the over-arching point I am attempting to make is that whatever gun you have, it will have involved a large number of component suppliers, each providing specialist parts. They will each have been chosen by the gunmaker and used in the making of his gun.

It is no slur on the gun or the maker to acknowledge this fact. For a commentator to make the judgmental leap from observing that a gun contains component parts from a number of sources to asserting that it is, therefore, a mere assemblage of off-the-shelf parts, is common, but wrong.

E.C.Hodges with his wife Emma, 1865. Hodges was making guns for the trade throughout the late 1800s.

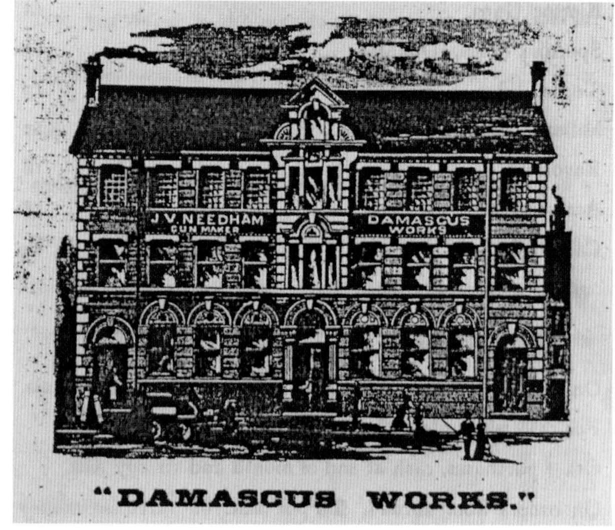

Needham's factory in 1879. Greener produced trade guns from here after taking over the business.

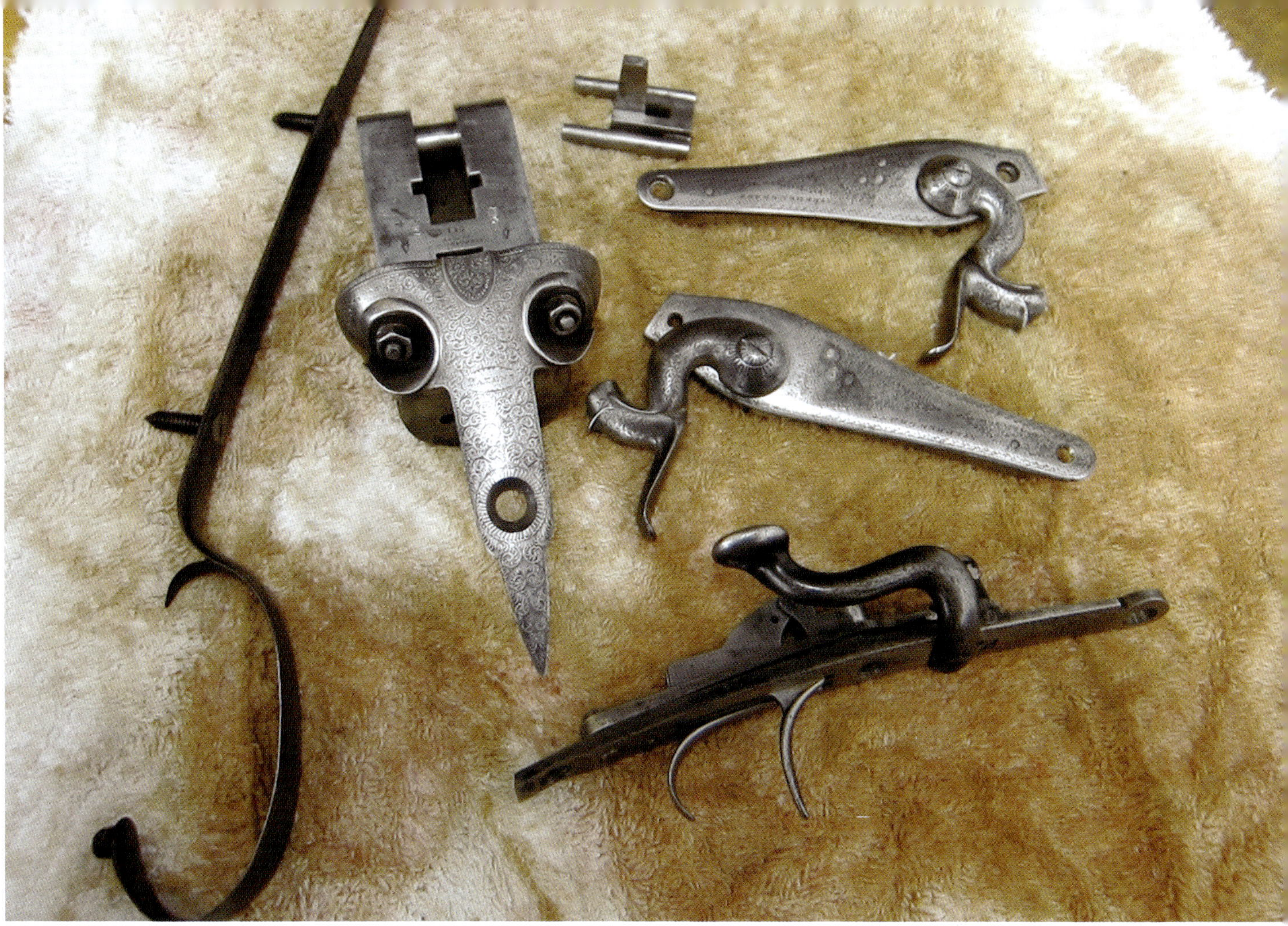

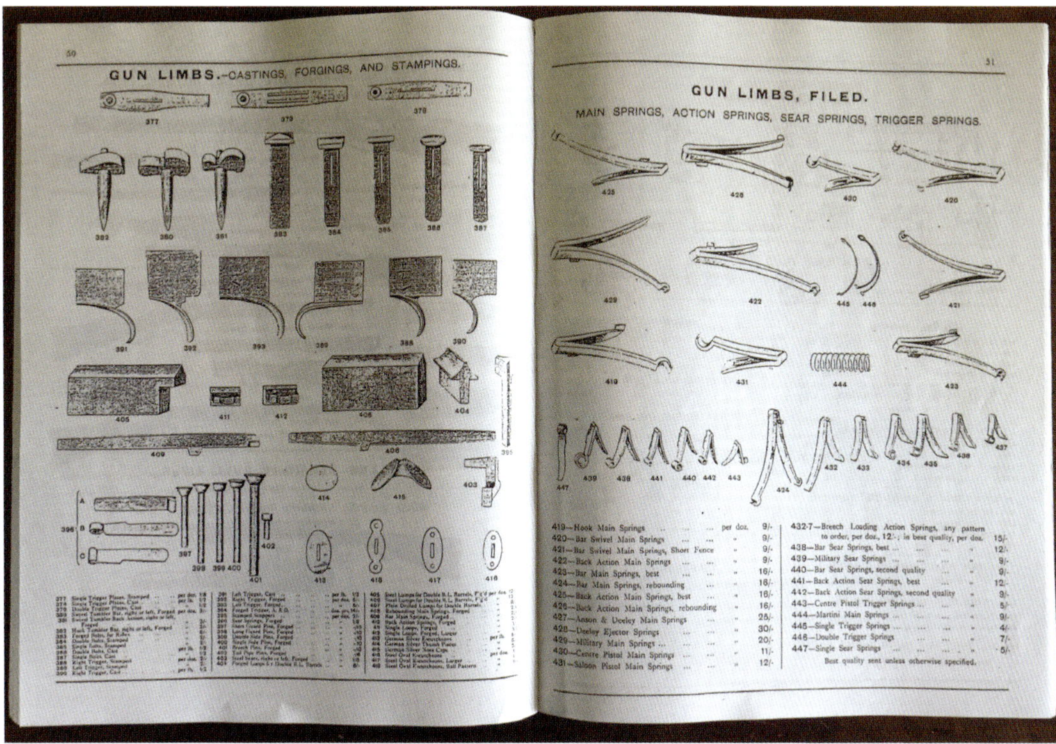

50

GUN LIMBS.—CASTINGS, FORGINGS, AND STAMPINGS.

31

GUN LIMBS, FILED.

MAIN SPRINGS, ACTION SPRINGS, SEAR SPRINGS, TRIGGER SPRINGS.

419—Hook Main Springs	per doz.	9/-
420—Bar Swivel Main Springs	"	9/-
421—Bar Swivel Main Springs, Short Fence	"	9/-
422—Back Action Main Springs	"	9/-
423—Bar Main Springs, best	"	16/-
424—Bar Main Springs, rebounding ...	"	16/-
425—Back Action Main Springs, best ...	"	16/-
426—Back Action Main Springs, rebounding	"	16/-
427—Anson & Deeley Main Springs ...	"	25/-
428—Deeley Ejector Springs	"	30/-
429—Military Main Springs	"	20/-
430—Centre Pistol Main Springs	"	11/-
431—Saloon Pistol Main Springs	"	12/-

432-7—Breech Loading Action Springs, any pattern to order, per doz., 12/-; in best quality, per doz.		15/-
438—Bar Sear Springs, best	"	12/-
439—Military Sear Springs	"	9/-
440—Bar Sear Springs, second quality ...	"	9/-
441—Back Action Sear Springs, best ...	"	12/-
442—Back Action Sear Springs, second quality	"	9/-
443—Centre Pistol Trigger Springs	"	5/-
444—Martini Main Springs	"	9/-
445—Single Trigger Springs	"	4/-
446—Double Trigger Springs	"	7/-
447—Single Sear Springs	"	5/-

Best quality sent unless otherwise specified.

Above: A Hodges-made Stephen Grant sidelever stripped. The gun is built on Hodges' best-known patent action, which has become something of a classic.

Left: Osborne's wholesale catalogue shows component parts of differing quality and degree of finish available to the trade at large.

American Exceptionalism: the unheralded heroes of US gun-making

The American (sportsmen)... cannot or will not discriminate between the first and second classes (of guns) and are slow even to see the difference between the second and third.

W.W. Greener *Modern Shot Guns* (1888).

Writing about American guns is something I generally avoid. There are good reasons for this. The guns favoured by American collectors are invariably factory produced guns of recognised grades and their histories and variations are very well covered in print by some highly knowledgeable writers. It would be, I feel, impertinent to write on a subject about which I know so comparatively little.

American frontiersmen demanded reliable, robust guns that could stand up to abuse and harsh conditions.

The other reason I avoid the subject is that, little though I know about the minutiae of the output of American factories in the 19th century, I know enough about quality to recognise that they are crude and uniform, when compared to the variety and sophistication of the 19th century output of Birmingham and London. American factories, like Parker, produced hammer guns that would be considered third quality or lower, had they been the products of the Midland Gun Co, or Charles Osborne. They were serviceable and generally agreeable but no more. I hesitate to be as forthright as the combative Greener, who lamented 'Strange to say, those keen people inhabiting the United States of America appear less able to discriminate between a good and a bad gun than any civilised people', but the market for quality sporting guns was certainly dominated by British, German, Russian, South African and French customers.

My own observations will not, I hope, be seen as a side-swipe at American prowess, it is simply an observation of fact in this sector. Parker collector Ron Kirby explains, for example:

The product of the Parker Brothers Company was utilitarian in nature. While other goods produced for the consumer may have reflected some taste for opulent decorations, the Parker shotgun did not. The highest grade had fancy wood in the stock, and engraved scenes on the metal surface.

There was good reason that most American output was factory made, inexpensive, over weight

Tonks of Boston made some very high quality guns for the discerning American sportsman.

and limited in variety. The US market was overwhelmingly one of hardware store outlets and guns were tools. Greener, who had business interests in selling to overseas markets, lamented that he 'can hardly believe that the astute American will sacrifice everything to cheapness', but that was the demand. The higher-grade American side-by-sides that were produced prior to 1900 were polished and engraved versions of the standard, basic models and still crude by English standards.

Demand for quality, and the necessary competition to produce that quality, was far higher in England. Where America excelled was in innovation, engineering and mechanisation; qualities nowhere better personified than in the genius of John Moses Browning. If there is a true American classic shotgun, then surely it is the Browning semi-automatic?

The East coast styling married English, Irish, German and Bohemian influences.

However, American gunmaking was, at one time, bespoke, individual and innovative. For a brief period, between 1850–1890, the early gunmakers of Boston and Philadelphia were immigrants from the Old World, first generation Americans, if you will. They came from Germany, England, Ireland, Belgium and Bohemia and sported names like Mullin, Schaefer, Tonks, Abbey, Kirkwood and Sneider. This pool of talented and time-served gunmakers mingled, set up workshops and began to make the first American sporting shotguns in the manner of their old systems. Greener briefly acknowledges their existence, referring to

> *The better-class (American) gun, made by some American-born or emigrant gunsmith, whose production is limited...*

Their work puts the factory output of the well-known American firms decidedly in its place. However, output was small and surviving examples are few.

With trade routes delivering from Europe regularly, the necessities of the gunmaker: action forgings, barrelled actions, barrel tubes, parts and accessories, were easily secured from old contacts in the 'home country'. We see some American makers producing guns with clearly English actions, often half-a-decade or so after they were considered obsolete in their country of origin. A good example would be a Dougall 'Lockfast' type 12-bore made by American maker Charles Mills, which we renovated recently. One can speculate that Mills bought-up obsolete barrelled actions inexpensively and used them as a basis for production. The American market was less exposed to new developments and the Dougall is a strong, reliable action, which would have served well.

I am indebted to my friend Bill McPhail for allowing me access to his wonderful collection of some real American gun-making heritage. His collection encompasses muzzle-loaders, pin-fires and centre-fire hammer guns. What they have in common is that they were all made in America, by American citizens in the very best traditions of British and European bespoke bench work.

The most interesting observation when appraising these guns is the mix of British and continental styles. Some look very English but are engraved in a Germanic manner, others have a W&C Scott action, with the trademark 'Tower' stamp but lever work or bolting such as never graced a gun by that firm.

One can uncover historical references to the artisan gunmakers in early sporting literature and news reports. Patrick Mullin is mentioned in an 1860 volume called *Frank Forester's Field Sports*. The author, H.W. Herbert, writing under a pseudonym, advises:

> *For the heavy duck guns, I earnestly recommend Mullin of Barclay Street, New York, as the best and cheapest maker in the United States... I will back... a gun of his make.. to beat any imported gun... for the same price...*

Some Mullin guns may well have been delivered from Birmingham in a close-to-finished state. Patrick Mullin is recorded as early as 1850 in New York City, a time of high-volume Irish immigration due to the potato famine. Mullin is likely to have apprenticed with an Irish gunmaker and was reported to have worked in Dublin and London before crossing the Atlantic, taking his skills to America with him. John Mullin was operating in NYC at around the same time and was a relative of some kind, possibly his father. He left Patrick and set up in business on his own account in the mid 1850s.

Both Mullins made high quality guns, which bear similarities to each other. These Mullin muzzle-loaders and later breech-loaders are almost certainly Birmingham guns and Mullins would have done various degrees of finishing in the US. Mullin's shotguns could cost as much as $600 and he is known to have sold guns in 12-bore, 10-bore and 8-bore. He was known for big bore muzzle-loaders in the early years of his business. His 1870s guns often bear Birmingham proof marks and feature typical English patents, like the Jones double grip. Guns marked 'P Mullin' appear to have been largely Birmingham made but those which were his own work, probably from imported barrelled actions were fashioned 'Patrick Mullin'.

Forest & Stream, a news sheet for fishermen and hunters, dated December 1893, reports:

> *...Mullin sent out guns which had a deserved reputation, for he put into their making honesty, skill and pride. The duck shooter who had in his blind a Patrick Mullin gun was accustomed to feel the utmost confidence...*

Mullin guns varied in price from $400 to $1000; very expensive for the place and time. The *Evening Post*, in an obituary, said of Mullin:

> *He was plain mechanic of the old fashioned type, working for himself with no journeymen, and with no ambition but to make his work perfect and to give it that finish and beauty which come from perfect adaptation to the purpose designed. No money could tempt him to turn out a poor piece of work, or to accept anything more than a fair and reasonable price for the best.*

Another American whose work stands proudly alongside the high-end English gunmakers of his day was Joseph Tonks of Boston. Tonks was born in Warwickshire in 1827, into a family of lock filers. He however, is listed as a 'gun stocker' in the 1851 census. It seems probable that Tonks arrived in the US in 1851 as a skilled gunmaker and he became an American citizen in 1867.

Tonks, like Mullin, is referenced in literature of the day. *American Wildfowl Shooting* by Joseph W. Long discussed the feats of Fred Kimble, who is widely credited as a pioneer of choke-boring, (which did not receive a patent in England until 1866 by way of W.R.

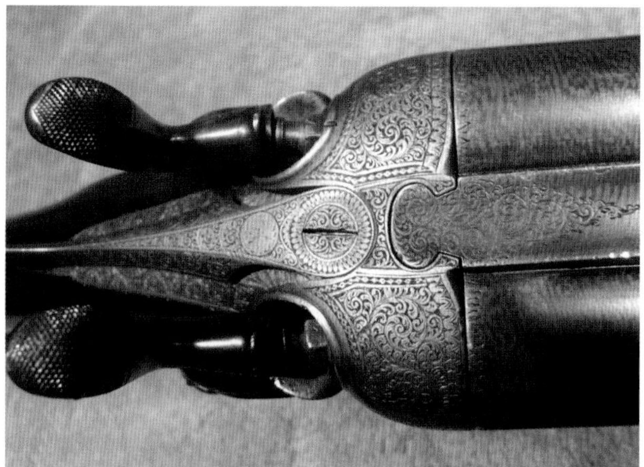

Barrelled actions were often sourced from Birmingham by the better quality American makers.

Pape). Writing on choke-boring, Long recounts an 1869 wager between himself and Kimble as to who could produce the best shooting gun. Tonks made Long a breech-loader, rather than the muzzle-loader he desired, with the promise that it would be a gift if it did not satisfy the writer with its performance.

While making Long's gun, Tonks lent him a 10-bore pigeon gun he had made for Jack Haywood. Long patterned it and sent the results to Kimble, who circulated the quality of the patterns to his friends, spreading the word about what would become known as choke-boring and popularised in Britain by W.W. Greener in the mid 1870s. From Long's pen, it is apparent that Tonks, W.R. Shaefer and probably other American gunmakers were applying choke to their guns prior to 1830.

Another gunmaker, Kirkwood Brothers, commented on Tonks in an obituary in 1924, reflecting on the old master's talents:

> *...Mr Tonks turned out splendid guns, both muzzle loading and breech loading, importing his barrels or barrels and actions from England, stocking and finishing the guns here.*

Tonks had a career of high and low points and travelled widely, eventually returning to England, possibly in financial difficulty. Of his guns remaining, of which there are a significant number, the general quality is very high and the quality of choke-boring equally impressive and consistent.

Examination of early US guns is a worthwhile activity and there are some genuinely interesting pieces doubtless still to be uncovered and appreciated. I would encourage American readers to seek them out and be proud of what they represent.

The high quality of these early American guns can rival the work of European makers in a way that few later American makers can claim.

James Foster showing Purdey bolts and a form of split cross bolt.

Lawrence of New York showing Scott 'C' Share Hammers.

Hammer Ejectors

Hammer gun enthusiasts often talk in hushed tones of the rare and elusive (not to mention expensive) hammer ejector gun. Ejectors found favour following Needham's work and subsequent patent in 1874, but this was a period in which hammerless guns, led by the Anson & Deeley and its derivatives, were developing alongside the ejector mechanism.

Most of the efforts of the best inventors gravitated towards providing ejection to hammerless guns. Greener bought Needham's firm, largely to get hold of the ejector patent (1205 of 1874), which he then applied to his hammerless guns in the form of the 'Self-acting', then the 'Unique' types of ejector. It would appear that the majority of gunmakers saw hammerless guns as the future and the hammerless ejector as the target for perfection. Hammer ejectors were something of a side-show.

Split extractors on a hammer gun? A sure sign it is an ejector. This is an ultra-rare Boss side-lever ejector.

Crudgington & Baker *(Vol.2)* show a number of ejector patents, the drawings of which use hammer guns as illustrations of the mechanism at work. The last of these is Rosson's patent 15313 of 1889. Donald Dallas records a 12-bore by Cogswell & Harrison fitted with Edgar Harrison's patent ejector 16214 of 1886, known as the 'Avant Tout'.

Of the actual guns I have encountered, the Phillipson & Baker patent (8323 of 1889) and the Perkes ejector in one of its 1887 guises appears more common. Interestingly, provincial maker George Jeffries of Norwich appears to have made a fair number of hammer guns on his own patent ejector systems of 1885 and 1886. I have seen several examples of this. Perkes 1887 patent ejectors appear to have been used quite widely on guns converted to ejector. Purdey seem to have made general use of the Wem ejector when making their hammer

This Holland & Holland was converted to ejector.

Perkes patent ejectors are commonly used.

Maker	Type	Ejector System	Year of Manufacture
Purdey (S.N 16598)	Back action, 12-bore, top-lever	Wem	1902
Boss (S.N 4016)	Bar action, 12-bore, side-lever	Perkes 1889	1889
Purdey (S.N 9886)	Bar action, 12-bore, top-lever	Unknown, converted 1877	1877
Purdey (S.N 7245)	Back action 12-bore, rotary under lever	Perkes (converted) 1866	1866
Boss (S.N 2574)	Back-action, 12-bore, rotary under lever	Unknown, converted 1868	1868
Boss (S.N 4175)	Bar action 12-bore, top-lever	Unknown, converted 1891	1891
Jeffries (nvsn)	Back action, 12-bore, side-lever	Jeffries (7895 of 1885) 1887	1887
Jeffries (S.N 10)	Back action 12-bore, side-lever	Jeffries (7895 of 1885)	1885
Grant (S.N 4161)	Back action, 12-bore, side-lever	Unknown, converted	1876
Purdey (S.N 17841)	Back action, 12-bore, top-lever	Wem	1903
Atkin (S.N 768)	Bar-action, 12-bore, side-lever	Boss (likely conversion)	circa 1885
Holland & Holland (S.N 6469)	Back-action, 12-bore, side-lever	Perkes (12176 of 1887) converted	1883
Jeffries (S.N 122)	Back-action, 12-bore, side-lever	Jeffries (7895 of 1885)	1885
Purdey (S.N 2389)	Back-action 20-bore, top-lever (pair)	Wem	1929
Purdey (S.N 15948)	Back action,12-bore, top-lever (pair)	Wem	1897
Purdey (S.N 15082)	Back action, 12-bore, top-lever	Wem	1894
Purdey (S.N 22182)	Bar action, 12-bore, top-lever	Wem	1922
Purdey (S.N 15030)	Back action, 12-bore, top-lever (pair)	Wem	1894
Purdey (S.N 14982)	Back-action, 12-bore, top-lever (pair)	Wem	1894
Boss (S.N 4181)	Bar action, 12-bore, top-lever	Boss	1893
Purdey (S.N 16598)	Island lock 12-bore, top-lever	Wem	1902
Cogswell & Harrison (S.N 14747)	Back action, 12-bore, top-lever	Harrison patent 162164 of 1886 'Avant Tout'.	Unknown
Cogswell & Harrison (S.N 14750)	Back action, 12-bore, top-lever	Harrison patent 162164 of 1886 'Avant Tout'.	Unknown
Boss (S.N 4016)	Bar action, 12-bore, side-lever	Perkes patent 12176 of 1887 (first version)	1889
Purdey (S.N 9886)	Wood bar, 12-bore, top-lever	Unknown, converted	1877
Purdey (S.N 7245)	Back action, 12-bore, rotary under-lever	Perkes (12176 of 1887)	
Boss (S.N 2574)	Back action, 12-bore, rotary under-lever	Unknown, converted	1868
Boss (S.N 4175)	Bar action, 12-bore, top lever	Boss (converted)	1891
B. Norman (n.v.s.n)	Bar action 12-bore top lever.	W. Ford & J. Clifford patent 9348 of 1888	circa 1889

A hammer ejector by B.Norman of Framlingham.

A reliable ejector system is essential.

A Purdey hammer ejector with unusual relief engraving.

A Henry Atkin hammer ejector.

Boss ejectors on the Atkin.

ejectors. This was the first design used on their 1880 Beesley patent side-lock ejector as well.

Few genuine hammer ejectors were made by anybody. Boss record only fourteen, though others have been uncovered, which are conversions. Henry Atkin, Stephen Grant, Alfred Lancaster, B. Norman, Charles Lancaster and James Purdey all made hammer ejectors. Purdey made them in both bar-action and back-action style, most of the back-action guns having typical Purdey 'island' locks, but at least two were made with the less common 'peninsular' locks. By the late 1890s, a large proportion of the hammer shotguns Purdey made were fitted with ejectors and were made for some very prominent people, such as Sir Harry Stonor, King George V, The Marquis of Ripon, Lord Walsingham and many well-regarded competitive live-pigeon shots.

Prices for these are always strong and, in a market driven by rarity, they are likely to continue to hold value. The table on page 85 outlines some hammer ejectors encountered in London sales, or listed in publications in recent years.

In addition to the hammer shotguns listed on page 85, Holland & Holland are known to have made four identical hammer ejector 'Royal' quality 12-bore

Andy Lloyd's Lancaster hammer gun with Perkes patent ejectors. It is one of a pair.

'Paradox' shot and ball guns. They were destined for the Indian firm Walter Locke in Calcutta and were made around 1910 at a cost of £78.9s.0d. Holland & Holland made no hammer guns after that year.

Converted hammer guns with ejector systems added later are potentially difficult and may pose safety and reliability problems. While managing Atkin, Grant & Lang, I recall one by Stephen Grant, which we had to convert back to non-ejector, as the system proved impossible to regulate correctly. The extra pressure it put on the mainsprings made the gun liable to accidental discharge when relieving the hammers. It was unsafe and I refused to release it until we had resolved the issue.

With prices of Boss hammer ejectors in good condition in excess of £20,000, unless you are an investor with cash to park, I don't think they represent very good value as practical pieces. A converted example by Holland & Holland recently appeared with a valuation of £9,000. Had the gun been a non-ejector, its value would have been £3,000. Ejectors are an added complication. Many of the patents used on hammer guns were short lived and troublesome. They do offer a little more speed, a talking point and, perhaps, bragging rights; if that is what motivates you. However, if modern performance is what you are looking for, you probably won't be shooting with a hammer gun anyway.

England ZZ team regular Andy Lloyd prefers to shoot game with his Lancaster hammer ejector, despite having grown up with modern trap guns.

Self-cocking Hammer Guns

In the quest for speed, gunmakers worked tirelessly on the opening and closing mechanism, as we have seen, with slow inert actions giving way to fast snap-actions. They also looked at the cocking process. If a manual operation could be removed, or combined with another, then the time required to reload and fire the gun each time would decrease.

In most hammer guns the operation that opens the gun by unbolting the barrels from the action, and the one that cocks the hammers, are separate. If a gun could be configured so that one movement dually opened the gun and cocked the hammers, it would offer an edge over the competition. A number of gunmakers worked on this idea during the hammer gun period.

Of course, quality modern hammerless guns cock the locks automatically and, because the hammers are inside the body of the gun, we neither notice nor ponder the issue. However, back in the early 1870s, there were two avenues to this destination being explored. Either the lever could be used to release the bolt and cock the hammers, or the barrels themselves could be used as a lever, once they were released and gravity caused them to fall open.

The first gunmaker to successfully attempt barrel cocking was Needham, quickly followed a year later, in 1875, by Anson & Deeley. However, the mechanisms to which they applied their patents were

The Daw lever was popular on self-cockers.

A Norfolk self-cocker in action shooting Texas doves.

hammerless and a subsequent wave of patents followed applying both systems to the cocking of hundreds of variations of sidelock and trigger-plate action hammerless guns. Details of these are covered extensively in *The British Boxlock Gun & Rifle*.

Our interest here, however, is the hammer gun. We will, therefore, pause to consider some of the self-cocking systems to be found on hammer guns. They are rarely encountered and it is likely that very few were made, as the automatic cocking of the locks was a necessity in a hammerless gun and once it was achieved, the hammerless types proliferated and hammer guns began a steady decline.

Early attempts at addressing the issue of self-cocking can be traced back to the era of the non-rebound lock, when two distinct movements were required: half-cock and full-cock. Needham's 1862 patent and Harrison's, of 1864, both achieved automatic setting of half-cock. However, Stanton removed the need for a mechanical operation to achieve this when he incorporated the rebound feature in his 1867 patent. From then on, guns fitted with Stanton locks were effectively set to half-cock automatically after firing. However, in order to fire the gun, the hammers still had to be pulled back to full-cock.

Crudgington & Baker refer to the Gibbs & Pitt patents of 1873 making provision for a hammerless, a semi-hammerless and a hammer gun, all self-cocking. I have not encountered one to date. In 1875, Edwin Hughes, the manager of Joseph Lang at the time, patented a self-cocking hammer gun (patent No.1290). It features a snap under-lever, which is pushed forward.

A self-cocking bar-lock, showing the stud, acting on the lever, which cocks the lock.

When operated, studs on the tumblers are forced backwards by the lever, which also releases the barrel bolt.

James Woodward patented his well-known self-cocking gun in conjunction with Thomas Southgate, who is best known for his over-centre ejector mechanism. Patent Nos.117 and 600 of 1876 cover the mechanics, which are very similar to the Lang gun, with the addition of another lever between the under-lever and the tumbler stud. I have seen examples of this gun by Woodward, Norfolk and Jackson. I used one for dove shooting in Texas for several days and found it to be reliable, convenient and easy. A firm push on the under-lever is all that is required to set the gun to full-cock and open the breech. This was the precursor to the successful Woodward 'Automatic' lever-cocking hammerless gun, which worked in the same manner but with internal hammers.

THE LOADING/FIRING CYCLE: HOW HAMMER AND HAMMERLESS GUNS COMPARE FOR SPEED

The test employed to compare the speed of various actions was taken using a clay trap at Griffin Lloyd Shooting Ground in Knighton, Powys. The stand chosen was a driven pheasant target, firing two clays simultaneously, directly over the shooter, in the normal 'driven' manner.

Each test began with the timer started upon the first shot. Clays were, thereafter, released upon the gun being closed and cocked. The shots were taken as normal, aimed, attempts to kill the 'bird', rather than the gun simply being discharged aimlessly. The purpose of the test was to discover how many aimed shots per minute each type of gun offered the shooter in a realistic shooting situation.

The shooting in each case was carried out by the author and the timing by Tom Waite, with roles then being reversed and repeated for comparison. When re-loading, this was done by the shooter, loading from a pocket, much as would happen at the peg on a driven day.

GUN TEST DATA			
MAKER	Locks	Operation	Shots in 60 seconds
Purdey 12-bore	Rebounding back-locks	Second pattern thumbhole	14
Henry Egg .410	Non-rebounding back-locks	Jones under-lever	8
W&C Scott 12-bore	Sidelock non-ejector	Top-lever	12
Cashmore 20-bore	Rebounding bar-locks	Top-lever	12
Lang 12-bore	Non-rebounding back-locks	Lefaucheux type	10
Atkin 12-bore	Sidelock ejector	Top-lever	16
R. Watson 20-bore	Sidelock ejector	Side-lever	15
Bonehill 20-bore	Boxlock ejector	Top-lever	16
Rosson 12-bore	Boxlock non-ejector	Top-lever	14

Interestingly, both shooters achieved identical results with all guns tested. The poor gape on the Scott hammerless side-lock hindered loading.

Strikers without springs to retract them automatically slowed closing of the gun, as evident from the Egg. The top-lever was expected to be the fastest to operate, since it is considered the most 'modern' system. However, it was beaten by the thumbhole lever for speed,

Lang forward-facing under lever. 10 shots per minute.

Jones lever, 8 shots per minute with non-rebound locks.

Cashmore with top-lever and Purdey bolt. 12 shots.

Purdey thumbhole: 14 shots per minute.

Scott non-ejector, top lever. 12 shots per minute.

perhaps because of the proximity of the thumb lever to the operating hand.

Without the aid of automatic ejection, there is little operational speed advantage between the hammerless and hammer guns of snap-action operation. The addition of ejectors clearly speeds up the cycle significantly.

Non-rebounding locks appear to reduce the firing cycle by 2 shots per minute, compared with rebound locks. However, in modern terms, if I were to be killing pheasants at a rate of fourteen per minute, I would be far exceeding my norms.

Interesting Asides

There are certain features observable in individual guns which make them unusual. They may appeal today because they have something the average hammer gun does not. These features may be a peculiarity ascribable to a particular maker, a short-lived, ingenious, but ultimately unnecessary modification or a trademark of one maker, who patented it and then found its usefulness did not out-live the patent protection.

Some ideas that gunmakers had were applied to a few guns only before failing to prove useful, or perhaps being too expensive to make, while offering only marginal advantage over more widely adopted patents. They remain with us today and their very variety offers the chance to make an interesting collection. Many are beautifully engineered and filed and, in some cases, may unlock the workings of an obscure patent that one may only have read about. We shall examine some of these over the next few pages.

SELF-RETRACTING STRIKERS

Early hammer guns in the centre-fire era suffered from a tendency for the strikers to stick in the soft caps of the cartridges, effectively bolting the gun closed after discharge. There were three avenues to explore to

A big bore Greener with self-retracting strikers.

A Morrow with self-retracting strikers.

A 10-bore Pape with self-retracting strikers of his own patent.

alleviate the problem. The first was to move the angle of the firing pins from horizontal to oblique. Many makers also started filing ramped grooves into their extractors to push the pins back into the fences when the gun was opened.

Another advance was the inevitable improvement in the quality and consistency of the caps themselves, leading to fewer punctures. While the problem persisted, gunmakers sought a mechanical solution, involving the attachment of a retracting lever to the striker, which pulled it out of the cap automatically, using the force of the barrels dropping, or the hammer cocking. There are several such patents. Personally, I find them attractive and interesting relics of their time. All the examples I have used proved perfectly effective and were beautifully made. They quickly became an unnecessary complication, once the early problems ceased to prove on-going and the self-retracting striker faded into disuse.

LOADED INDICATORS

One can see with a quick glance if a hammer gun is cocked or not, though it is not always immediately apparent whether the gun is at half cock or full cock, if it is a non-rebounder.

Devices indicating the presence or absence of a cartridge in the chamber are more widely associated with early hammerless guns, when the issue of a loaded or empty gun was significantly more of an issue. However, hammer guns with loaded indicators will occasionally be encountered.

Loaded indicators - these are covered by a shroud when the gun is empty.

In closed and empty position.

A Purdey showing the activating projections.

EXTRACTORS

Extractors for breech-loaders were in the experimental stage in the 1860s. By the mid years of the decade, they had settled, largely into the pattern we recognise today, with a single piece extractor face, lifting both shells clear when the gun is opened. A lower (thicker) and upper (slimmer) extractor leg move with a camming action, when the barrels drop or rise.

Early centre-fire guns may have encountered strikers sticking on the extractor, so frequently they can be found with inclined grooves, designed to slide the pins back into the detonating as the gun is closed.

Once it became usual practice to insert small springs into the striker holes to withdraw them automatically and rebounding locks were the norm, this ceased to be necessary.

Early extractors often worked on an externally fitted slide arrangement.

External extractors required more complex cut-outs in the bar to accommodate them.

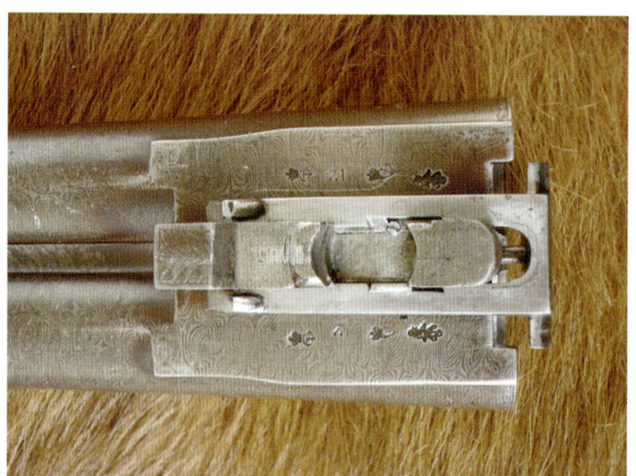

Another external extractor, this one by Sylven of the Strand.

The bar of the Sylven gun, showing the rails cut out of the bar.

MUZZLE-LOADER AND OTHER CONVERSIONS

The mid 19th century must have been quite tough on the bank account of any gentleman who wanted to keep abreast of the gunmaker's every improvement. It must have seemed that every couple of years, his 'new' gun became obsolete and required replacing. Reluctant to scrap a good flintlock, owners had their favourites converted to percussion-cap ignition. I have even encountered one flintlock/percussion cap gun made with both ignition systems. The gun, by Charles Jones, could be fired by either means, or both!

Later, good percussion guns were converted to breech-loading and later still, pin-fires were converted to centre-fire.

Occasionally one uncovers a gun that started life as a flintlock, became a percussion lock and was eventually converted to pin-fire or centre-fire breech-loader. Some gunmakers, like Thomas Sylven of The Strand, in London, patented conversion plans and specialised in doing the work. One sometimes finds a gun with the name of the firm converting it engraved on the rib, alongside the maker. It is often clever work, beautifully carried out and can be less than obvious when first examined.

Lever work can vary, Jones screw-grip and Purdey thumbhole with Purdey bolt are examples I have encountered recently.

The Purdey (above) was converted from muzzle-loader to pin-fire, then to centre-fire. The Blanch (below) shows the filled-in pinfire holes in the barrels.

BOLTED HAMMERS

Bolted hammers were used mostly, but not exclusively, on double rifles. Generally, they are sliding external bolts, which slot into a gap in the hammer, adjacent to the screw holding it to the lock plate. When engaged, with the gun at half cock, it prevents it being inadvertently cocked to 'full' and made 'live'. This is a useful feature when crawling through thick bush in pursuit of game. One can imagine that faced with a sudden charge, remembering the hammers were locked and having the mental fortitude and physical dexterity to free them, cock the hammer and take the shot under pressure would be a challenge that may have proved many hunter's undoing!

Hammer bolts of the rebounding lock era tend to be made so as to hold the gun at half cock. In the rebound era, they prevent the gun from discharging while at full cock. They may be made to engage from the front of the hammer or the rear of the hammer.

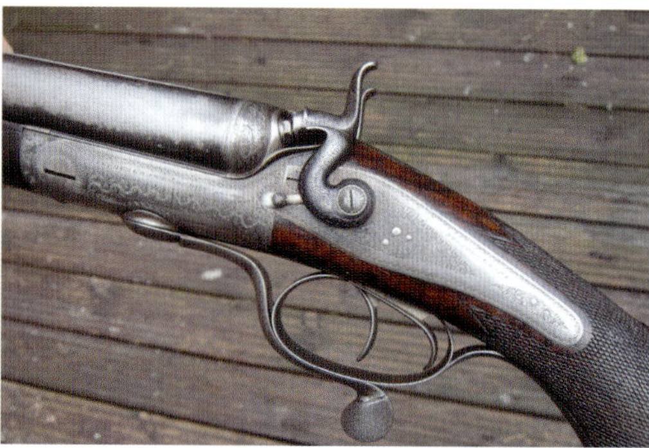

Non-rebound locks with forward mounted bolts.

Right: a rear-mounted bolt on a Beattie double rifle.

Below: An Alex Henry rifle wih forward bolts holding the hammers at rebound.

"I fired both barrels at once, and leaped sidewise."

PATENT STAMPS AND OTHER MARKS ON GUN ACTIONS

It is not uncommon to see various stamped references to a gun's origins on the surfaces not visible when the gun is closed. These may be initials, they may be Patent numbers, or references to a patent. They may be patent use numbers, from the days when patent protection was still in place and royalties being paid to the patentee by other makers who wanted to use it.

Other stamps may be the trade marks of firms involved in the making of the gun. A monogram or symbol could be a mark of a particular model or grade of gun. Whatever they indicate, it pays to give these marks a little attention and to decipher them. If nothing else, they shed a little light on the gun you own: at best, they may show you some important provenance or indicate something of the construction process, or confirm the gun of being higher quality than you thought.

This Adsett 14-bore shows his trademark stamp on the bar.

'AH patent action' is actually Purdey's bolt! Alex Henry being a bit naughty.

Stamps sometimes name the patentee and the patent number.

F.T. Baker used this as a marker on his best quality guns.

Early steel barrels were often stamped with the source material, in this case Whitworth's.

Chambers, Bores and Barrels

The ordinary double-barrelled modern shot gun is composed of 95 pieces, of which the most important are the barrels. W.W. Greener *Modern Shotguns*

Barrel construction underwent some important changes in the breech-loader era. Barrel makers had to fix the two barrel tubes together and they also had to fit the lumps, which are very important as they form part of the hinge for the break-open action and they are the location of the bites in most locking systems. They need to be secure.

Barrel maker's stamp. The names of most of these men are lost to history.

When hammer breech-loaders first appeared, barrel tubes were invariably made from some type of ‘twist’ construction; either intricate multi-iron ‘damascus’ or single iron ‘scelp’. Steel barrels do overlap the heyday of the hammer gun but not until the mid 1890s did Whitworth’s ‘very expensive’ steel tubes become established as the barrel material of choice.

In order to fix lumps onto a pair of damascus tubes, the normal method was by ‘dovetail’, much like a cabinet maker fitting a wedge shaped piece into a cut-out. Dovetail lumps are fitted tight and brazed into place. They occasionally work lose but are generally very sound; even a hundred or more years and tens of thousands of shots later. Dovetail attachment of the lumps is not, as I have found to be commonly supposed, a single, uniform, process. Greener illustrates five different types of attachment (including chopper-lumps) as options in 1871.

FIVE DIFFERENT METHODS OF AFFIXING BARREL LUMPS

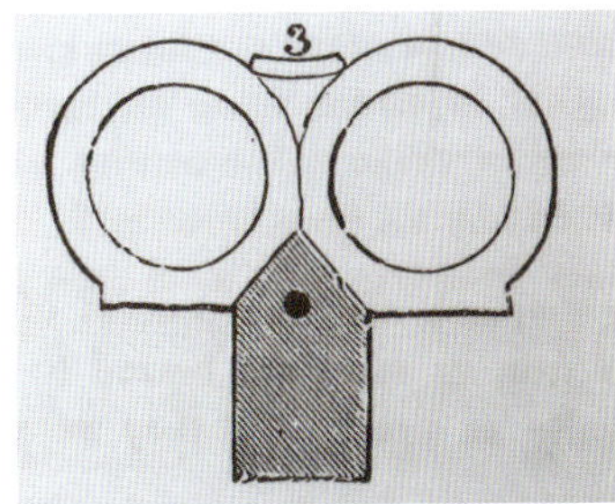

Simple brazed lump without dovetail. Can be weak in early centre-fire guns but generally sound if correctly brazed.

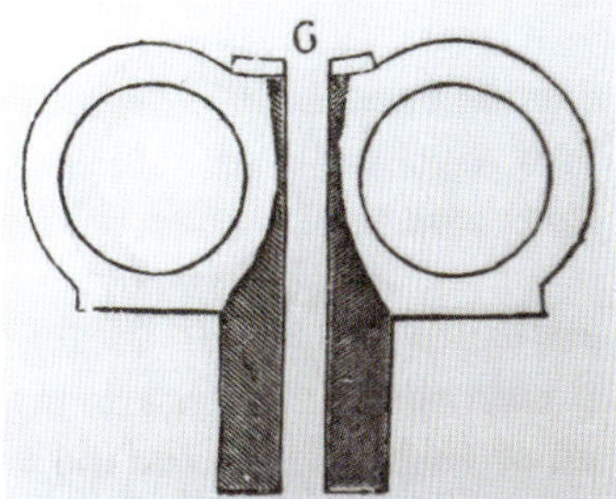

Parsons' patent 'chopper-lump' barrels. Occasionally of damascus but really found favour used with steel barrels, becoming 'best practice'.

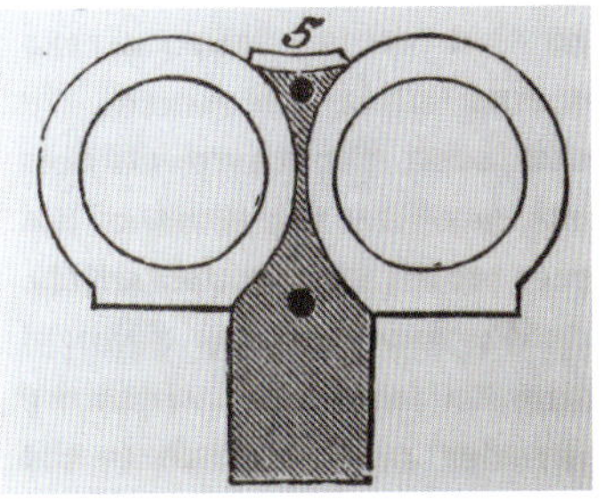

Solid steel lump extending between barrels to top rib. Soldered rather than brazed. Very strong but slightly widens the breech.

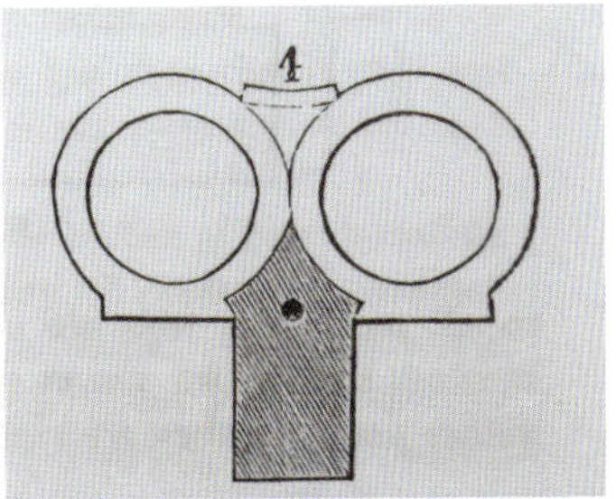

Classic dovetail lump; brazed in place and the preferred method for attaching damascus barrels. Very rarely fails.

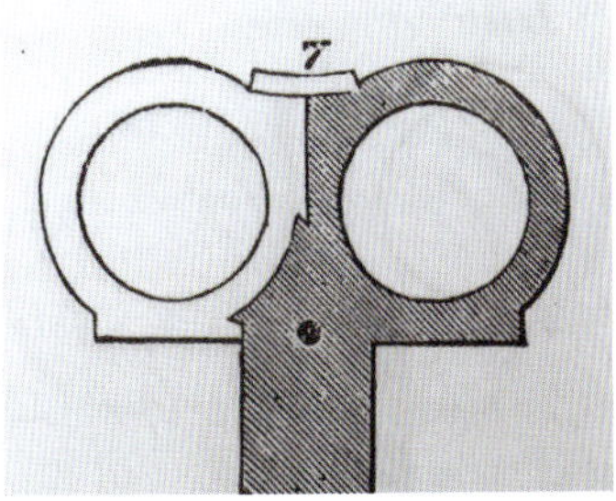

One lump welded to one barrel, the second dove-tailed in place and soldered or brazed. Very strong. Not very commonly employed.

The barrel making process for damascus barrels involves brazing the lumps into place, by which process the breech ends are fixed, then packing pieces are placed to hold the tubes uniformly and they are, in turn, soldered ('tinned') together at various intervals. The ribs (top and bottom) are also tinned into place, as is the forend loop. This explains why loops and ribs are commonly found to have worked loose or become detached but lump failure is so rare.

An alternative to common brazing of the lumps was the use of 'spelter', which is a copper braze, rather than a brass one. It is even tougher, is very unlikely to come loose and withstands very hard wear.

Greener remains our best reference in print, writing as a first class gunmaker of late Victorian period. His own comments on his preference for affixing lumps are interesting. They reflect his developing attitude to changing technology and he expressed a preference for the methods in the examples illustrated earlier, numbered 3 and 5, when writing in 1871.

Gunmakers continued to experiment with barrel construction well into the 20th century (in fact, experimentation continues) but the Victorian and Edwardian hammer guns, in which we are principally interested, will generally be found to have barrels assembled on one of the principles illustrated here.

DAMASCUS BARRELS

Much has been written on the process of making damascus barrels; Greener's *The Gun & its Development* provides very detailed explanation and I provide a comprehensive commentary on the subject in *Vintage Guns for the Modern Shot.*

I would, therefore, direct readers to these two volumes if their interest in damascus barrel production and evaluation is deeper than I intend to go in this one.

Damascus steel used in English gun making dates back to 1806, when a Mr Jones took out a patent for 'scelp', which is the basic form of twist barrel, hammering a strip of metal around a mandrel to make a tube. Rigby is known to have been producing damascus tubes in Dublin by 1817 and Birmingham firms Wiswould and Adams are recorded as being active from around 1820.

Charles Lancaster was one of the first 'branded' barrel makers to the trade, supplying numerous London firms with his 'CL' stamped damascus barrels in the early and mid 19th century. W. Fullard, of Clerkenwell was another maker revered for his fine damascus barrels, until he ceased producing them in 1844. From 1845 to 1855 John Dive in Birmingham and John Marshall in Staffordshire were major suppliers of barrel tubes to the Birmingham gun trade. Thomas Kilby & Son of Steelhouse Lane, in the heart of the Birmingham 'gun quarter' also produced damascus barrels for the wider trade.

Many British makers sourced their damascus barrels in Liège, where very finely figured tubes could be found. Purdey certainly used Belgian tubes for a time and, as the 19th century wore on, gunmakers often lamented the erratic quality control at some of the English tube makers, the presence of 'greys' being principal among the complaints.

Very little English damascus was produced after 1903 but stocks were used for many years beyond

Lord Walsingham changed his steel barrels for damascus, complaining he got 'gun headache' from the new material.

that date. I had a Stephen Grant 12-bore, made in 1922, with damascus barrels and I occasionally encounter other, similarly late-production guns with the same original equipment. Some gunmakers continued to offer damascus barrels as an option in their catalogues well into the 1930s.

Here, I shall concentrate on the practical issues for the buyer and user of vintage hammer guns, such as how to recognise different types and qualities, how to recognise faults or damage and how to ensure barrels are properly maintained.

BARREL MATERIALS AT A GLANCE

Ironically, any barrels marked 'Best London Damascus' or 'English Fine Twist' etc are, almost certainly, Belgian forgeries of poor quality. British makers did not adopt this practice, as a general rule. The various types of damascus, or twist, tubes used by British makers were successfully employed through the flintlock, percussion, pin-fire and centre-fire eras. It is often supposed that forged steel succeeded them because it was a superior material. However, many sportsmen of the day disagreed.

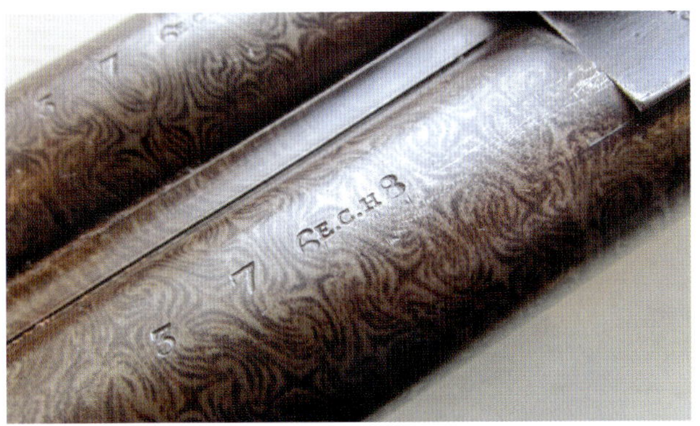

Most barrels will have a barrel maker's stamp. In this case, another example of 'ECH': Edwin Charles Hodges.

Beautifully polished and browned barrels on a Purdey, showing great figure.

These early twist barrels lack the intricacy of finer damascus but they are long-lived and well made.

Acid etched barrels like this were a speciality of Rigby and are a beautiful, distinctive feature of his hammer guns.

Lord Walsingham was prominent among the nay-sayers. He wrote, after shooting a record bag of grouse to his own gun, actually using number of guns he then owned: '*Whitworth steel barrels are not desirable for a heavy day's shooting. The explosion in them makes quite a different sound from that given off by Damascus barrels: there is more ring about it, and I can imagine that this might prove a serious annoyance to anyone who minds the noise of shooting. Moreover, the Whitworth barrels became hot much more rapidly than the Damascus, and this is a serious drawback...I am replacing them with Damascus as in all my other guns.*'

Damascus barrels of all the main types encountered in English gun making will prove serviceable. Many now sold will have been subjected to a modern proof test at either the London or the Birmingham proof house.

The tests for re-proof are the equal of the tests imposed on brand new guns submitted by current makers, be they American, Turkish, Japanese, English or wherever in origin. Therefore, any damascus barrelled gun with new proof marks can be used with the appropriate modern ammunition with absolute confidence.

Parts of the Hammer Gun

SIDE VIEW

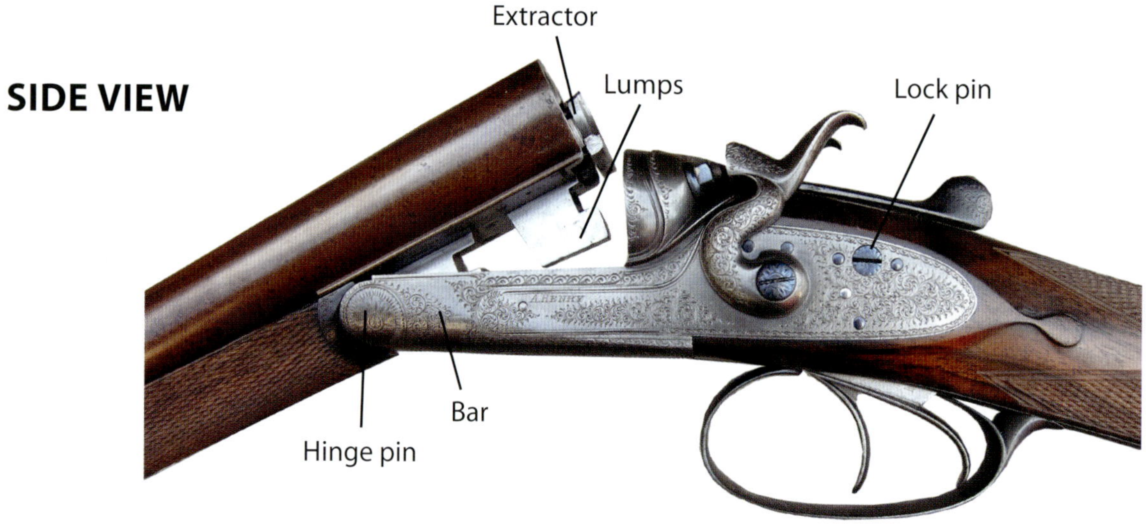

FROM ABOVE

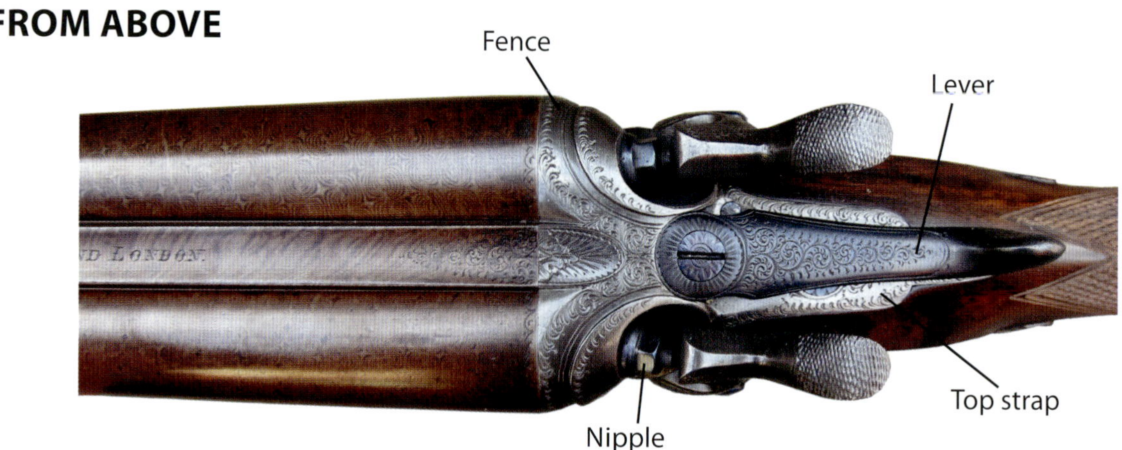

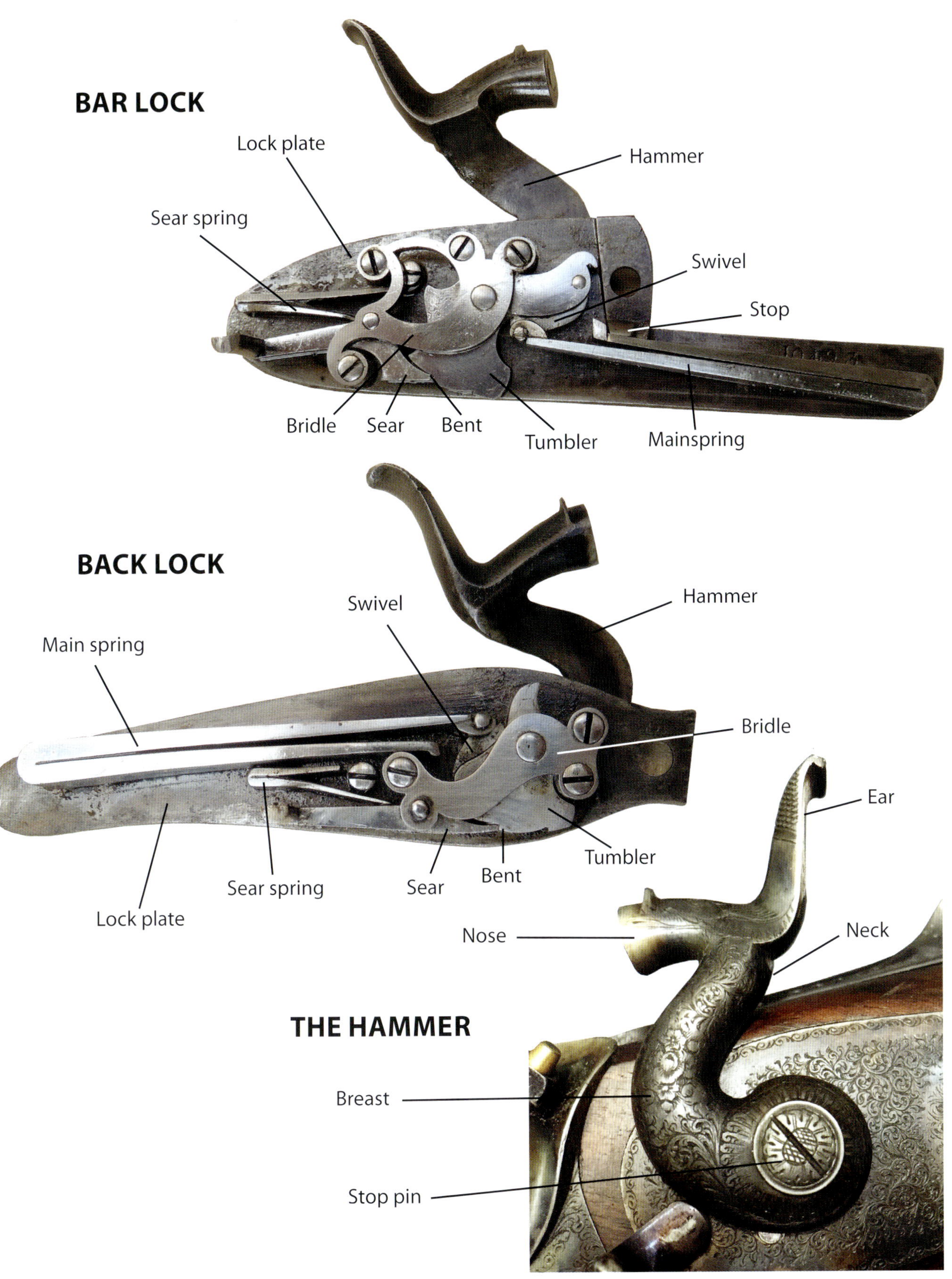
BAR LOCK
Lock plate
Hammer
Sear spring
Swivel
Stop
Bridle
Sear
Bent
Tumbler
Mainspring
BACK LOCK
Swivel
Hammer
Main spring
Bridle
Ear
Tumbler
Sear spring
Sear
Bent
Lock plate
Nose
Neck
THE HAMMER
Breast
Stop pin

CHAMBER SIZE

With proof marks, we can trace the reaction of the Proof Houses of Birmingham and London to the introduction of the breech-loader and the need to test the new type of gun. By the time we reach the centre-fire era of the 1860s, we find ourselves with a starting point of the 1855-1868 rules of proof, which, of course related to the use of black powder, as 'smokeless powders' had not yet become workable. Modern shooting men, perhaps used to seeing a chamber size stamped on the barrels may be perplexed to find no such clear marking on many early hammer guns with original proof marks.

In fact, no chamber size indication was provided by proof stamping until the 1887 rules of proof came into force, at which time a diamond was stamped on the barrel flats with the bore size and an indication of chamber length by the following key (we shall use 12-bore as an example):

1. A diamond with '12' inside indicated a 'chamber-less' gun. (Made for thin brass cartridges)
2. A diamond with '12' and 'C' inside indicated a 2½ inch chamber.
3. A diamond with '12' and 'LC' indicated a 3 inch chamber.

Where service loads are indicated, under the 1896 rules of proof, a 12-bore load of 1⅛oz indicates a 2½" chamber and a stamp showing 1¼oz indicates a 2¾" chamber. This rather difficult system persisted until 1925, when the new rules required explicit stamps to show chamber length clearly. Here can be found either a 2½" or 2¾" or 3" stamp, which needs no further explanation. These rules were in force until 1954; well past the manufacture date of any of the hammer guns of interest to readers of this book. However, they are useful to know because many guns will have been re-proofed one or more times and will bear 20th century proof marks.

In 1954, the imperial mark of 2½" could be stamped as an option in the metric equivalent of 65mm, the 2¾" equivalent was 70mm and the 3" corresponded to 76mm.

In 1989 the imperial option was dropped in favour of the metric and in 2005, the terms 'Standard' and 'Superior' proof were coined to indicate proof pressures. The test for the 65mm and 70mm Standard ('STD' with crown above) Proof became the same pressure (850 BAR). The long-chambered 3" or 2¾" guns, previously considered 'Magnum' could be tested at a higher level (1200 BAR) and stamped 'SUP' with two crowns above for 'Superior Proof'. Superior re-proof stamps will not be common on old hammer guns.

The vast majority will have been made with the standard British chamber length of 2½". Black powder era guns (made earlier than the 1887 rules of proof came into force) will often have been re-proofed for nitro and therefore bear re-proof marks from a later date.

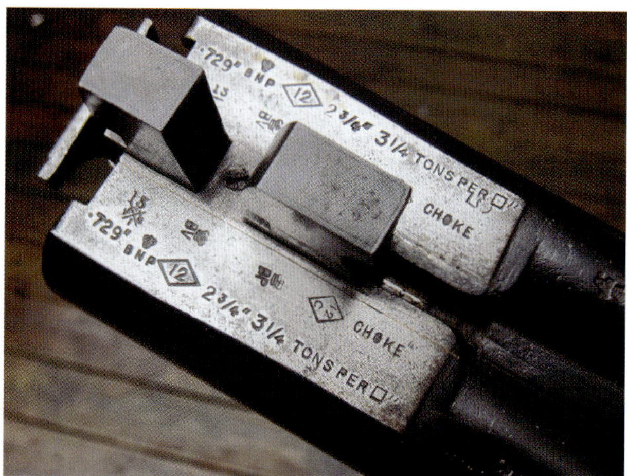

A steel barrelled Pape with 2¾" chamber stamps. Note the 3¼ TON pressure stamp.

Chamber gauges of the modern Triebel type used by the Proof Houses.

CHAMBER LENGTHENING

British proof law requires that guns be subjected to re-proof if the chamber is lengthened. Therefore, a hammer gun made in 1880 with 2½" chambers which has had chambers lengthened to 2¾" is legally out of proof unless it bears new proof marks indicating the new chamber length. It is technically illegal to offer such a gun for sale in the UK or Europe. Gunmakers in Britain know this and such problems are very rare.

However, guns that have been repatriated from the USA (or which are still there, for American readers) are often found to have had the chambers extended, sometimes competently, sometimes incompetently. In either case, the gun's value outside the US will have plummeted, as re-proof prior to sale will be a legal requirement and re-proof is not an inexpensive or risk free business. Modern proof tests are set at 25% in excess of maximum service pressure and two proof charges are fired in each barrel (it used to be one).

Chambers are measured best with plugs of the correct size and length. Chambers lengthened (from old 2½" to modern 70mm for example) and submitted for re-proof at the London or Birmingham Proof Houses will be expected to conform to the current CIP standard dimensions in all respects, including head space, rim shape, diameter and length. Be careful to ensure that your gunsmith has the correct cutting tools and gauges to perform the task accurately, otherwise getting the gun through re-proof could become difficult.

Bore Size

Bore size is much easier to determine than chamber length, as it has always been stamped clearly. Well, I say 'clearly' but we are talking about the British gun trade here, so a little work is still required in order to decipher the stamps accurately.

The stamping of bore size goes right back to the 1855 rules, so all our breech-loading hammer guns will have them. The 'whole numbers' are clear: '20' means 20-bore (.615") and '12' means 12-bore (.729"). However, to determine the size of the bore when the barrel was considered ready for proof, gunmakers used plug gauges. They dropped one in from the breech and when it stuck 9" from the breech end, that size was stamped on the tube. It may well be that the right barrel was made at .719" and the left at .729", in both cases they fall into the nominal 12-bore range and the chambers would be cut for 12-bore cartridges, but the difference is one proof size.

Fraction of an inch (calibre)	Bore Size Stamped on Tube	Designation
.740 .729 .719 .710 .701 .693	12/1 12 13/1 13 14/1 14	Nominal 12-bore with 12-bore chambers
.669 .662 .655 .649 .637	16/1 16 17/1 17 18	Nominal 16-bore, with 16-bore chambers
.626 .615 .605 .596	19 20 21 22	Nominal 20-bore with 20-bore chambers
.556 .550 .543	27 28 29	Nominal 28-bore with 28-bore chambers
.415 .413 .411 .410 .409 .407 .405	65 66 67 .410 68 69 70	Nominal .410 calibre with .410 chambers

It is very important to assess what the original bore size was, as proof status depends on it. In the example discussed, one could easily fall into the trap of assuming the 12-bore to be originally .729" in both. When measuring both bores, finding the left now to be .732" and the right .734", one could think the gun in proof, when, in fact the left barrel would be out of proof by three thousandths of an inch.

The above table shows the possible bore sizes within the range of commonly encountered nominal bore designations for hammer breech-loaders.

Bore size is measured with a bore gauge and the reading is always taken at a point 9" from the breech.

Damascus barrels spanned from the flintlock era, right through percussion, pin-fire, centre-fire and into the modern hammerless age. They are very durable and only gave way to steel because they were relatively expensive to make and required highly skilled craftsmen. This Charles Lancaster is as serviceable today, with modern ammunition, as it was when it was built in the 1860s.

Whitworth one-piece steel barrels

I once examined a 12-bore hammer gun by Edward Paton, a good gunmaker, from Perth, with whom I was familiar. It was shown to me by auctioneer Gavin Gardiner prior to one of his London sales. Firstly, I noticed the apparently swamped rib, with odd-looking, visible breech face, lacking the ramp to the rib usually encountered. Then the absence of a bottom rib became apparent. Finally, the penny dropped; the barrels were actually made from a single piece of steel, including the central 'rib' and were engraved 'Joseph Whitworth & Co'.

This 19th century hammer gun's barrels mirrored the current over & unders of modern gunmaker, Longthorne, who describe them thus:

'Solid construction... the barrels involve an innovative method of manufacture which utilises neither chopper lumps nor mono blocks. The high specification material we use to manufacture the barrels results in them being extremely strong but also light…'

In a nutshell; one piece barrels. Whitworth to Longthorne: history is repeating itself.

Joseph Whitworth is well-known to gun collectors for his steel tubes and, especially, for his rifling. He was an engineer who brought mechanisation to many craft processes and in doing so helped modernise British gun making. Damascus barrels, of various types and quality, had been used since the days of flintlock, but quality control had always been a problem and craft techniques in a mechanical age were out-dated.

The problem with using early homogenous steels for barrel making was in the process for casting ductile steel, as it tended to leave air pockets, which made the steel weak. Whitworth's patented solution in 1874, was an adaptation of Bessemer's principle of hydraulic pressure casting and it is the reason we see many old gun barrels inscribed with the words: 'Made from Sir Joseph Whitworth's fluid-compressed Steel'. The process was observed during a visit to the factory in 1877 by former US president, Ulysses Grant and described in a report: 'An immense loop of red-hot steel was lifted from the furnace and quickly reduced to one half its size by hydraulic compression, so as to fit it for its purpose in breeching a gun.'

While this may be well-known, Whitworth's earlier patent number 1645 of June 1857 is often overlooked. It refers to the milling of two barrels from a single piece of fluid steel. The process leaves the two tubes joined by a thin central rib. In the Paton gun, the top rib is laid only at the muzzle, to site the bead. The proof marks are London and denote pre-1875 proof as a 12-bore. The Paton records do not help much, only indicating manufacture between 1875 and 1887. Two other observations: firstly, Whitworth was knighted in 1869 and later barrels referred to 'Sir Joseph Whitworth' and, secondly, Joseph Whitworth & Co was formed in 1874. These different styles can help with dating a gun.

Gavin had catalogued it with the following notes:

'The gun has one-piece barrels made by Sir Joseph Whitworth, patent number 1645 of 1857. The patent specification mentions numerous improvements and mentions specifically "also in making double barrel guns I bore both barrels out of a solid piece of metal leaving the requisite thickness of metal in certain parts to give the necessary rigidity, the object being to make the barrels shoot parallel without making the piece unnecessarily heavy."'

Edward Paton back-lock 12-bore. It looks conventional enough at first glance.

The breech end shows the rib-less profile.

At the muzzle, the bead is mounted on a simple insert.

So, the Paton's steel barrels were probably made around 1874, using Whitworth fluid-pressed steel and conforming to his 1857 patent for one-piece barrels. But what is the point of the single-piece barrel? If it is such a good idea, why did it not gain popular acceptance? For an answer, we come back to 2012 and Longthorne Gunmakers, who told me they believe it was a combination of high cost and inferior available materials back in the mid 19th century.

The modern Longthorne's gun barrels are made from much harder steel than Whitworth had available. Their 30" barrels weigh just 47 oz with ¾" chokes and a minimum wall thickness of 37 thou'. Whitworth steel was softer and with a less favourable weight-to-strength ratio (though traditionalists will tell you that steel which is 'too hard' is very difficult to work if you do have to raise a dent). Today, with more sophisticated machinery and better materials, Longthorne claim to have made Whitworth's 1857 idea practicable and cost effective.

One may legitimately wonder why Whitworth felt the need to differ from the status quo at a time when barrel making was a well established process. Traditional barrels are made from two tubes with either dovetail or chopper-lump construction. The ribs and loop are then soft-soldered in place.

Any barrel's potential weaknesses are the points of assembly. Dovetail lumps can work loose, as can loops and ribs. Solder can fail and allow moisture to collect, rusting the barrels from the hidden valley between them. The ribs and solder add weight to the barrels and the various heat treatments applied when brazing, soldering and fitting barrels can affect the straightness and qualities of the tubes.

A one-piece construction avoids all these problems: the ribs won't rust out, the loop won't work loose, the lumps won't fail and the barrels can be made lighter, straighter and closer together. Longthorne believe the benefit of straight tubes is a reduction in recoil, and shot patterns which converge much better.

Sir Joseph Whitworth was a man well ahead of his time; in gun making and other industrial disciplines. It was a fascinating experience to link his idea, dating from the year in which Darwin published his treatise on evolution, with cutting-edge gun-making technology.

The Paton hammer gun with Whitworth barrels and the modern Longthorne over & under are cousins, showing that modern gunmakers are still looking back to the days of the hammer gun for ideas, and that very few 'new innovations' in gun making are truly novel.

The barrels are browned, with a mottled pattern.

Lumps are integral with the barrels.

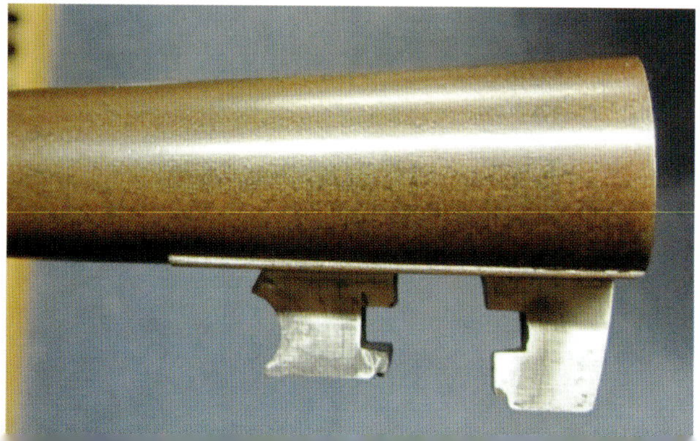

DAMASCUS CHOPPER LUMP BARRELS

One frequently encounters comparisons in barrel construction, when such things are discussed; the conventional wisdom being that chopper lump barrels are the quality choice, employed in the best guns. Lower quality guns, made where a cost saving was desirable, would generally employ the dovetail lump method. Gun making factories experimented with other variations of fixing the lumps into the breech section, like Bonehill's 'clip-lump' patent, which was used extensively by the firm in the late 19th century and variations of the idea were used by other firms well into the 20th century. However, many of these options emerged in the era of steel barrels, which began to make inroads during the 1880s and became very popular in the mid 1890s.

Parsons' patent chopper lump damascus barrels.

In the era dominated by the hammer gun, spanning the years from around 1860-1880 the materials of choice were various combinations of 'twist' or 'damascus' steel. Damascus barrels will almost invariably have tubes and ribs of damascus steel with dovetail lumps; the harder steel needed to minimise wear on the hinge pin and hook differing from the softer damascus tubes, which were more forgiving and elastic, as befits the purpose to which they were employed.

However, very few ideas in 19th century gunmaking went unexplored. The chopper lump system of forging the tube and lump for each barrel out of a single piece of steel, then fitting them together with a single, central joint, will, very occasionally, be found on guns with damascus barrels.

Chopper lump barrels may have become the choice of the best gunmakers in the steel era but the patent pre-dates that. It can be attributed to Henry Parsons, of 2 Hanley Street; another of those Birmingham gunmakers who provided the inventive spark that London firms applied and took much of the credit for. He patented ejector and safety mechanisms but his major legacy is the chopper lump barrel. His patent symbol of a hammer with one pointed face can be found stamped on damascus barrels with chopper lumps conforming to his patent (No.201 of 20th January 1868). Early guns, made while the patent was still in force, will be stamped with a use number as well.

W. Richards with chopper lump damascus barrels.

I have handled a small number of guns fitted with chopper lump damascus barrels, by makers such as W. Richards, Henry Egg and James MacNaughton. Most of them date from the late 1860s or early 1870s.

A quality composition, the gun cased with accessories.

CHOPPER LUMP DAMASCUS BARRELS ON A W. RICHARDS WOOD-BAR HAMMER GUN

I have no reliable data on comparative wear resistance between solid steel lumps and chopper lumps made of damascus. Theoretically, the softer damascus steel should wear faster at the hook. This could be overcome by a harder steel shim being dove-tailed into the hook, which is a process that was commonly applied when guns were re-jointed in the past, before welding technology reached its current heights. Modern spray welding produces a harder bearing surface than the original one once re-jointing has been completed.

Damascus tubes can be made with differing degrees of hardness; the amount of hammering involved is the key to this. Typically double rifle damascus barrels will be significantly harder than shotgun damascus. It may be that the damascus used in Parsons' chopper lumps was produced with this hardness requirement under consideration. It is likely that the lumps, of the desired hardness, were welded onto the damascus tubes.

Discussions with one of Britain's best actioners revealed that it is preferable to have a harder cross pin and a softer hook; that way the hook alone wears and routine replacement of the hinge pin in subsequent years is not required when the gun shoots loose.

Interesting as it is to note, there really is no qualitative difference in practical terms between chopper lump and dovetail lump steel barrels,when both are made to the same standards of quality and workmanship. Even in the hammerless era of side lock ejectors with steel barrels, the top London firms all made best guns with chopper lump and with dovetail lump barrels, until the idea became set in the collective mind of the trade that chopper lumps were to be preferred for best guns.

Chopper lump damascus barrels on hammer guns can be viewed as an interesting feature and they can be a good talking point or serve as an example of an historical gun-making practice but they are no advantage and should not be taken as an indication of superior quality to guns with more conventional dove tail lumps.

Most damascus barrels have steel lumps brazed on with a dove-tail.

Hammer Guns for all Occasions: Wildfowling

The epitome of the hammer gun as a wild-fowling tool, but one of quality that defies its ostensibly plain exterior, is probably the double 8-bore by J&W Tolley. Those on the foreshore needed something muscular to kill big birds at long range and upping the bore size was the original answer to the question of how to do this. Of course, the pursuit of water fowl with shotguns was not restricted to the large bores, but to evoke the true essence of the foreshore, these behemoths of the salt flats are the ones which still create a stirring in the belly of a select few.

A 10-bore or 12-bore duck gun was modification of the basic game gun principles. The modifications being designed to extend the range, to withstand the severe conditions to which it was likely to be exposed, and to absorb the recoil of the heavier charges normally fired. Conversely, one could argue that, as 'fowling preceded game shooting, the differences should be viewed in reverse.

In the pre-choke years before 1875, range was addressed by loading duck and goose guns with heavier charges of bigger shot. An 8-bore was expected to deliver killing patterns of consistent quality at 80-90 yards. Normal game gun ranges for a 12-bore were closer to 30 yards. With the advent of choke, 12-bores with tightly constricted muzzles began to appear with greater regularity. Even the larger bores could be made lighter and with shorter chambers once choke was proven effective.

The retention of slower but simpler and more reliable mechanical devices was a feature of the wildfowler's gun. There was no need for very fast re-loading or automatic ejection. As a result, the Jones under-lever continued in use, even on hammer guns of high quality, well into the 20th century. Guns with side-nail attachment of the forend, gradually gave way to more convenient methods, like the Anson pushrod or snap-actions of the Hackett type or similar. As with other types, the non-rebound lock was dropped in favour of the rebound lock.

Unlike game guns, which were often carried to a peg and handed to the shooter by a loader, wildfowling guns are frequently found with sling eyes, to enable a heavily encumbered sportsman to carry it on his shoulder while making his way over rough ground. The stock itself may well be shorter than the average and be for semi, or full pistol grip type. These grips provide more strength as well as sure purchase with wet hands. The reduced length reflects the heavy clothing the foreshore inhabitant had to don out of necessity in the cold, wet, muddy domain of his quarry. A vest, shirt, thick sweater and greatcoat added an inch or two to the perceived length of the stock, when used.

Most wildfowling hammer guns will have damascus barrels, though Whitworth steel made inroads, as it did with game guns. In addition to the plain, but well-made 'fowling pieces for the UK market, far more elaborate examples remind us of the demands of the wealthy Indian princes, whose duck shoots were of monumental scale. Tom & Jim Purdey recorded one in *The Shot Gun* as *'quick work and hot work... your wash-leather glove is dripping in oil and you cannot tough your barrels.... as for the fore-end, it is oozing oil!'* They go on to explain the flight accounted for 800 birds to 20 Guns: *'a very nice shoot but by no means a really big day'*. The maharajahs in the time of the Raj were essentially British puppets, but they were kept in lavishly gilded cages, allowing them almost unfettered wealth to expend on whatever luxuries they desired. British gunmakers did very well indulging their whims and the legacy includes some sumptuously elaborate and unique wildfowling pieces.

However, we digress. The mainstay of the foreshore was the single or double 4-bore, the single or double 8-bore and the double 12-bore. Most firms would make a gun of this type but some firms specialised in them, J&W Tolley, Bland and Greener foremost amongst them. There is a great deal of variation in weight of wildfowling hammer guns of all bore sizes. Examination of these guns, which appeared in London auctions relatively recently, illustrates this.

LIST OF GUNS AND WEIGHTS

4-bores			
Maker	Barrel Length	Chamber Length	Weight
W.M. Watson & Son	42¾"	-	14lb 1oz
Holland & Holland	41¾" (single)	4½"	13lb 2oz
J&W Tolley	48" (single)	4"	15lb
J. Rosier	34"	3¼"	13lb
Rodda & Co	37¾"	4"	15lb
W&C Scott	36"	4"	15lb 14oz

8-bores			
Maker	Barrel Length	Chamber Length	Weight
E.M. Reilly & Co	29½"	–	13lb 0oz
E.M. Reilly & Co	34"	3¼"	13lb 0oz
E. Whistler & Co	39½"	3¼"	12lb 2oz
Mountstephen	36"	3¼"	11lb 12oz
W. Gallyon	34"	3½"	12lb 7oz
E.M. Reilly & Co	34½" (single)	3¼"	10lb 12oz
Cogswell & Harrison	37¼"	–	13lb 8oz
J&W Tolley	31¾"	3¼"	13lb 8oz

10-bores			
Maker	Barrel Length	Chamber Length	Weight
Ward & Sons	32"	2⅝"	7lb 10oz
J. Purdey & Sons	30"	–	6lb 14oz
J&W Tolley	30"	2⅝"	8lb 8oz
J&W Tolley	30"	2⅝"	7lb 15oz
Lincoln Jefferies	26"	2⅝"	6lb 11oz
G.E. Lewis	31½" (single)	2⅝"	7lb 7oz
E. London	29"	2⅝"	8lb 8oz
J.V. Needham	38"	2⅞"	8lb 12oz
George Gibbs	32"	2½"	8lb 10oz
J&W Tolley	32"	3¼"	9lb 14oz
J. Blanch & Son	28¼"	3¼"	13lb 8oz

Along with different chamber lengths, brass cases were developed for wildfowling in the 1880s and were available for the next three decades or so. The idea was to produce a waterproof cartridge case, but these new shells offered the other advantages of reducing the need for a forcing cone and providing more space for shot and powder, due to the thinner case walls.

This resulted in more powerful-for-bore guns and produced better patterns, with less recoil. One occasionally encounters these 'chamberless' guns and it is important to understand what one is looking at – otherwise the chamber size, bore size and cone shape will appear totally wrong for the type of gun under examination.

Cartridges of 3" length for the 12-bore appear to have become popular with wild fowlers from the late 1890s, with Tolley's introduction of the 'Altro' cartridge of that length, with guns made to match. As hammer guns gave way to hammerless types, like Greener's 'Empire' and the ubiquitous Anson & Deeley, nitro powders, effective choke boring and more powerful loads made the heavy 12-bore a more common sight in the hands of a duck hunter as the 20th century progressed.

The use of big guns declined steadily, though always attracted a small but dedicated following, which persists to the present day, though American wild-fowlers are restricted to hunt with guns no larger than 10-bore, due to legislation introduced to discourage the large scale commercial slaughter of wild birds for the market.

After several decades in the doldrums, big bore guns made a huge come-back in popularity during the early 21st century as a small number of collectors began to seek out the best.

All markets can be affected by a glut and in 2015 Christie's sold a large collection of 4-bore and 8-bore guns from the USA, rather flooding a small market. However, these guns are unlikely to come onto the market again for quarter of a century so anyone seeking one will again have to look carefully among the guns that are available.

4-BORE DOUBLE

A gun of this type would be expected to fire a 3oz load. 4-bores can weigh up to 20lbs.

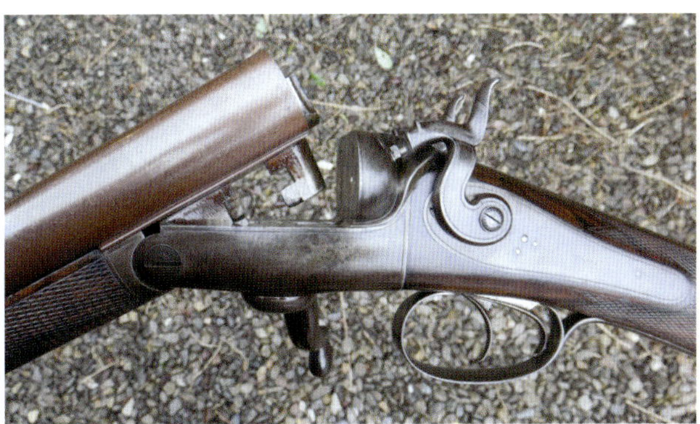

8-BORE DOUBLE (Purdey)

An 8-bore of 12lbs can handle a shot load of 2oz. They can weigh as much as 21lbs and be chambered for cartridges of 4½".

10-BORE DOUBLE (Purdey)

Typically weighing 9lbs and firing 1½oz loads, the 10-bore offers greater performance and comfort for shooting long range ducks than a 12-bore.

BRITAIN'S ONLY SHOOTING INDUSTRY PUBLICATION
GUN TRADE NEWS
WARNING

Pigeon Shooting

In the early days of live pigeon competition shooting, bores larger than 12 were quite common, many of them being light 8-bore or, more commonly, 10-bore guns designed to shoot the regulation load.

The determination that a gun may have started life with the pigeon ring as its intended domain, rather than the foreshore can be clouded. Generally, pigeon guns will be more profusely engraved and finished with more delicacy than their wild-fowling brothers. Few serious 'fowlers bothered to have their guns elaborately detailed because they knew they would very likely see a lot of cold, wet, muddy evenings and that function had to determine form. Even very high quality 'fowling guns were often plain, though fit was top class.

The pigeon gun, conversely, was more often than not found in an environment which allowed for a good deal of third party admiration. The fashionable gentleman attending a pigeon match would often like his gun to reflect well on him as a person of means and taste. This is the reason we encounter large bore guns of especially fine quality and finish. The other reason is that a very wealthy sportsman could afford the finest embellishments on his duck guns, as on everything else and was not concerned about the cost. These clients were generally foreign royalty.

Pigeon guns do not have to have side clips, though many do. They do not have to be pigeon guns if they have flat ribs, though many pigeon guns do have flat ribs. Pistol grip stocks became a standard feature of pigeon guns in the hammerless era but most hammer pigeon guns will have straight hand stocks well into the 1890s. In short, there are no sure-fire ways to perform a tick box operation and determine if a gun is pigeon gun, a wild fowling gun or a heavy pheasant gun. Visual cues will need to be observed in tandem with one another to make a balanced evaluation as to the likely original purpose of the gun.

The examples illustrated will serve to indicate some of the pigeon gun features readers may encounter on guns of the hammer era.

Shooting live box pigeons in North Carolina.

Above, a 19th century magazine feature on live pigeon shooting in London with Edward VII in attendance.

Facing Page: Howard Dixon of Christie's sold a huge collection of big-bore guns in December 2015.

A blue rock pigeon engraved on a W.P. Jones 12-bore.

An F.T. Baker pigeon gun with full choked steel barrels. Patterns are outstandingly regular and even.

An ivory bead on the muzzle of this pigeon gun helps find the target in difficult light.

Side clips are a common feature of pigeon guns.

A W.P. Jones pigeon gun with patent single trigger. Single triggers are very rare on hammer guns.

This Scott has 'Improved bolt' and side bolsters to enhance the strength.

Pigeon guns today find favour with many competitive shots. This is a scene from the 2014 Hurlingham Cup ZZ competition in Kent. ZZ (Helice) is the closest British competitors can get to live pigeon shooting on home soil.

Double Rifles

One cannot help but fall for the beguiling qualities of the 1870s double hammer rifle.

The beauty of the old, heavy bullet, medium game rifles, for that is what they were (dangerous game in those days was tackled with 'bore rifles' at close range), and the sheer quality of construction and attention to detail is breathtaking.

For many Victorian hunters, utility required them to adopt military weapons or commercially available repeating carbines. Martini action rifles were common, as were Winchester lever-action repeaters. However, for the discerning and wealthy gentleman heading out in search of 'soft skinned' dangerous game (lions, tigers and bears) or for tackling red deer or exotic ungulates of a decent size, nothing would do but a double rifle.

It is remarkable how many of these rifles still exist and appear to be in very good condition, considering the relatively small numbers that were made and the work they were intended to undertake. The key decades are the 1870s and early 1880s. Smokeless powders developed in the 1870s, like Schultze, were more easily applied to smooth bore guns than to rifles, until refinements allowed for their wider adoption into rifle ammunition. Vieille's 1884 'Poudre Blanche' was promising, followed in 1888 by Nobel's 'Ballistite' and in 1891 by 'Cordite'. This heralded the advance of 'nitro express' rifles.

One must not confuse these later 'N.E' rifles with the 'BPE' guns of the 1870s and 1880s. While both types appear in various .400, .450 and .500 calibre guises, the BPE versions are medium game rifles and the NE versions designed for thick-skinned dangerous game, like elephant and rhino.

Performance characteristics of .500 NE and .500 BPE will tell the tale: original performance with black powder propels a 440 grain bullet at 1,500 fps and a muzzle energy of 2,198 ft-lbs. The .500 (3") BPE, loaded with nitro-for-black powder, fired a 440 grain bullet at 1,900 fps, delivering 3,530 ft-lbs of energy. The .500 (3") NE, loaded with Cordite and firing a 570 grain bullet, achieved speeds of 2,150 fps and 5,850 ft-lbs of energy. A .500 BPE is likely to weigh in the region of 8½ to 9 lbs, whereas the nitro version will tip the scales at 10½ to 11½ lbs.

Classic Stephen Grant .500 BPE, made in 1871.

Clearly, the rifles are very different, despite the bores being equivalent sizes. The .450 and .500 NE express rifles carried by elephant hunters in Africa in the early 20th century are very different to the . 450 and .500 BPE rifles used for tiger in India in the late 19th century.

The double hammer rifles of the '70s and '80s are the epitome of hand crafted precision implements. They were made at a time in which craftsmen in the gun-making factories and workshops of Birmingham and London were at the zenith of their skills and ingenuity. Handiwork predominated, every surface was made to its exact final shape and contour from a forging by a supremely talented and experienced gunmaker. Different parts of the process were specialised and undertaken by specialists.

1902 Holland & Holland Royal de luxe .450 BPE.

The skills required to make a double rifle hold 'on point' effortlessly, despite its weight, come to rest with a perfectly steady sight picture through the leaf and ramp sights and group acceptably at set ranges are exceptional. Considering the technology (or lack of it) available to the gunmakers of the day, what they produced in terms of functional perfection and artistic beauty is remarkable.

For most rifles of this type, knowledgeable gunmakers appear to have favoured the combination of back-action locks, often with bolted hammers, rounded bars and the 1859 Henry Jones screw-grip (also called a double-grip) action. Barrels are usually of damascus construction and the forend held by a wedge and escutcheon in earlier versions and a lever-grip in later ones. Both provide a very secure fastening.

In rifles, security and stability were more important than speed, whereas with shotguns, speed of re-loading was increasingly important to sportsmen, as driven game shooting became more popular.

As an example of the type, we can examine a .500 Stephen Grant rifle, built in 1871. It conforms to all the build attributes listed above, with Jones grip and under-lever, wedge-attached forend and leaf sights.

• The stock has a curved pistol grip, which felt immediately comfortable and secure in my hands, the guard-strap extending into the steel grip-cap, providing a subtle but effective bolster to strengthen the wood.

• The rib is full-length, flat and filed to reduce glare, much in the manner of a live pigeon gun. It has a standing leaf sight for 50 yards and a further two, folding options for 100 and 150 yards.

• The action has a short top-strap and is filed flat to the rear of the rib. Engraving is generous coverage of fine scrolls. Despite its 190-year age, the rifle is in fabulous condition. It retains a lot of original case colour hardening, including on the lever, which, restorers should note, was originally cased-hardened, not blacked.

• The non-rebounding locks are bolted, in this case with bolts placed forward of the hammers, to hold them at half-cock. This prevented inadvertent cocking of the rifle, when carried loaded but not required for

Purdey with guard lever and bolted hammers.

imminent discharge. It functions as a very secure, but early, form of individual safety catch for each lock. Most conventional safety catches merely lock the triggers, so the bolted hammers are actually safer, though slower to operate.

• Ammunition is relatively easy to find. Kynoch provide nitro-for-black ready-loaded in new brass cases. Re-loading is still popular with owners of BPE rifles, as they can experiment with loads and bullet weights. Many of these rifles come with loading data on the cases or sometimes engraved on the rifle itself. Cases often contain bullet moulds and powder measures.

As for the cost of collecting one of these beautiful rifles: the Stephen Grant illustrated here was sold for $6,000 in the US. Holt's listed an 1872 Purdey .500 (3") in March 2016 with an estimate of £3,000–£5,000 and an Alexander Henry .500 (3") made in 1873 with the same estimate.

If one considers £5,000 a typical purchase price for a very good example, these rifles are exceptional value for money. They are probably the hardest thing to make. In fact, nobody could make you one today approaching the finesse and featuring the apparent alchemy required to make these engineered masterpieces look, feel and operate the way they do. If they could, they would want to charge you close to £150,000.

A best Purdey .500 with island locks, bolted hammers and lever-over guard.

Notable Provenance

Provenance. Much is made of it by vendors and collectors, perhaps too much at times. I once had a Purdey 20-bore hammer gun that belonged to Lord Lilford, the Victorian aristocrat who introduced the little owl to these shores. He was an interesting, historically significant gentleman. I enjoyed researching his life and times, and owning his Purdey was a pleasure enhanced by the knowledge I had of its original owner. When I sold it, the provenance made no difference to the buyer; the gun sold on its merits.

I often have would-be sellers waxing lyrical about the fact their gun was made for General This or Admiral That. Unfortunately, the nature of these very expensive items is that the only people who could afford them were 'somebodies'. The top end of the Victorian gun-buying public consisted of British royalty, aristocracy, captains of industry and their foreign counterparts.

Practically every Purdey sold in the 19th century went to a 'person of quality'. This makes provenance a hard sell when it comes to pushing up the price of a gun. To have a real impact, the original owner had to be somebody really important.

Shooting, like most walks of life, has its own higher echelons, its own icons and superstars. Add to these the great political and literary figures of the day and the major European and Asian royal families and you start to arouse interest beyond the merits of the gun involved.

Publications like Jonathan Ruffer-Garnier's *The Big Shots* and more recently, Rupert Godfrey's excellent *Olly*, which charts the life and times of the 2nd Marquis of Ripon, Frederick Oliver Robinson, have provided modern enthusiasts with insights into the world of the heyday of the country house shooting parties that dominated the social scene in a manner now impossible to truly recreate. What this does, however, is create interest in possessing the guns once used by the shooting stars of the day.

Auctioneer Gavin Gardiner snared a lovely collection of these coveted objects during his winter travels and presented them in his April catalogue in 2015. The collection included fifteen guns and rifles, once owned by the shooting superstars of the second half of the 19th century. The impressive roll-call names: The Duke of Cambridge, King Edward VII, Lord Ripon, Lord Walsingham, and Prince Albert. Some of the guns were presents to her family from Queen Victoria. Another gun, a double 8-bore was made by John Dickson for the eccentric collector Charles Gordon (his life story is well told in *Magnificent Madness* by Donald Dallas).

Now this kind of provenance is something that will make serious collectors sit-up and take notice. Only very rarely does one get the opportunity to buy the guns of the royal shooting set. Their exploits are well recorded

Below: Gavin Gardiner sold this group of guns with royal and aristocratic provenance in 2015.

Capt. Charles Dundas V.C.

and their photographs widely available. To buy into this kind of history is very appealing.

Some years ago Holt's sold a pair of Stephen Grant under-lever hammer guns, gifted to the then Prince of Wales by Queen Victoria in 1871. They made £50,000, if memory serves. European royalty and nobility don't quite garner the status of the British Royal Family when it comes to adding collectibility to a gun. The exception would be the Russians; as the newly wealthy elite compete to gather the trappings of the Romanov dynasty.

It helps that the guns of the rich and famous are generally of the finest quality and by the best makers of the day. Examples include the Duke of Cambridge's 12-bore hammer gun, Lord Walsingham's 12-bore Purdey hammer gun, Lord Ripon's Purdey self-cocking hammer 20-bore and one of his early (1868) Purdey hammer 12-bores, which were apparently, his favourite guns.

An interesting observation, which shines a light on the relationship between the friends Ripon and Walsingham, is the timing of the delivery of the two smaller bore Purdeys. Ripon's 20-bore was made with 33" barrels and was, perhaps, a point of discussion during the season, as Walsingham took delivery of his 16-bore just nine months later, also with 33" barrels. He evidently did not get on with it, as he subsequently had them shortened to 30". We also see that, as choke-boring became all the rage, the Prince of Wales's set all ordered guns with high degrees of choke, but mostly had them altered later, or reverted to using their open-bored guns.

Of course, collecting is cyclical. A collection is amassed during someone's lifetime and then liquidated when age requires it, hopefully netting the collector a few thousand pounds for his dotage and enabling a number of new enthusiasts to take pleasure in the ownership of these interesting items. Who would not like to be afield and make passing comment to his fellow gun that he just happens to be shooting Lord Ripon's favourite Purdey?

Another gun with collectable provenance I saw recently is a 20-bore H.Holland hammer gun, once the property of Lady Randolph Churchill, Sir Winston's rather colourful mother. Churchill, like Teddy Roosevelt, is one of the few politicians whose status is sufficiently iconic to raise the value of an item significantly.

In my own collection is a Lang converted pin-fire with forward facing under-lever. It was sold to a Lt. James Dundas of the Bengal Engineers. I have no idea what level of sport Dundas enjoyed with the Lang on his Scottish estate, but I do know that he won a Victoria Cross in the Bhutan War of 1865. He was killed in action in Afghanistan in 1879.

The provenance in this case adds no monetary value to the gun but my Army friends, especially the Royal Engineers, appreciate it and I try, once a year, as close as I can to James Dundas' birthday on 12th September, to load some black powder shells into the pitted old barrels and kill a partridge or two in his memory.

For some, provenance is about money, for me, it is about a tangible link to the past and the ghosts that still walk the fields with us.

The Lang 12-bore, made as a pin-fire and later converted to centre-fire. The mechanism is Lang's forward facing under-lever, inspired by the Lefaucheux.

Famous Hammer Guns and their Owners

LORD RIPON

Born Frederick Oliver Robinson, in January 1852, 'Ollie', as he was known, started his shooting career aged nine. His first gun was a 28-bore single muzzle-loader and he started with feral pigeons on the farm buildings at his Studley Royal estate in Yorkshire. By thirteen he was shooting grouse, partridge and pheasant and counting his scores among the highest in the line of Guns.

Wealthy aristocrat that he was, Ripon (he took the title in 1909 but was known as Lord de Grey for most of his life) was provided with fine guns from the beginning. It is not surprising that his local gunmaker, Thomas Horsley of York made him a pair in 1866. In 1868 he ordered his first trio of Purdeys. Early promise as a natural game shot flowered into adulthood as the most famous and admired game shot in the country.

The 2nd Marquis of Ripon (centre) in action.

His prowess at shooting moving targets was legendary. Whatever the situation, whatever the quarry, Ripon was an avid participant. He excelled in competition; shooting 'running deer' exceptionally well and was a top live pigeon shot, though not quite on a par with the finest trap shots of the day. His element, however, was the grouse butt, the pheasant covert or the partridge drive. When driven game shooting was the pinnacle of social sport among Britain's elite, Ripon stood at the top of the tree. Between 1867 and and 1923, he killed over five hundred thousand head of game to his own gun.

Teasdale-Buckle, author of *Experts on Guns and Shooting* noted in response to a 'Top Shots' list in *Baily's Magazine* in 1903,

> *'Lord de Grey is the only shooter who is as good as his reputation. No doubt he is as good, for many of those who voted for him put him "in a class by himself", and more particularly when the shooting was extra difficult, as in strong wind and when the birds were far out'.*

Ripon owned many guns during his lifetime. He used hammer guns until his death in 1923 and some survive to this day. I have examined a number of them. Ripon favoured 30" barrels and seems to have been comfortable with the classic Purdey 'island lock' back-action guns that were very much in vogue during his formative years. An example of his taste is embodied in Purdey 12-bore number 14981, built in 1895. It has ¾ choke in both Whitworth steel barrels and is one of a pair. They were made without chequering on grip or forend. The locks are rebounding. However, they have a manual 'half cock' between the rebound 'half cock' and 'full cock'.

Ripon's self-cocking Purdey 20-bore with 33" barrels.

Although most associated with Purdeys, Ripon owned and used guns by others. We have noted the Horsleys of his youth. I examined another of Ripon's Purdeys recently, one of his first trio, built in 1868 with 30" damascus barrels, no choke, non-rebounding back-locks and no chequering. Weight is 6lbs 9oz with a 14½" stock. Another Purdey indicates Ripon, like other sportsmen, experimented. Serial number 10395 is a 20-bore self-cocking hammer gun with bar-action locks and 33" barrels, choked ¾ in both. Weighing 6lbs 3 oz and with a stock length of 14¾", this would have been an attempt at making a lighter gun for high birds. When I handled it, the gun seemed little used considering its age and one can surmise that it was not considered a success. Ripon's surviving Purdey 12-bores are very much worn.

Among collectors, Ripon is the real superstar of the Golden Age of driven shooting. His guns fetch a premium and demand is high.

LORD WALSINGHAM

Walsingham, of Merton in Norfolk, cut a dashing figure in the heyday of the driven shoot. Considered second only to Lord Ripon by his contemporaries, this lean, moustachioed aristocrat, born Thomas de Grey, still holds the record bag for driven grouse. He killed 1070 to his own gun in August 1888, shooting on Blubberhouses Moor. He was one of a handful of exceptional shots who graced the Victorian era's premier sporting estates in the last third of the 19th century.

One of Walsingham's guns, a Purdey 16-bore made in 1882 with 33" Whitworth barrels and weighing 6lbs 2oz, with rebounding bar-locks and 14" stock closely resembles the 20-bore Purdey owned by Ripon. He shortened the barrels to 29½", suggesting the long-barrel small bore experiment did not suit him. Interestingly, the top lever has a left-hand operation.

Apparently not one for new inventions, Walsingham ordered the last muzzle-loader Purdey made, in 1888. He changed the Whitworth steel barrels on some of his hammer guns for damascus after his record breaking grouse shoot, complaining that the new steel caused a 'gun headache' in a way that damascus did not.

Walsingham owned this 16-bore Purdey and had the barrels cut down from 33" to 29½".

Lord Walsingham in action with loader.

Walsingham was an intelligent and interesting man with a passion for science and nature and was a director of the British Museum. His prowess as a shot rested not only on his accuracy, but his speed. The ability to shoot quickly was very much admired, especially when gathering a team to shoot a record bag and Walsingham was the quickest of his set.

Sadly, his wealth, grand though it would seem to most readers, was insufficient to maintain his shooting commitments. Two of his three estates were sold and he lost the site in London upon which The Ritz hotel now stands. He died in relative poverty in 1919, having lived abroad for the last seven years of his life.

SPORTING ROYALTY

Probably the best-known royal sportsman, Edward VII spent most of his life as the Prince of Wales. Such was the length of Victoria's reign. The Queen never allowed Edward a defined role so, without much of a job to do, he spent his time leading society at play and where Edward led, the rest followed, at least those who could afford it.

Apart from food and women, preferably other people's, he seemed to enjoy shooting more than anything else. His Sandringham estate became the hub of a continuous round of country house shooting parties of ruinous extravagance, hosted in turn by the sporting lords, earls and dukes of the realm.

Edward's sporting life began in the early days of the breech-loader and his guns traversed the course of history covered in this book. It is impossible to be sure how many guns he owned as he was sure to have been gifted a great many by admirers, visitors or those seeking to commemorate an event with a suitable gift.

Edward was considered a decent shot, but certainly not amongst the top rank. What he lacked in talent, he made up for with enthusiasm.

I encountered a pair of his guns a few years ago. They were Stephen Grant 16-bore hammer guns, built for him as gifts from his mother, the Queen. He received the first for his birthday, in November and the second for Christmas, in 1870.

The guns were just a little more highly finished than standard guns, though not any more flashy. Everything was just perfect, down to the individual oak and leather cases, with special red leather and gold trade labels. They came to light via a Scottish estate, where Edward had reputedly swapped them for another pair of guns with his host, while a guest on the grouse moor.

Later photographs of Edward show him with Purdey hammerless ejectors, so he moved with the fashion as hammerless guns were perfected.

Edward's second 16-bore gun by Stephen Grant, received as a Christmas present from Queen Victoria. The first was a birthday present earlier in the year.

Edward's No.1 gun, wih P.O.W. feathers and his birthday 'Nov, 9th 1870' engraved in the gold oval.

Edward's son, later King George V, was a far better shot than his father and regularly ranked amongst the top shots in the country. He was present in 1913 when the record bag of over 4,000 pheasants was shot by a team of guns on one day; an excess he reflected upon to his own son, Edward VIII, as they departed for London.

Unlike Edward VII, George used Purdey hammer guns throughout his life, being pictured as late as 1923 shooting grouse with a back-lock 12-bore, of which he had several.

George had a distinctive shooting style, with his left hand thrust straight out in front. This was much copied by other sportsmen, keen to emulate His Majesty. It can help draw the weight over the front foot and the face onto the comb, which is helpful when shooting forward. However, it can cause a check in the swing if used on crossing birds or those over the 90 degree angle overhead and is not recommended by modern shooting instructors.

Guns that belonged to the royal family of this country and others emerge on the auction market with surprising regularity, as do accessories like cartridge magazines and gun cases.

Some of the history of these items can be accounted for as gifts, swaps or lost bets. Others, one has to speculate over. The gun room at Sandringham has a huge collection of guns owned and used by the royal family through the years. Clearly, some escaped.

If you can find a gun or accessory with genuine royal provenance, it can be a good investment as well as a lovely keepsake. You can be assured it will be of extra special quality and the market prizes these items above almost all others.

The other sporting royalty of note were the Indian princes. In return for their loyalty to the British Empire, they were granted great wealth and autonomy, though little real power outside their own feifdoms. Many were avid sportsmen and collectors, patronising the best British gunmakers from the 1860s until WWII. These guns are often very highly embellished and beautifully presented with tools and all kinds of accessories.

King George V shooting grouse in 1923 with a Purdey 12-bore hammer gun.

The Intrinsic Qualities of the Hammer Gun

It is a reasonable question to ask, in these days of reliable, versatile, modern, inexpensive over & under guns, why anyone would choose to encumber himself with a slower, less convenient, more fragile, harder to shoot field companion. As one who has shot most of his game over the past twenty years with a hammer gun, perhaps I should try to explain why.

STRENGTH

The boxlock is the strongest lock mechanism. Its few parts allow each to be very robust and unlikely to fail in use. Hammer guns have all the smaller parts that a hammerless side-lock has. More space is allowed in the lock because the hammer is on the outside rather than the inside. However, the hollow body makes the action of the boxlock weaker than a hammer gun or a hammerless side-lock.

Whatever the theoretical strengths and weaknesses of various actions, as discussed at great length by the grand of expert in such matters, Sir Gerald Burrard, time has taught us that a well made hammer gun's mechanical parts will last indefinitely if properly cared for, even with hard use. Each part was made of a grade of steel appropriate, and hardened or not according to the optimum degree desirable for its use and wear characteristics.

Without ejectors, extractors are stronger; without a safety mechanism, the hand is stronger; without internal hammers, the head is stronger. Each gun was made to do the job specified. While marvelling at the amazing robustness of 150-year-old hammer guns, one must consider the correct load for which they were designed and select ammunition accordingly.

SIMPLICITY

The majority of British hammer guns will be of either bar- or back-action format. They consist of the lock parts and the bolting mechanism, with an operating lever of some kind. The mechanisms are essentially simple. In a quality gun every part is optimised for best work. Each part does its job and will continue to do it ad infinitum. Breakages are infrequent, most commonly a striker may crack, a swivel might break or a spring might eventually fail. It it happens once every hundred years, in a moderately well cared for gun, you have been unlucky.

Even the most complex hammer guns lack complexity. The solutions to gun-making problems were generally cleverly engineered, beautifully executed and ergonomic. Snap-action guns have an extra spring (potentially a weakness) compared with inert actions, like the Jones. Apart from this, there are none of the irritations that we encounter with later guns; especially those of the early hammerless era, as superfluous niceties, such as single triggers and ejectors, added potential banana skins for the gun to trip over when exposed to repeated use in various hands and different conditions and climates.

There is very little to go wrong on guns without single-triggers, ejectors or snap-actions, like this Grant.

EASE OF MAINTENANCE

Your classic hammer gun has neither ejector nor single trigger to malfunction. The inert actions, like the Jones screw-grip have no springs to break. Every part of a quality hammer gun will be internally polished and burnished and so closely fitted that moisture and dust

Guns made to the order of royalty could be just a little better than the norm. This E.M. Reilly was made for Alfonso XII of Spain as a prize for a competition he organised. It is a 12-bore with rifle and shotgun barrels, cased with Dickson, Hawksley and Reilly loading tools and accessories, all presented in a blue velvet lined oak and leather case. It was made in 1880.

have very little chance to penetrate and do damage. Some hammer guns I dismantle after a century of inconsiderate storage, gleam like new once the old grease has been cleaned off the lock-work.

Damascus barrels are easy to remove dents from; it is also easy to strip them and to re-lay the ribs. Every part of their construction can be replicated with basic workshop facilities.

AESTHETIC APPEAL

The fact that a hammer gun does not need to accommodate hammers within the action body means that it can be made narrower across the fences, and immediately behind them. This makes for a more graceful gun, in my opinion. The hammers themselves are artistic sculptures and blend form and function to perfection. The individual and beautifully hand-crafted finish applied to many of these guns has, to my mind, never been surpassed in taste, proportion or quality.

Every gun seems to have a unique quality, even a personality; something that even the best modern guns lack. One can almost feel the hand of the artisan reaching through the years and connecting the two of you, as you cradle your 130-year-old 'fowling piece in anticipation of an evening flight of mallard or a steady stream of September pigeons folding their wings and dropping towards your decoy pattern, heads into the wind.

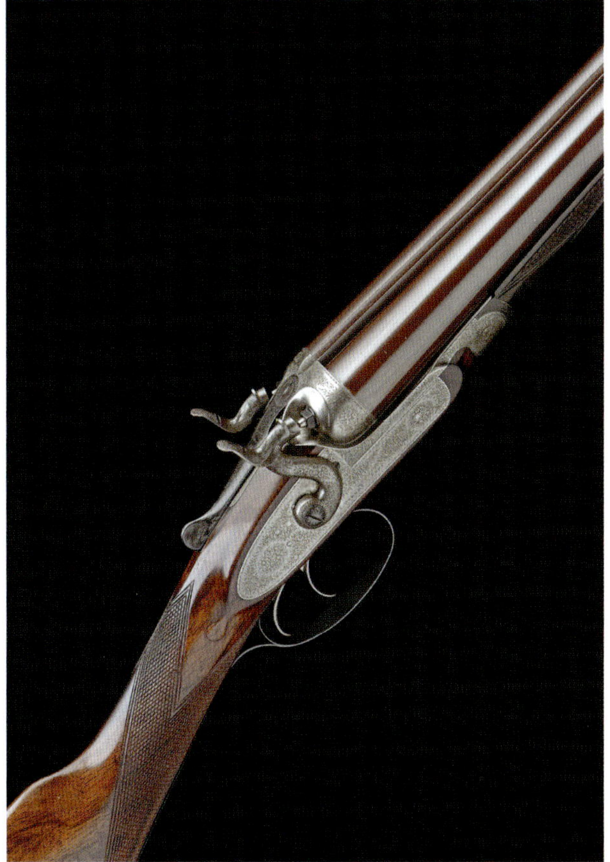

The elegance, balance and grace of a well-made hammer gun cannot be denied. This is a wood-bar Purdey.

BALANCE

This is a personal issue. Some prefer barrels to be slightly heavier to aid swing, others want weight in the butt to accelerate the gun from static faster. Balance is a science and an art. Gough Thomas once suggested that theoretically a pole with a one pound bag of sand at either end would 'balance' perfectly in the centre. Yet, we would not consider a gun with this weight distribution to be at all desirable. Somehow, a best quality hammer gun has the balance and proportion in-built in a manner that only time and experience can teach.

The old gunmakers knew how to make them right and those almost magical qualities remain with their offspring into old age.

SAFETY

A safety catch is a nothing more than a trigger block in most guns. Higher quality British hammerless sidelocks, and some boxlocks, will have an intercepting safety sear or block. In either case, the gun is cocked at all times when loaded and cannot be uncocked.

A hammer gun may be loaded with cartridges but remain incapable of discharge for as long as the shooter decides not to cock the hammer, with a deliberate, manual action. When walking over rough ground or sitting in a hide, the gun can be considered much safer than a fully cocked hammerless gun with a safety applied. This is not a substitute for muzzle awareness, which is the only absolute guarantee of safety, but all other things being equal, a gun which is not cocked is less risk than one which is cocked.

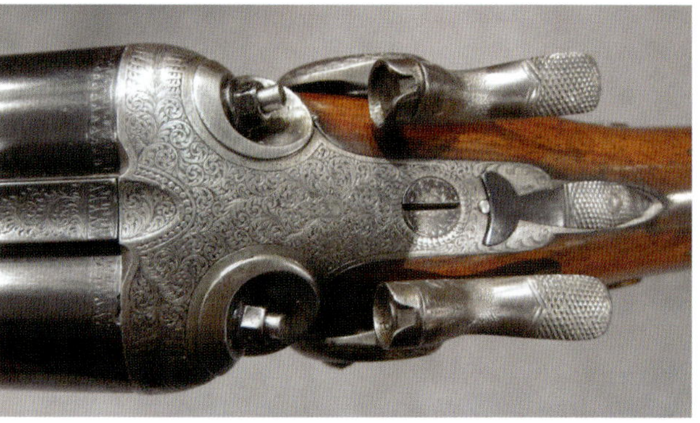

Hammer guns rarely have safety catches. However, never say never when talking about old guns. Modern Purdey hammer guns have incorporated a safety for legal reasons.

Below: The grip safety was once widely used but many deactivated in later life, as on this Morrow 12-bore.

The Glory of the 'No Name'

W. Thorn 12-bore in its element. Walked-up 'rough' shooting in Wales, where the slow re-loading cycle is irrelevant.

People are predictable. In the 21st century, the marketing-driven manipulation of the public's subconscious is so well developed that most people want what they are told to want, indeed, they appear to want to be told what to want. It is with depressing regularity that I'm asked by a tyro to the English gun scene to get him a "Purdey, Boss or Holland & Holland". He has little idea of what they are but it has been ingrained into him that nothing else will do.

I take my pleasure elsewhere. For me, the thrill of the job I now do and the passion I have for all that is fine in 19th century gun making is best embodied in an unexpected, yet exquisite gem, unearthed from some dusty cupboard or from under an old man's bed. Don't get me wrong, I'm as happy as Nick Holt to be handed an unused Purdey muzzle-loader, but what I both enjoy and can afford are the guns of equal quality that bear the name of some provincial maker, a Birmingham out-worker or a short-lived London firm, now largely forgotten.

The delight of the 'no name' is that few others appreciate the quality when it is there, based on its own merits. They can only recognise what they have been told to appreciate. It is easy to see a pretty piece of wood and a household name on the locks. It is harder to recognise true beauty of proportion, form and function when the object may be dirty, unconventional and unheralded.

I'm often asked what I shoot with. Surely a man with almost unlimited access to the finest guns in the world must be seen afield with the best of the best. I am indeed lucky to have the option to take guns off the rack by the famous makers, in their hammer and hammerless forms. The guns I choose to own are different.

W. Thorn 12-bore, with beautifully convex metal parts, put to use on the grouse moor.

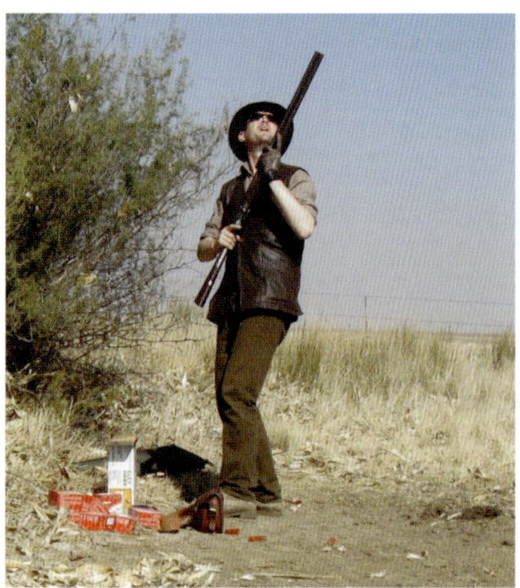

Driven pheasants in Kent, duck shooting in Hertfordshire in the snow or tackling African pigeons in the dry, dusty sunflower fields of the Free State, the author knows his 'no name' guns will out perform modern kit.

Purdey, Boss, Holland & Holland? Try Cashmore, Thompson, Thorn. I know they don't trip off the tongue quite as well and telling the chaps at the beginning of the day "I shoot with a Cashmore, you know" won't quite get them bowing with impressed deference but I find you grow out of that kind of thinking if you appreciate other qualities in a gun.

However, before we get carried away with whimsy, let me describe the guns I have on my personal shotgun certificate and which I take with me when I have pheasants to shoot at, grouse to bother or pigeons to annoy. It started with the Thompson. I know not which Thompson, although the initial 'J' narrows the choice of potential makers a little. The gun appears to have been re-barrelled early in its life, as it has London 'View' marks on the action, but Birmingham proof marks on the barrels. Unhelpfully, there is no address on the rib, nor a name.

The gun was unearthed from a widow's cellar, handed to a Midlands gun shop and bought by me for £50. I thought the action pretty but the gun was a basket case. Following a good bit of work, we rescued the whole thing, not just the action. Re-proof for 70mm and a thorough overhaul provided what I thought would be a good gun for travelling with. Something that would be able to accept rough treatment and which, if the worst happened, I'd not be too worried if the stock got broken or the barrels dented. I was, at the time, shooting predominantly with a Purdey side-lock ejector.

Three years later, I sold the Purdey. For some reason, it was getting left in the cupboard, while I shot the Thompson in preference. It seemed silly to have £15,000 worth of gun unused while I banged away with something that cost less than £500.

Since then, I have fired tens of thousands of cartridges through the old Thompson. She has shot spur-wing geese in South Africa, guinea fowl in Botswana, quail in Romania, woodcock in Wales and grouse in Scotland, not forgetting thousands of pigeons in England and Africa and wildfowl of all descriptions. Even on formal days, this has been my preferred gun. She has graced 400 bird driven pheasant shoots in the grounds of stately homes and lowly 70-bird walk and stand days around the family home in Shropshire, killed partridges at Six Mile Bottom and was once even loaded with buckshot in case of unwanted attention from lions while sleeping in a tent in the Okavango Delta. We have been close!

A beautiful old Morrow sidelever bagging woodpigeons with style.

Simply put, I shoot the gun because I like her. Because I shoot her a lot, I have learned to shoot her quite well. I have never had a fitting or adjusted the stock. I know it is ½" to ¾" shorter than I would recommend for myself. What choke she has is accidental, 3 points and 7 points. You may be surprised at her effective range with quality ammunition.

This choice of gun is not rational, it is sentimental. I love the fact that I rescued the old girl from the scrap heap, that my first two shots, taken while the proof house marker pen was still clear on the struck-up tubes, dropped wood pigeons right and left. We have history and to me that is worth a lot. However, it is not an affectation. I shoot the gun well. I feel confident when afield with the Thompson and if I had to go out and kill birds because my life depended on it, this is what I would take.

For years, the Thompson and I were a team. 'Trusty Rusty' as my friends disparagingly mocked her from Kent to Kroonstad. Many guns came and went through my hands during that time. Beautiful guns by all manner of maker. Some tempted me, but none stayed. Until the Thorn arrived.

Not a no-name of no fixed address like the Thompson, but not exactly a household name. One of my gunmakers sent it to me: "I've had this for years, I think you might like it" was the message at the end of a phone conversation about other repair work. The gun arrived a day or two later and I unpacked it without any trepidation, I expected something ordinary.

The biggest game bird in the world; the spurwing goose, taken without chokes.

Thorn was a lock-maker by trade and a gunmaker by profession, with London premises in The Strand in 1876. To most people this 12-bore with Jones under lever would be unremarkable. To me it was outstanding. Nothing is flat. The locks are slightly convex on the outside, as is the bar, the top strap, the lever work; everything. The skill with a file and the eye for subtlety required to make a gun this way is breathtaking. It is like nothing I have seen before. So subtle that one wonders who appreciated it other than the maker.

At home, woodcock and pheasants are my more common quarry.

Externally, the gun was grubby but original. As with the Thompson, too short and with too much drop for me. Never mind, I took it grouse shooting and did very well, the natural inclination of the gun to shoot low worked a treat, as driven grouse tend to be missed above. On driven pheasants it took a bit of mental adjustment to get used to, as these tend to be missed below and the gun was not helping!

So far, I have only cleaned up and re-browned the barrels and stripped and cleaned the mechanism. I will keep the gun forever but will do some head scratching before undertaking any radical refurbishment or re-modelling. She cost me £600.

Small bores have never been my thing. I like a gun to swing: both the Thompson and the Thorn weigh

7lbs. Victorian 20-bores are too light for me – I forget that the front arm has to work hard and when I switch to a 20-bore, I shoot badly. It has been pointed out that one can learn to shoot any kind of gun. This is true indeed but experience has never warmed me to small bores, pretty as they are. However, in the 2014-15 season I decided to shoot almost exclusively with a 20-bore.

The gun came with an unexpected phone call from a man in his late eighties. He has a 20-bore hammer gun by Cashmore, which he had owned since 1941 and occasionally used to shoot pigeons. He was giving up his guns and wanted to find a home for the Cashmore. Conversation turned to appointment and he came to see me with the gun.

I picked it up, checked it over and noted the dirty exterior and pitted barrels of a 'sleeper'. Black powder proof marks were original and the gun had clearly never been serviced. It was not worth the £2,000 I paid for it but I wanted to honour my verbal indication of probable worth and I wanted the gun. Somehow, I felt I could shoot with it and that was all that mattered.

The maker, William Cashmore, was a well regarded Birmingham gunmaker situated in Steelhouse Lane in the old Gun Quarter. He is best known for his pigeon guns and is revered in Australia, where he was one of the principal providers of quality guns, through his distributors there. In England he is considered by most as just another modest Birmingham maker.

The gun is unusual. Given that 20-bore guns were made in tiny quantities compared with 12-bores, it is quite rare. When one considers that most Victorian 20-bores were made with 26" or 28" barrels, the fact

The author with his 20-bore Cashmore in Scotland, tackling driven pheasants and driven grouse on alternate days.

The 20-bore Cashmore proved quick and effective on driven grouse.

that this has 31½" damascus barrels is very remarkable. The pistol grip stock is well proportioned and close to 14¾". Drop was about right for me, actually showing little more rib than I like, which should make it a good driven pheasant gun.

Like the Thorn, I baptised the Cashmore on the grouse moor. The wind was blowing, the grouse were fast and the shooting was quick. I could not have had a better companion. Early success with the Cashmore on the grouse was, sadly, a case of flattering to deceive. When the pheasant season began, I struggled in a manner that has become predictable for me when shooting small bores. I felt I lost contact with the gun. When engaging pheasants in open sky, the light gun developed none of the momentum of my 12-bores. I found myself 'poking' or trying to put on lead mechanically, rather than naturally. All this led to failure and by January, persisting as I did, I had endured the worst shooting season of my life.

Frustratingly, when at the clay ground and under no pressure, I found I was able to break the driven pheasant targets. So, the solution to the Cashmore problem has yet to be reached. It will involve a careful gun-fit session in the close season and some serious thinking and practising resolutions. It does underline the importance of muscle memory and familiarity with your gun when in a hot spot.

My total outlay amounts to about £4,000 in the three guns. Forming a personal bond with your firearms is, I think, a huge part of the pleasure of ownership. Instant gratification is not what is important, it cannot be rushed.

The Scottish grouse moor, Cashmore in hand. Possibly the most exciting bird shooting there is.

Selecting Appropriate Ammunition

British based owners of Victorian hammer guns are well catered for. Using a typical game gun, weighing between 6lbs and 7lbs and made with the normal chambering of 2½", today's sportsman can select a far wider range of loads, each well-suited to whatever task he may have for the gun on any given day.

Victorian gunmakers considered an ounce and an eighth to be a normal game load, this was shifted down in the early twentieth century to an ounce and a sixteenth, when it was found that it performed equally well with modern powders.

For many British game shooters, an ounce of No.6 or No.7 was considered a 'gentleman's load' and sufficed for the vast majority of sporting driven birds encountered on a traditional shoot and engaged with a classic side-by-side. This load became exemplified by the, once iconic, Eley 'Impax' cartridge, which was a favourite of the Guns when I was a young beater.

A quick check of the proof marks will indicate what your gun is chambered for.

A) The presence of one of the following marks will indicate the gun has 2½" chambers:

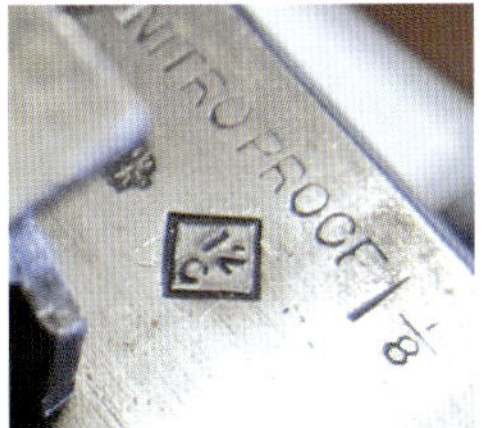

Some of these marks will be original to your gun, others will indicate later re-proof. These guns can be used with any CIP ammunition cased in 65mm, 67mm or 67.5mm shells. Caution should be exercised when using shells of the latter two lengths, guns with steep chamber cones may shred the extremities of the cases and produce greater felt recoil. A true 2½" chamber will favour 65mm hulls.

B) The presence of one of the following marks will indicate the gun has 2¾" chambers:

These guns can be used with any CIP ammunition cased in 70mm shells (not including those marked 'Magnum').

C) The presence of one of the following marks will indicate the gun has 3" chambers:

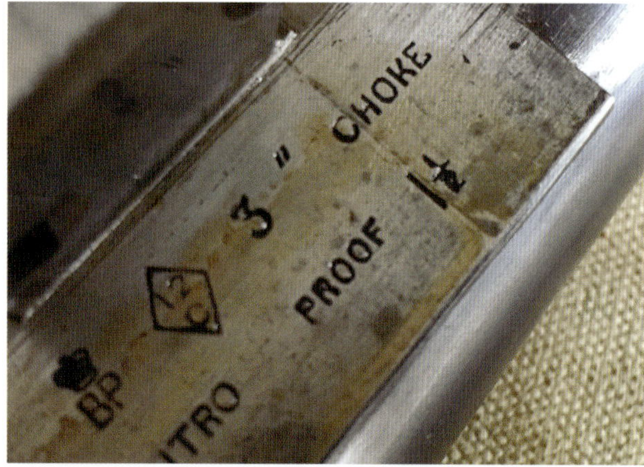

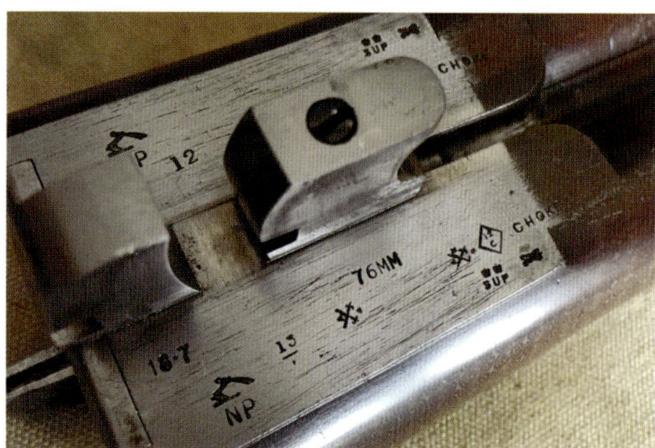

These guns can be used with any CIP ammunition cased in 76mm shells (not including those marked 'Magnum').

The British have always matched their guns to the ammunition they wanted to use, whereas American guns typically had to be able to digest whatever happened to be available. This attitude led the average British sportsman to be far more discerning in his choice: Purdey records, for example, regularly show guns made to order and intended for use with a specified load. The characteristics and weight of the gun would be calculated accordingly. They were tested and patterned with the desired load before dispatch to the customer.

As manufacturers, like Purdey, loaded the ammunition specified for a new gun, they would, thereafter, be able to supply a season's worth on demand and have it carried to the nearest railway station. I recall an 1889 Purdey side lock I once owned. That had been regulated for one ounce cartridges loaded with No.6 shot. This proved a useful guide as to what to use in the gun and it is what I generally chose.

American and continental users, however, often appear to have taken the view that if an ounce is good, then and ounce and a half is better. I still see this when visiting Italy and Cyprus, where 36g is considered a walked-up pheasant or partridge load.

In Romania, we were given hyper-punchy Italian 33g loads of No.11 shot for walked-up quail. I'm not sure if the quail suffered as much as the shooters did!

Conversely, when outfitting the annual bird safaris we organise in Africa, some of which are aimed specifically at users of vintage hammer guns, I order a variety of loads depending on the quarry. For pigeon shooting over crops or on flight lines, light, fast shells

Cartridges in the past were not made with the same standard dimensions as demanded by modern CIP treaty conventions.

A pair of damascus barrels fresh from the proof house, where the new (metric) chamber size and bore sizes are written in permanent marker.

deliver excellent patterns and save the user from the effects of heavy recoil. This is advantageous when a typical afternoon might require the shooter to expend between 250 and 500 shells.

Typically, I would recommend 24g loads of No.7 shot. Eley 'Trap' or Express 'HV' have been used with great success. Staying with 2½" shells, when a slightly heavier load is required for larger birds, modern game cartridges perform well. Eley 'High Flyer', Hull 'High Pheasant' and Gamebore 'Pure Gold' have been my choices for several years. Shot size choice is a personal one but for convenience, I generally buy No.6 as the best all-rounder.

Eley produce their excellent 'Maximum' cartridge as a heavy 34g load for the user of 2½" chambered guns and they are very effective. I invariably use these loaded with bismuth as my waterfowl load, when lead is not permitted.

As an habitual user of 2½" chambered guns, I never buy ammunition for the longer 2¾" chambers, even when I use guns designed or adapted for them. There really is little to be gained and 2½" ammunition is so good these days that it is not a compromise in performance to use it. It certainly makes life easier not to have to keep checking that you have not mixed two types in a cartridge bag.

Personally, I am very little concerned with choice of cartridge. Modern ammunition is generally so good that I have every confidence that its performance is certainly better than that of most sportsmen. When I see particularly good displays at the peg, I never think to myself "that chap must have better ammunition than the rest of us", it simply registers that he is a better shot.

Ego and performance errors in the field tempt one to blame ammunition where the fault is really the operator. Of course, the ammunition manufacturers feed this insecurity and urge us to buy their ever more advanced, faster, 'harder-hitting' creations. Amongst all the 'Extreme Game' and 'High Pheasant' brands, why do we not see any called 'Average Pheasant' or 'Low Partridge'? The answer is easy, nobody would buy them. We all think we need extra hitting power and extreme performance.

Most driven birds shot at and not killed are missed off line or behind. If a pellet on the edge of a misplaced pattern extracts a few feathers, the sportsman thinks he centred the bird and the cartridge let him down. Ego prefers to blame the kit. The number of times I hear people say what a tough bird the pigeon is; largely because he has so many small, dense feathers.

One pellet raking the chest or rump will leave a cloud of them floating in the breeze. Proof to the average shooter that the bird flew, like an A10 Warthog, through a wall of lead. Again, not the cartridge, nor the gun, but operator error.

Experience shows that 24g of No.7 shot, well-placed, will dump pigeons at 40 yards every time. My philosophy is to keep things simple. Find a cartridge you find comfortable to shoot in your gun, buy lots of them and never give it another thought.

If you like, have a light load, a normal load and heavy load. Then you have something for every occasion. What feels good on your shoulder is probably the most important thing. If your gun kicks you in the face every time you pull the trigger, you won't shoot well with it.

Many experienced users of British hammer guns in the United States, have of late fallen into the trap of believing that ultra-light, low pressure loads have to be used in them. They do not. An 1870 hammer gun with 65mm nitro proof will just as readily absorb modern factory-loaded 65mm cased ammunition as will a new side lock with the same proof marks.

While this low-pressure tendency is a welcome antidote to the old one of trying to put very heavy shells through everything, there is no need to fear: an old

Tight forcing cones will 'rag' longer cartridge cases. All these are nominally 2½" shells.

hammer gun in good condition can still do its work. For example, a 2½" cased performance game load, like 30g Hull 'High Pheasant' or Eley 'VIP' will have a muzzle velocity of 1450 feet per second and these are generally perfectly comfortable to use in a Victorian hammer gun which weighs around 6¾lbs or 7lbs.

Commercially loaded black powder shells are less easy to obtain than they were a decade ago.

I offer my own selection of ammunition here, not as an indication that it is the best choice, simply because it represents the, currently easily available, choice I have found works for me, and because I am often asked what I use in practice.

I offer the full list for the sake of accuracy but in reality, I shoot 90% of my UK game with Gamebore 'Pure Gold' 30g fibre-wad, No.6 shot.

For game shooting, it is increasingly required in the UK that fibre-wad versions of the above are chosen. Most manufacturers are well aware of this and provide fibre wadded versions of their popular loads. Photo degradable shot cups are sometimes allowable but they take a very long time to degrade and livestock farmers will still object to them, despite their 'green' credentials.

Despite the advocacy of certain well known and respected writers in the USA, I cannot and do not advise users of British guns of any kind, which are chambered and proved for 2½" shells, to use any ammunition with longer cases. If the box lists the ammunition as 65mm, 67mm or 67.5mm then it is safe to use in 2½" chambered guns.

Any cartridge in a case of 70mm or longer should not be used in these guns. For the record, I have never noticed that my scores at game shooting increased with the use of heavier loads than my 'norm' of 30g, nor decreased with the use of lighter ones.

More important is that the cartridges are good quality and comfortable to shoot in your gun and that you are shooting ranges within your ability and that of your kit. If you are going to take on 60+ yard pheasants in Devon or Wales, a sub 7lb game gun with open chokes is not the right tool.

Personally, I do not want to take a goose gun on a pheasant shoot and let 40g of No.3s off in an attempt to bring them down. If that is your sport of choice, it requires specialist equipment and training, which is outside the realm of this book.

Many shooters get hung up about ammunition. I am relaxed about it. If I'm not killing my birds, the chances are I am to blame, not my shells.

MATCHING LOADS TO QUARRY

Pigeon & Dove	Express HV 24g No.7	Eley Trap 28g No.7
Sporting Clays	Express HV 24g No.7	Eley Trap 28g No.7
Pheasant	Gamebore Pure Gold 28g/30g No.6	Hull High Pheasant 30g No.5
Partridge	Gamebore Pure Gold 28g No.6	Eley VIP 28g No.6
Grouse	Gamebore Pure Gold 30g No.6	Hull High Pheasant 32g No.5
Ducks	Eley Maximum 34g Bismuth No.4	Eley High Flyer 30g Lead No.5 (in Africa)
Geese	Eley Maximum 34g Bismuth No.3	Eley High Flyer 34g Lead No.3 (in Africa)

NON-TOXIC SHOT

Steel shot should not be used in any vintage hammer guns, regardless of proof status. We shall consider the use of lead, and lead alternatives, later in this chapter. The law in Scotland differs from the law in England and Wales and overseas readers will need to be mindful of local restrictions.

We can expect the ammunition manufacturers to continue making progress with available loads and perhaps in the near future a steel load for 'normal' guns will be available, rather than one requiring steel shot proof.

RE-LOADING

Re-loading is a popular pastime in the US, many shooting men becoming quite expert at the process and producing loads that suit their needs or preferences, as well as saving a few dollars.

In the British Isles, it is far less common. I have friends who re-load black powder ammunition for their more fragile old guns. I also know sportsmen who re-load pin-fire ammunition in order to keep their guns in service despite the absence of anything commercially loaded.

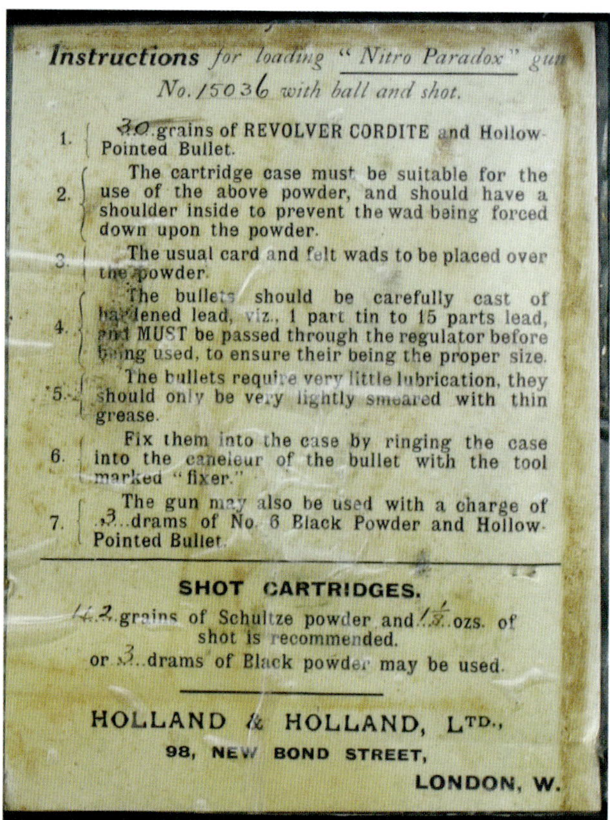

Instructions *for loading "Nitro Paradox" gun No. 15036 with ball and shot.*

1. 30 grains of REVOLVER CORDITE and Hollow-Pointed Bullet.
2. The cartridge case must be suitable for the use of the above powder, and should have a shoulder inside to prevent the wad being forced down upon the powder.
3. The usual card and felt wads to be placed over the powder.
4. The bullets should be carefully cast of hardened lead, viz., 1 part tin to 15 parts lead, and MUST be passed through the regulator before being used, to ensure their being the proper size.
5. The bullets require very little lubrication, they should only be very lightly smeared with thin grease.
6. Fix them into the case by ringing the case into the caneleur of the bullet with the tool marked "fixer."
7. The gun may also be used with a charge of 3 drams of No. 6 Black Powder and Hollow-Pointed Bullet.

SHOT CARTRIDGES.

42 grains of Schultze powder and 1⅛ ozs. of shot is recommended.

or 3 drams of Black powder may be used.

HOLLAND & HOLLAND, LTD.,
98, NEW BOND STREET,
LONDON, W.

The label above is loading data from the case of a Holland & Holland hammer 'Nitro Paradox' showing load data for both 'smokeless' and black powder.

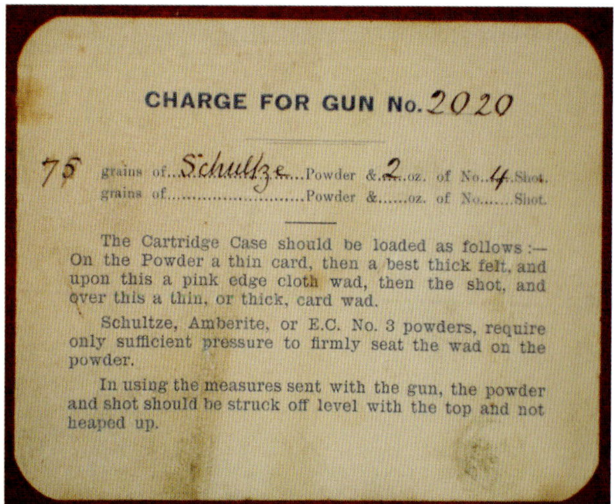

CHARGE FOR GUN No. 2020

75 grains of Schultze Powder & 2 oz. of No. 4 Shot.
grains of .... Powder & ...... oz. of No. ...... Shot.

The Cartridge Case should be loaded as follows:— On the Powder a thin card, then a best thick felt, and upon this a pink edge cloth wad, then the shot, and over this a thin, or thick, card wad.

Schultze, Amberite, or E.C. No. 3 powders, require only sufficient pressure to firmly seat the wad on the powder.

In using the measures sent with the gun, the powder and shot should be struck off level with the top and not heaped up.

Loading data from old gun cases is invaluable to the home loader. This is for a Leeson 8-bore shotgun.

Of course, if you are the owner of an early 4-bore, 8-bore, 10-bore, 14-bore, 32-bore or 24-bore then re-loading is one way of keeping the gun in service.

If you want to re-load using black powder, the correct licence must first be obtained from the police to own and store it.

Owners of obsolete calibre black powder hammer rifles benefit today from the re-launch of cases and bullets, as well as loaded cartridges, by Kynoch, after years of drought. This has made many old classics viable once more.

Home re-loaders also have fantastically precise data available for their old rifles, thanks to the exhaustive work of Graeme Wright, published in *Shooting the British Double Rifle*.

Kynoch, above, are once again making loads for many 'obsolete calibre' rifles, both in black powder and 'nitro-for-black' alternatives. Below, for home loaders, finding the right recipe to make your old rifle or shotgun pattern to perfection is all part of the fun.

1875 and all that (or who needs choke anyway?)

WHAT IS CHOKE?

Choke is a means of reducing the spread of the lead pellets in the discharged cartridge from what it would be if fired from a barrel which was an even bore diameter from chamber to muzzle (True Cylinder).

The means of effecting the desired reduction in spread is achieved by restricting the muzzle diameter, over about 1½", so that the shot is condensed as it exits the barrel. The greater the constriction (within limits), the tighter the pellets will be kept in flight and the further from the muzzle the effective 'killing pattern' of the load will be. In short, choke extends the killing range of the gun.

Before choke boring was perfected, range was extended by the use of 'shot concentrators', which were paper enclosures with fine wire inside, held rigid with plaster of Paris linings. They were filled with the shot charge and held it together. The wire basket would be dragged back by air resistance in flight but would hold the shot together for some distance, thereby extending the effective range of a gun with cylinder bores.

WHAT IS A 'KILLING PATTERN'?

A killing pattern is a 30" circle in which the pellets are evenly distributed enough so as to not let a game bird escape without sustaining mortal injury, if placed anywhere inside the circle. Since penetration is also a key factor in killing your bird, each pellet must retain sufficient energy to do the necessary physical damage at your normal range.

Ideally, the optimum killing pattern for your gun will be achieved with your desired load at the range at which you will usually engage your chosen quarry. This would be set at 30 yards for most driven game shooting. If you achieve your killing pattern at 30 yards without any muzzle constriction, using an ounce of sixes, you have a good all-round game gun.

However, if your typical target is a duck at 45 yards, then you need your killing pattern to be reached at that range, not 30 yards. A 30-yard circle will be far too open by 45 yards to deliver good results, the pellets

It is a worthwhile exercise patterning your gun with different ammunition.

This is the penultimate Boss hammer gun: a pigeon gun with full chokes, made in 1902.

will be too far spaced. A strong bird like a duck at that range also needs a bigger pellet, which retains greater striking energy, in order to be effective.

So, your ideal load for the duck at 45 yards would be a No.5 shot size. Bigger shot means fewer to the ounce. To make the pattern denser, the muzzles can be constricted until your killing circle at 45 yards equates to the ounce of sixes at 30 yards. This is the essence of choke. It helps gunmakers regulate any gun they make so that it can be suited to the job for which it will be used. This explains why different guns built for different types of shooting will be choked differently.

WHEN DID CHOKE BECOME COMMON?

Before 1874, choke boring was not a science. Barrel borers practised what were seen as dark arts and some built formidable reputations. First Fullard and then Lancaster were well-known for the quality and shooting regularity of their barrels. Pape introduced the first patent showing a muzzle constriction (in 1866) but the idea was also being experimented with in America (certainly by Fred Kimble), which Greener acknowledged when he quoted J.H. Walsh, editor of *The Field* writing; *'We cordially congratulate both Mr Greener and Messrs (W&C) Scott on the result of their labours, and whether or not they can fairly claim any improvements upon the American system (of choke boring), they, and especially Mr Greener, are entitled to the thanks of English sportsmen for bringing it prominently forward'.*

Mr Walsh, editor of *The Field*, was instrumental is addressing the benefits of choke in the 1870s.

Following experiments that he began in the spring of 1874, Greener caused a huge uproar with an advertisement he placed in *The Field* on December 5th of that year, in which he stated that he could build guns to order that would deliver a shot pattern far tighter than any other gunmaker would dare to claim. The actual figure was 210 pellets in a 30" circle using a gun weighing under 7¼lbs and firing 1⅛oz of No.6 shot, ahead of 3 drams of powder. To the sportsman, this offered the holy grail of being able to kill farther out than he had been able to do with regularity.

In an inventive and competitive atmosphere, where everyone was trying to make everything stronger, faster, farther, harder etc, where boundaries were being pushed in every human endeavour, the 'far shooting gun' was sure to be a hit. It would take a while for sportsmen to realise that there was a downside, but we shall consider that issue later.

The circumstances in which the efficacy of choke boring was proved beyond doubt are well chronicled, perhaps in most detail by Greener himself in *The Gun and its Development*. I will not, therefore repeat them here. However, the effects of the 'Field Trial: Choke Bores v Cylinders' that settled the matter were widespread in gun-making circles and, after 1875, we begin to see choke being applied throughout the gun trade.

Hammer guns pre-dating 1875 will invariably be bored 'cylinder', though in practice, some variation between muzzle and bore is often in evidence, some of which may be due to later lapping of the barrels to remove pits.

A cylinder bored gun can be expected to perform very well with modern cartridges. In tandem

W.W. Greener, who popularised choke boring in Britain. His barrels were bored by William Ford.

with the improvement of gun design and manufacturing in the mid-nineteenth century, we saw a vast improvement in the powders available to the sportsman. It is useful to note the importance of the latter and not become too focussed on the former.

Greener wrote, in 1871 in *Modern Breech Loaders*, of a gun of his manufacture and its shooting qualities: '*We introduce the representation of a target thirty inches centre and four feet square, with the diagram of the shooting of a good gun at forty yards, with a charge of 3 drams of powder and 1⅛ oz of No.6 shot. There are 146 pellets in the 30-inch circle, 114 on the outside, making 260 on the whole target. This was with a load consisting of 310 pellets.*'

Greener goes on to say '*For long ranges we recommend 2¾ drams of powder and about 1⅜ to 1½oz of No.4 shot and concentrator. This will kill game at sixty yards clean....No.2 and No.3 shot will be found equally effective at duck at about seventy or eighty yards.*'

To the modern sportsman, this makes surprising reading. Heavier loads, larger pellets but less powder, to kill at range in what Greener calls 'a light game gun'. It is interesting in these days of high speed loads that they are the opposite of what Greener tells us deliver best down-range energy. However, his is not a lone voice. Burrard writes convincingly about low-pressure loads and their effectiveness in *The Modern Shotgun*.

The 2nd Marquis of Ripon, well-known as the best shot in England during the hammer gun period and beyond, came to game shooting before the advent of choke, having his first trio of guns built by Purdey in 1868, naturally without any choke. He had further trios built in subsequent years (1876, 1881, 1890 and 1894) and in these he experimented with choke.

The 1881 guns were full-choke bored, the 1890 guns were also full-choke in both barrels and the final trio were cylinder in the right and ¾ in the left. He had the choke in the left barrels reduced in 1902. Despite having his later guns choked tightly, Rupert Godfrey, his biographer, reports that 'Olly' used the first set of guns he owned in preference to any of the subsequent ones. Perhaps Ripon found that, in practice, he killed more game with open bores than with tight ones.

I digress slightly, but the basic point is that in the days before choke, cylinder-bored guns were used to kill cleanly out to 40 yards with normal game loads and could deliver lethal patters out to seventy yards with heavier loads of larger pellets. Many modern shooters think that beyond twenty yards, a cylinder bored gun is ineffective. They are wrong. My own experience of using pre 1875 cylinder-bored guns concurs with Greener's evidence. With the right loads, they are very effective, even at longer ranges.

It was into a competitive and thrusting world that choke-boring arrived. With it, sportsmen started claiming wonderful long-shot kills and ordering guns with choke became the norm. The amount of choke and the barrels to which it was applied varied, as one would expect, with the purpose of the gun.

We can assess the difference experienced by sportsmen by tabulating some of Greener's reflections on the shooting of a cylinder bored gun and a choke bored gun (what we would now consider as 'three quarter' or 'modified' choke).

Table 1 shows pellets present in the pattern within the 30" circle, from a load of 42 grains of Schultze (smokeless) powder and 304 pellets of No.6 size, 12-bore gun.

Table 1						
Boring	inside 30" at 10 yards	Inside 30" at 20 yards	inside 30" at 30 yards	inside 30" at 40 yards	inside 30" at 50 yards	inside 30" at 60 yards
Choke Bored (¾)	304	304	278	233	160	100
Cylinder Bored	304	264	172	130	76	61

The distribution of pellets outside the 30" circle but inside the 30-48" periphery look like this:

Table 2						
Boring	inside 30-48" area at 10 yards	inside 30-48" area at 20 yards	inside 30-48" area at 30 yards	inside 30-48" area at 40 yards	inside 30-48" area at 50 yards	inside 30-48" area at 60 yards
Choke	304	304	278	233	160	100
Bored	0	0	24	90	90	95
Cylinder Bored	0	38	90	103	86	57

Victorian hammer guns now encountered may be bored as follows:

- Open (or True) cylinder in both barrels.
- Some choke constriction in both barrels.
- True cylinder in one barrel and some choke in the other.

Where choke is in evidence, it will usually be found in the left barrel. One can speculate that this is to suit the walked-up game shooting scenario, where the first shot at a rising covey will be close and the second, a longer, going-away shot.

Some guns are choked the reverse, with choke in the right barrel and less (or none) in the left. Logic suggests that for incoming targets, like driven grouse or driven pheasants, the first shot, taken well in front, will benefit from a tighter pattern at 40 or 50 yards, and the second, as the bird comes closer, will be more useful if the pattern is more open. For walking-up, the reverse is usually the case, the first bird in a rising covey may be at 20 yards and the second at 40, making a better case for a choked second (left) barrel.

As a practical measure, I recommend testing your guns with a variety of modern ammunition. It generally patterns tighter than many of the Victorian tests suggest did the ammunition of the day, even in open-bored muzzles. With modern powders, wads, crimps and shot, penetration is also better and more dependable. The difference in performance between different loads in the same gun is noteworthy. By swapping loads, you can effectively alter your choke.

In conclusion, I would argue that the modern user of a hammer gun with cylinder bored barrels need not worry that he is ill equipped to shoot on even terms with users of later, choke-bored guns. My most regularly used 12-bore hammer gun has no choke in either barrel but I have used it for years with utter confidence in its ability to kill game from walked-up snipe to flighted spur-wing geese, driven grouse or driven pheasants. My attitude to choke is so disinterested that when selecting a gun for purchase for use, I pay no attention to the choke it may or may not have. If asked to express preference, I

Many hammer guns in use today were made before choke boring was popularised. With modern ammunition they are very effective. True cylinder is a great option for most game and pigeon shooting.

would probably opt for light Improved Cylinder in both barrels (around 7 points of choke).

The current fashion for shooting extremely high pheasants in the UK is something of a departure from the sport the Victorians and Edwardians normally experienced.

When the average bird on a drive is between 50 and 60 yards distant, the gun and ammunition makers are reporting modern sportsmen favouring heavy over & under guns with full choke and loads of 34g to 36g of shot in size No.5 or No.4. If this is your sport, you are unlikely to be selecting a century-and-a-half-old hammer gun with open bores and will find any light or medium game gun firing civilised charges not quite up to the job. These are special circumstances and require specialist tools.

I experienced the practical benefits of choke at long range when shooting ZZ in England. With a 7lb weight, 30" barrelled game gun without choke, my scores were significantly lower than when using a 32" barrelled W&C Scott live pigeon gun of 8lbs in weight with ¾ and full-choked barrels. If all your shooting is long range, choke will improve your averages, if not, open bores will prove more effective game getters.

When shooting pigeons on a fast wind, open chokes and small shot can be deadly.

IS BARREL LENGTH IMPORTANT?

At the time many of our hammer guns were made, the prevalent thinking on the subject of barrel length largely mirrored Greener's recipe. He wrote: For 12-bores: 30" is considered 'general', while 28" 'quite long enough' and 26" about the 'shortest desirable', especially if longer range shooting is intended. For 16-bores, Greener recommends 30" barrels. Interestingly, he suggests larger bored guns may be shorter of barrel, but that the ideal 8-bore duck gun would be 12 lbs and have 30" barrels.

The 'XXV' revolution, prompted by Churchill and taking effect from around 1914 onwards, maintaining some hold on the shooting public well into the 1980s, was a clever exercise by a shrewd businessman and innovative gunmaker. Churchill established the benefits of a properly set-up and light 12-bore with 25" barrels as a general covert gun. With Churchill's style of shooting, the short barrelled 12-bore is a fast, effective killer on a partridge drive or a woodland pheasant shoot, where most of the shooting is within 30 yards. For our purposes in a book concerned with hammer guns, however, this debate comes rather too late in the historical narrative. By the time Churchill got started on the XXV, hammer guns were well out of fashion.

We find ourselves, in the second decade of the new millennium, with the trend having swung back towards longer barrels. It appears to have steadied somewhat from the days when George Digweed, perhaps the best competitive shot these islands have ever produced, bullied lesser mortals with a monster 34" Perazzi. He eased back to a 32" gun, but the days of 26" and 27" barrelled game guns seem to have largely passed, such guns being rather harder to sell than those with 28" or longer barrels.

The general attitude has softened in recent years, however. Those whose shooting is primarily walking behind dogs and shooting flushed game, appreciate the faster handling characteristics of shorter barrels and perhaps enjoy the greater availability of such guns at reasonable prices. In this respect, American sportsmen have led the way in reminding others that to discount the short barrelled gun out of hand is passing the opportunity to own and use some wonderful firearms that do their work beautifully.

In the days of black powder 30" barrels were the norm for a 12-bore. The BP burns all the way up the barrel.

While, as we have seen, Greener was making guns with barrels of 26" and under in the 19th century, most 12-bore guns of our era will have the then-common barrel length of 30". Smaller bore guns will generally have shorter barrels but exceptions are relatively common, bespoke as the trade then was. I have owned 19th century hammer guns in 20-bore with damascus barrels of 26", 28", 29", 30", 31" and 32", for example.

Most people buying hammer guns today will favour the original barrel length, corresponding as it does to the modern ideal; 30" seeming to be about where most people want to be. However, 28" barrels are very similar with regard to handling and sight picture and always sell well.

One must be careful to check for barrels having been shortened, it is sometimes easy to spot – look at the muzzle end and see if the end piece is absent from the rib: often these are forgotten when the barrels are cut. Sharp edges or oddly placed or mis-aligned beads can also give away the cut. Shortened barrels will have no choke, but many hammer guns will have no choke anyway, dating as they do from before the 1875 trials made choke boring popular.

If the gun is properly balanced, barrel length is a personal issue. I find longer shots easier with 30"

Bob Mills on a sporting clays target. Many experienced shots prefer longer barrels and heavier guns for this discipline.

barrels than with 25" ones but if you are familiar with your gun, you will learn to kill with it. I recall a trip to Africa to hunt birds with an American friend, Alan Tuck. He arrived with a 'vierling' (a 20-bore side-by-side with a 7mm rifle barrel between them on top and a .22 Hornet under-slung). Despite the barrels being a mere 24" in length, I can barely recall Alan missing a walked-up bird, be it twenty yards or sixty, and he littered the ground with pigeons on the sunflower fields and with ducks when we flighted the big pans.

When selecting your hammer gun, be aware that fashion may make the gun you are considering more or less expensive according to the length of the barrels. Currently, longer barrels are very much in vogue, though I detect a slight cooling in the market in this regard. My advice is to ignore the prevailing trend and choose what suits you and works for your shooting context.

A word of caution; many hammer guns, originally with 30" barrels or longer have been shortened over the years. Don't buy one un-knowingly, as the truncation will be detrimental to value and will affect balance and patterns in ways that will be hard to predict without testing.

The Proof Houses and Re-proofing Hammer Guns

There are two major questions to ask oneself when considering re-proof of a hammer gun. The first "Is it necessary?", the second "Will it survive the process?"

For a British enthusiast, buying and selling guns requires attention to the law of the land. To offer a gun for sale which is out of proof is an offence. It is not an offence to buy an out of proof gun, nor is it an offence to own and use one. It would appear, from a legal point of view, that it is not an offence to give someone a gun which is out of proof, as long as no money changes hands.

Considering the advanced age of most hammer guns, many will be in need of careful examination to ensure that they are still in proof. Many will have been re-proofed in the past. It will not be unusual to encounter guns that have been proofed a number of times since the original submission.

The proof of antique guns under current regulations is exactly the same as it is for new guns. The Birmingham Proof House now houses the British Proof Laboratory, which provides the proof loads for Birmingham and London. The proof pressures are set at 25% higher than the maximum possible pressure of CIP regulated commercial ammunition. There is no

Shooting black powder is fun, but nitro re-proof is an option many choose.

provision for lower stress testing to allow for age. A century old Webley will have to demonstrate the same degree of strength as a new Beretta. Two proof charges are fired in each barrel. There must be no deviation in the barrels, the gun must not come off the face or otherwise sustain damage. If it does, it fails.

There are three levels of proof likely to be appropriate to the user of a hammer gun who is preparing a gun for re-proof. The British standard chamber length for most game guns was 2½". Today, most British guns are made with a 70mm (2¾") chamber. From the mid 1950s, 2¾" chambers became more commonly applied, even to guns not intended for extra heavy loads.

The current standard proof test for shotguns is the same pressure for both 65mm (2½") and 70mm (2¾") chambers. From that standpoint, it may be sensible to lengthen chambers to 70mm before submitting a gun for re-proof. This is inexpensive and ultimately allows for a greater range of cartridges to be used in future. Whilst not necessarily making any practical difference in the UK, if travelling abroad, it can be useful to have the option of buying ammunition at your destination and 70mm-cased shells are the norm in many parts of the world.

One last word on proof testing procedures being carried out in London and Birmingham, as of November 2014: The proof houses have introduced new chamber gauges for use in proof testing. They conform to CIP dimensions and are being used as the exclusive measurement determiner. These are now used regardless of when a gun was originally made or submitted for proof.

In practice, this means that all guns, new, sleeved or vintage, must have their chambers cut, or re-cut, to CIP dimensions, as provided in the schematic drawings on the organisation's website. Over recent years, proof has become increasingly traumatic as a process. The proof masters would argue that they are the guardians of public safety. Gunmakers are lamenting the old days, when they felt the proof houses worked in tandem with the industry to ensure guns made were fit for purpose. Now, some feel, they are making guns to suit the proof house and the CIP rather than the customer. The result may be that traditionally light and lively British game guns will mimic their American and continental cousins in becoming over engineered and over weight in order to withstand the ever increasing demands of proof.

For the vintage gun enthusiast, re-proof must be considered carefully and it is a process to be avoided

Tours of the Birmingham Proof House are most illuminating and the building reeks of history. Here a visitor examines the bench where proof stamps are applied to guns.

if at all possible, whilst being careful to adhere to all the legal neccessities. The increasingly stringent and inflexible rules that are becoming standardised across trade areas are a practical risk to the guns we all love and strive to keep in service.

New CIP compliant proof stamps at the Birmingham Proof House.

Damascus barrels are every bit as robust as steel barrels of the same age and most pass re-proof.

Auctions

London gun auctions provide a wonderful opportunity for enthusiasts to peruse a regular bounty of English guns being offered for sale to the highest bidder. I have written about auctions extensively in my previous books and articles but the auction scene is constantly shifting and one must be very careful when approaching them for the first time. While they may entice the enthusiast with lovely photos and temptingly low estimates, all is not necessarily as it first appears.

London gun auctions are becoming a retail environment, rather than a wholesale one. Arguably, the tipping point was reached some time ago. I no longer see some of the old trade regulars at the auctions of Holt's, Bonham's and Gavin Gardiner's, they simply don't provide the stream of stock that these dealers once relied upon.

One well-established dealer in vintage guns, who was a former auction regular, told me that auctions are now a waste of his time, as a trip to London hardly ever resulted in useful buying. Another, the proprietor of a large and successful provincial gun shop, confided that he now sits on any auction purchase for twelve months, at least, before offering it for sale.

The reason is the internet-search function available to, and employed by, so many prospective purchasers. A few minutes looking through the history of a gun's recent sales activity reveal that it was bought at auction for, say, £500 and is now for sale, a few months later, for £1,100. Savvy as they may be, people are one-eyed when it comes to processing this information. They see the hammer price, neglect to add the commission, VAT and the cost of renovation and they begrudge the trader any profit at all. Such an arena makes trade difficult.

So, where are all the guns going? In my experience there are now three main types of buyer: the foreign gun shop owner, the private collector or retail end-user and, finally, the dealer acting directly on behalf of an individual client.

The overseas gun shop may be able to operate in an environment sufficiently remote from the London auctions for their client-base to either not be in a position to do English-language searches of a history, or, more forgiving or accepting of the costs of gathering stock in another country and importing it in preparation for a retail sale.

The private collector or end-user either sources guns through auction because the rare or unique pieces that headline often offer one-off opportunities to buy, or because they think that they will under-cut the dealers and get a bargain. The dealer acting on behalf of a client is usually the 'wise head' who can advise the enthusiast and help ensure that he does not buy rashly and make a poor decision. We also have collectors who prefer to remain aloof and anonymous and have 'their man' act for them.

The buyer at most risk of running into trouble is the private individual seeking a bargain. 'Penny-wise, pound-foolish' may be a cliché but it is so often observable in the auction room that it has changed the market.

So, just what is it that the casual buyer overlooks when picking up a gun that has arrived in the auction

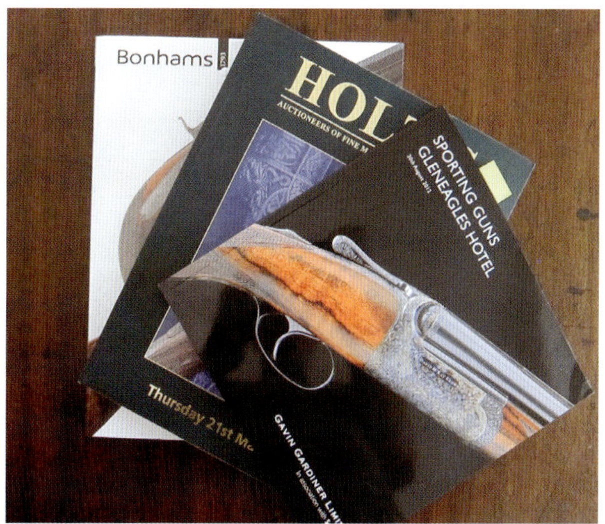

Guns sold at auction are often in poor condition and 'sold as seen'. However, they must be 'in proof' for the sale to be legally valid.

from the gun cabinet of a retiring shooter? Such guns typically have not been cleaned for decades. They look tired and perhaps a bit grubby but offer the fabled 'bargain' and in rush the fools.

The estimates are enticing and the bidding moves upwards, the bidder goes with the room and ends up buying over top estimate. Still, he tells himself, it is a quality gun and it must be worth it because someone else was bidding strongly on it too. Then he goes to the office to pay and takes a big swallow when he actually sees the calculation of commission and VAT. When it adds close to 30% to the hammer price, it starts to look like less of a bargain.

Still, what's done is done, the gun goes home with the buyer. What happens next can be a quick turnaround. I saw a Greener 28-bore single barrel gun at Holt's one summer, which had been in the previous sale and sold. The buyer had bought it blind, taken it home, found he missed the barn door from inside the barn and decided it had to go! So, back in again, Holt's were, doubtless, pleased to bag 25% of the sale price twice in succession on the same gun.

If not returned or chucked in the safe and forgotten, the auction gun will generally be in need of some work, which will rarely have been costed in at the time of purchase. Re-blacking the barrels will cost our hero £250; a strip, clean and service might run him up another £150. While there, the gunsmith tells him it is off the face and needs re-jointing, another £350 please. And did you notice the rib was leaking when we re-blacked it, we had to re-lay it; another £350. Once you are in, you have to keep going. With so much spent already, the gun looks a bit odd with nice barrels and worn chequer and dull wood, so, put it right, another £500.

The £1,000 bid has turned into a bit of a money pit; with the actual price paid being £1,300 and repairs running up a total of £2,900 in the gun. This is actually closer to the retail value that you would have had to pay in a shop, which would have done the work on trade terms, added a serviceability guarantee and peace of mind and made a small profit. Trying to get this reality into the mind of the auction amateur is a real trial. All they see is the headline figure.

A professional acting for a client can save him all of these headaches and can make end-user purchases worthwhile. He will be able to advise as to what work is necessary and how much it will cost. He will be able to have the work done well at trade prices and provide the customer with the gun post-refurbishment, with length and cast adjustments properly worked out and delivered accurately.

This way, a project can be planned and costed before the bidding begins, it will make the customer see

Above and facing page: Viewing day at Holt's in Hammersmith. A properly lit viewing room and good access to the guns is very helpful.

the true worth of the gun in both project start and retail finish terms.

One must always remember when bidding at auction that you cannot bid against stupid. The fact that someone else is bidding strongly is just as likely to be an indication of his ignorance of the gun's problems as it is of his appreciation of its qualities and value.

My own activities at the London gun auctions appear of interest to many readers, who frequently ask to peek at my notes or explain what I'm doing there. While many professionals in the trade remain secretive about their mode of business, I have always believed in sharing information and spreading knowledge and enthusiasm. Perhaps it comes from my years as a teacher in those, not so distant, days that now seem so very long ago.

It usually starts with an enquiry from a new or existing client. This may come in the form of general interest in acquiring a particular type of gun or it may be a more specific direction to a certain lot at a named auction. The client generally falls into one of two categories: either he lives abroad or sufficiently distant from the London viewing room that he cannot attend in the hope that the gun might be worth following up, or he lacks the expertise to assess the gun confidently enough to spend thousands of pounds on it. These two categories do overlap on occasion.

Once I have identified a likely candidate gun for the client, or he has done so himself, I compile a list of lot numbers that I need to inspect at the viewing. I highlight these in the catalogue in one colour for reports, then again in another colour if they graduate to becoming lots on which we will bid.

I then print out my pro-forma worksheet, on which I will note all the relevant issues and facts when I assess the gun. This prevents me from missing any

Auctioneer David Porter in action. The pace of a sale is faster than it appears to the casual observer and preparation is essential to avoid expensive mistakes.

key issues through oversight and it also formalises an assessment procedure, making the process faster and more efficient. For clients reading multiple reports, it also helps them to find the same information on each gun in the same section of each page, making like-for-like comparison easier.

The form is arranged logically, covering detailed assessment of major component parts, one section at a time. It lists crucial issues with each – when assessing barrels, for example, it notes the presence or absence of rusting, dents, pits or other material defects, it also specifies bore measurements, now and original, and notes minimum wall thickness. For the stock, any alterations, additions, defects and other issues regarding condition and originality will be covered.

The final part of the form covers the evaluative conclusion that clients want. After all, they want an opinion, not just observations. I summarise issues such as possible remedies for problems encountered, costs of repair or renovation work recommended and the final likely retail value of the gun, once all remedial work has been carried out. For me, the cross referencing process will feature an assessment of the original quality, the originality and the current condition of the gun, as well as practical issues such as functionality of mechanisms (single trigger or ejector type for example) and suitability for the client involved.

This enables the client to see the raw material but also to envisage the finished product in his hands and ready to take pride of place in his gun cabinet, along with a bottom line figure in order for that to happen. It takes the guesswork out of the process.

In the modern age we are fortunate with technology. When I first got involved in gun sales, back

Patrick Hawes of Bonham's auctioneers. in Knightsbridge.

Patrick started at Christie's before taking the reins at Bonhams and making their Sporting Guns department a success after a difficult period.

Having four auction houses in the capital is good for the gun trade. Most dealers converge every three months or so to see what might emerge onto the market.

in the mid 1980s, when, as a schoolboy, I assisted a local gun dealer in a small way by photographing the guns he had for sale and sending them to various potential buyers around the country, I had a Pentax SLR and had to develop the film at Boots.

Now, I have a digital camera, which plugs straight into the laptop and can send detailed macro photos to anywhere in the world in a few minutes.

I generally send ten or more such photos with each report, illustrating the examples of visible issues I have identified. It is one thing to mention a 'slight chip in the forend wood, adjacent to the bottom left side of the iron'. To be able to photograph the chipped wood and send that photograph along with the words, saves a great deal of description and subsequent conversation.

One caveat here. Very detailed macro photography can make any small defect look hideous. It is a skill to illustrate your points accurately without making every minor external pit look like a bomb crater. A gun that actually looks pretty tidy and will clean up can be made to look like a car crash if photographed too brutally.

Of course, the converse of this point is also true. The auctioneers are busy photographing their guns beautifully, with flattering lighting, in such a way as to make all but the very ugliest look like film stars. Legion are the remorseful buyers who have got excited over a catalogue photograph and bid strongly, 'winning' the gun, only to have a severe reality check when it arrives looking rather less fabulous in the less flattering daylight than it did in the catalogue.

Once the client has the report and the photographs, a brief conversation often follows. We may discuss pros and cons and usually quickly reach a decision as to whether or not the gun should be attempted as a purchase or dropped. In my experience 70% of guns assessed are discarded following the report stage. Those remaining are sometimes subjected to a second assessment and minor issues resolved.

Once a decision to bid has been made, either I will take instruction to bid for the client or he will do so himself by telephone. If I am to bid, I will make a clear note of the lot number, highlight it in red in the catalogue and note the maximum price to bid. I take care to calculate the auctioneer's commission and VAT on top of the figure agreed, so there will be no nasty surprises.

Bidding commences. If successful, I will collect the gun and pay for it, invoicing the client a few days later. I will generally then handle all the repairs and servicing work necessary and work out any export requirements. If export paperwork is required, Harry

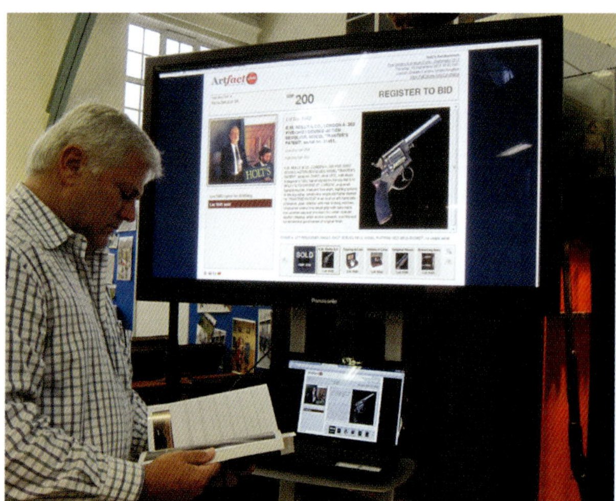

Auctions move with the times. Online bidding is a feature of the modern auction room.

Gordon, a specialist in such matters, takes care of that very efficiently, so I pass it on to him.

A number of trade professionals operate on a similar basis to the one on which I do. They can be seen carefully examining key lots and often reporting back by telephone to clients in hushed tones, lest anyone overhear them. It is a small but interesting part of the trade in old English guns in particular and the expertise of the people involved allows the wider public to buy guns at auction with rather more confidence than would be the case if left to their own devices.

Some may argue that activities like this are to the detriment of dealers who would rather buy auction guns and retail them to the public, than have the public buy direct. However, auctions have become retail environments, whether the trade likes the fact or not. Those of us who help safeguard the end user from the pitfalls are a necessary part of the modern auction scene.

However, as friends in the trade have noted to me on many an occasion, there are plenty of 'punters' too mean to pay for an expert appraisal. They may save themselves fifty pounds by forgoing one but these are the chaps who quietly put the gun back into the next sale, taking the financial hit, or approach their local gun shop a few weeks later with a rueful look, hoping the repair bill won't be quite as bad as looks likely. Auctions are still a minefield; glossy catalogues, canapés at viewings and snazzy websites notwithstanding.

Gavin Gardiner conducting a sale at Sotheby's in Bond Street. Bids are coming in from all over the world, via banks of telephones at the side of the room, as well as from the floor.

A Tale of Personal Provenance

Charles FitzGerald, 4th Duke of Leinster, was born in Dublin on 30th March 1819. On 13th October 1847, he married Lady Caroline Sutherland-Leveson-Gower, daughter of the 2nd Duke of Sutherland, and owner of Kilkea Castle. They were clearly rather happily married, as they had fifteen children.

Among those children were Lord Gerald FitzGerald and Lady Alice FitzGerald. Lady Alice married Col. Sir Charles FitzGerald. They were my grandfather's grandparents, while Lady Alice's brother, Lord Gerald FitzGerald became the 5th Duke of Leinster.

Gerald FitzGerald, 5th Duke of Leinster

In 1867, exactly a century before my birth, Purdey made a 30" barrelled 12-bore hammer gun on their 1863 'second pattern' thumbhole-lever action for Lord Gerald FitzGerald, who would have been sixteen that year. Perhaps it was a birthday present?

Having been passed through some honourable hands in the form of decorated army officers Capt. R.H. Fane de Salis DSC, OBE and Capt. H.R Westmacott, late of the SAS and a posthumous M.C, it appeared for sale in London at Holt's auctioneers.

I wonder how and when the Purdey passed into the hands of Capt. Fane de Salis, who was born in 1890 (three years before Gerald FitzGerald's death) and, presumably, unlikely to have got his hands on the gun until he was an adult; around 1910.

How the Purdey was passed to the next owner, Capt. Westmacott, is clearer, as he was Fane de Salis's great-nephew. The Fane de Salis family were, like the FitzGeralds, Anglo-Irish landowners, with estates in Limerick in the late 19th century, so the families would have known one another.

The Dukes of Leinster used Carton House, about fifteen miles west of Dublin, as their main residence and also owned Kilkea Castle in Kildare.

However, by the early 20th century they had lost most of their wealth and lands. Carton was sold in the 1920s and Kilkea Castle (where my grandfather was born in 1910) became the family seat under the 8th Duke until it was sold in the 1960s. It may be that during one of these moves that furniture and other items were sold off locally, the Purdey perhaps being among them.

I'm not one for superstition or numerology but there are some coincidences in this story which are quite notable. 1867 and 1967, exactly 100 years apart are the dates of Purdey 7580 being delivered to Gerald and my own birth year respectively. May 2nd was the day in 1863 when the patent for the Purdey bolt was registered. This was four years into its patent when Gerald's gun was built. It is also the day on which Capt. Westmacott was killed in action in Belfast in 1952. It also happens to be my birthday.

I headed to London on St Patrick's Day 2016 hoping this old Irish Purdey might find its way 'home' with a little bit of old Irish luck.

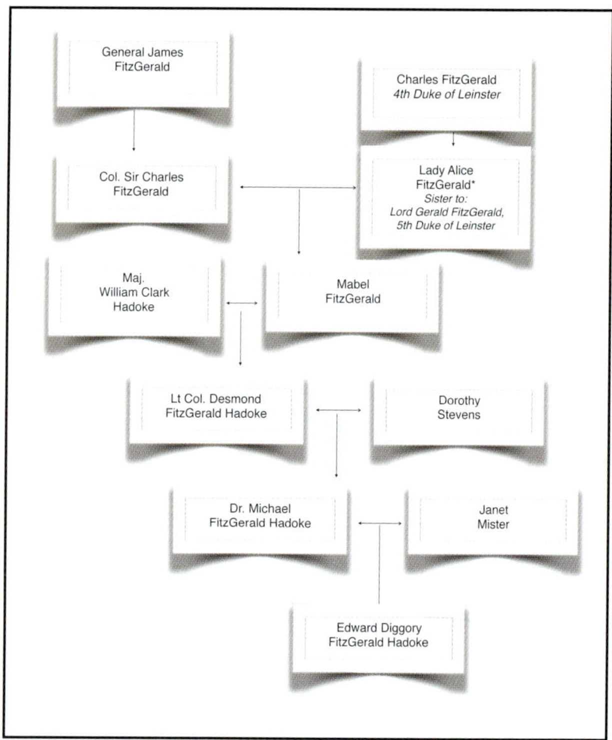

This slightly truncated family tree traces the link from Lord Gerald FitzGerald, the original owner of the Purdey, to the author, and current owner.

My great-great-uncle's gun was re-stocked some time in the distant past, and nitro-proved.

The sale takes place over two days of viewing with an auction on the third day. Lot 1800 was among the last items on sale that day and a few die-hards remained in the room as the evening gloom began to descend. Bidding began at £700 on the commissions bid sheet on the auctioneer's podium. I got my bid in next and the struggle was on. I had to fight off the bids on the book before it would be opened to the room to get involved. I went into auto-pilot. The decision had been made. I was going to buy the gun.

Had someone brought the Purdey to me in the state it is currently in and asked me to buy it from them, I'd have paid them £1,500. I may have offered £2,000 if I were feeling enthusiastic. That is without the provenance. With it, the figure was almost irrelevant. You get a chance like this once in a lifetime and I wasn't going to let it get away.

Eventually, the commission bids were exhausted and the room was opened to another bidder. For what seemed like an age the auctioneer appealed for more interest: finally, the gavel hit the block and I blinked.

Bidding had ended at £2,700. By the time all fees and commissions were settled, my bill was £3,500.

I also got the tatty old percussion gun case in which the Purdey was housed, all internals broken and detached but with a Purdey trade label and some handwritten notes starting, 'December 1867, Purdey gun No.7580...' in best copperplate handwriting. The two have clearly been together for some time.

So, having procured the old gun, what to do next? One can hurry into such ventures but really they deserve some contemplation. The barrels are shootable. They have some external pits and the browning has all but gone. There are some nasty gouges and dents but they will clean up tolerably. Someone thought to re-proof for nitro a few years ago and the action is sound, with good original hammers and island locks.

The gun was clearly re-stocked in the past and the job not quite Purdey quality. However, it fits me quite well and is strong and practical. I stripped it and re-finished it using my own red oil and finishing oils and had John Gibbs re-brown the barrels. I'll have to live with the external pits but I intend to use the gun, not just look at it and I need it in good operational order.

After stripping it, lubricating all the moving parts and re-assembling it, I'm ready for next season.

The Purdey attracted a lot of interest at Holt's, despite its shortcomings.

Chris Beaumont of Holt's presenting the author with his long-lost family Purdey, after some tense bidding.

Victorian Small Bores

Earlier in this volume, we explored the numbers of hammer guns made by several of the leading manufacturers of guns. Given the popularity of small bore guns and the desire of many collectors to buy a quality small bore hammer gun, it is interesting to consider the numbers of these made, and likely to be in existence.

This picture of two boys with a single hammer gun must have been a common sight between the wars. It shows my grandfather (holding the gun) and my great-uncle Gerry in Ireland, around 1920. The gun is a typical single back-action hammer gun of the type produced in Birmingham and sold by most makers. Light, inexpensive, well-made. They provided hours of fun and the basis of a sporting career.

The weights of guns made during the hammer gun era differ a great deal from modern trends and the shooter with an Italian over & under in 28-bore or .410, which he shoots well will find trading-up to a good Victorian or Edwardian small bore hammer gun will prove more of a challenge than he might imagine.

Weight is the crucial factor here. Let us examine some modern examples.

28-bore Browning o/u	.410 Beretta o/u	20-bore Browning o/u	16-bore Rizzini o/u
6lbs 7oz	6lbs 0oz	6lbs 4oz	6lbs 8oz

Now, let us examine the weights W.W. Greener advised for the manufacture of the various gauges:

16-bore	20-bore	28-bore	410
6lbs 4oz	5lbs 8oz	4lbs 0oz–4lbs 12oz	No comment

Finally, we can seek manufacturer's actual data by examining Greener's 1903 catalogue:

16-bore	20-bore	28-bore	410
6¼lbs	5lbs–5½lbs	4½lbs	No comment

William Evans offered 28-bores from 4½ lbs, 20-bores from 5¼ lbs , 16-bores from 5¾ lbs and light 12-bores from 6¼ lbs. These are listed in the range of best quality hammer guns, in their 1893 catalogue.

Finally, examination of small bore hammer guns which have passed through my own stock and

Right: A rare Cogswell & Harrison 360 gauge shotgun, used for collecting specimens of small birds.

25
·360
GAUGE
ELEY
GASTIGHT
CARTRIDGES

others recently examined for sale, illustrates nicely the weight ranges of the Victorian small bore hammer guns in circulation today.

One must make weight allowances for different barrel and stock lengths, and occasionally for chamber length (allowing for heavier 20-bore and 16-bore pigeon guns) but we can expect very different handling characteristics when comparing the average Victorian hammer side-by-side with the modern over & under small bore gun. The Watson Bros gun mentioned in the table is a very good example of how the 28-bore was often thought of as a gun for a child or a small lady. Made in 1885, it has 24" damascus barrels with ¾ choke in both, a 13½" stock with very little toe (suggesting it was fitted to a woman) and a weight of only 4 lbs 6 oz. A gun like this is going to be very difficult to adapt for an average size American male today, despite the attraction of its quality and condition.

Some makers listed .410 and 36-bore guns as 'collector's guns'. By this they mean adults hunting for taxidermy specimens of small birds and mammals while posted overseas. William Evans describe one as: '.410 bore, central fire, a miniature breech-loader

Above, a combination gun for overseas use: this Reilly had double rifle barrels and a set of 28-bore shotgun barrels. The re-stocking was a bit agricultural.

Below is a rare Holland & Holland 28-bore hammer gun of very nice quality and in remarkably unrestored condition. Small bore guns of best quality by top makers and made to adult dimensions are highly sought-after. A sleeper like this causes great excitement in the auction room. This one was discovered by Holt's.

with top snap action and extension rib, rebounding locks, low hammers, pistol hand stock Etc.'. They list a standard model at £7.10s.½d and a superior quality with better finish at £10.10s.0d. A case was an extra £1 and so was a service which involved packing it in a tin-lined case, insuring it and sending it by freight anywhere in the world!

16-bore	20-bore	28-bore	410
6lbs 2oz Alex Henry	5lbs 10oz Cashmore	4lbs 6oz Watson Bros	4lbs 13oz Cogswell & Harrison
6lb 4oz Westley Richards	6lb 1oz Cogswell & Harrison	5lb 2oz Holland & Holland	3lb 13oz James Burrow
6lb 0oz James Purdey	5lb 10oz W.W. Greener	4lb 10 oz W.H. Monk	4lb 4oz J.W. Rosier
5lb 12oz W.R. Pape	5lb 6oz W.B. Barratt	5lb 4oz Manton & Co	4lb 15oz F. Beesley
5lb 3oz Lincoln Jefferies	5lb 14oz T. Wild	4lb 14oz J.D. Dougall	4lb 7oz K.D. Radcliffe
6lb 5oz W.B. Barrett	5lb 4oz W.M. Agnew	4lb 12oz D. Murray	4lb 10oz Watson Bros
5lb 15oz James Purdey	5lb 5oz W.H. Pollard	4lb 10oz T. Bland & Sons	4lb 5oz T. Clough & Son
5lb 12oz John Dickson & Son	5lb 11oz Armstrong & Co	5lb 4oz (2¾") Charles Osborne & Co	4lb 2oz Watson Bros
6lb 11oz Westley Richards	5lb 7oz W.J. Jeffery & Co	5lb 2oz Army & Navy	4lb 6oz C.S. Rosson
6lb 0oz Williamson & Son	5lb 0oz W.R. Pape	5lb 2oz William Evans	3lb 14oz T. Wild
5lb 8oz Stephen Grant	4lb 7oz F. Beesley	5lb 4oz W.J. Jeffery & Co	4lb 6oz J. Booth

The first issue for adults with these light small bores will be lack of momentum. A heavier gun swings but a light one needs to be fully controlled by front arm movement. It is a very different style of shooting to learn and one which requires practice and concentration, especially when moving from a heavy 12-bore to a light 28-bore or .410. Many sportsmen find the idea of having a delightfully dainty small bore hammer gun as a field companion attractive but, in practice, they shoot very badly with one.

I am, perhaps, being overly negative with regard to the shooting qualities of light small bore guns in the hands of adult males. I know several very competent shots who use them effectively and stylishly. However, true as it may be that a good shot can learn how to shoot anything well, the work required to become adept with a gun of the kind described in this section is greater than most casual shooting men appreciate.

Small boys and small guns. In the 20th century the .410 became ever more popular. However, walking the hedges with a small bore shotgun was where many a country boy got his sporting education.

The author with old school friend Graham Clarke and his boys. Old small bore guns are handy for teaching children to hit moving targets. Many cannot handle a heavy gun and are too small for a long stock.

The issue of momentum becomes greater as the bore diminishes. A 16-bore of 6 lbs will be an easier transition to make, for the user of a 7 lbs 12-bore than will a 4½ lbs .410. I do, in fact rate the 16-bore as a long under-valued and very effective gauge. The beauty of the sixteen is that if a lighter gun is desired, a stronger, better balanced gun can be made in this size than in a 12-bore. Barrel length, wall thickness and weight distribution can remain optimal due to the naturally lower weight of the sixteen with its smaller action and slimmer barrels. Loaded with the ideal 'square load', which in a 16-bore is one ounce (28g), though I prefer a lighter (26g) cartridge, it patterns beautifully and is pleasant to shoot. For many years I used a Holland & Holland 16-bore hammer gun, made by Scott in Birmingham, with 30" damascus barrels and back-action locks and had some memorable and successful days with it.

The modern popularity of the Italian 20-bore over & under game gun can be attributed to the fact that it weighs what an old English 12-bore side-by-side does and people now fire a 12-bore load in it. Essentially, the trend towards over & under guns for game shooting, with their inherent tendency to out weigh equivalent side-by-sides has driven down the bore diameter to twenty but the desire to fire a 12-bore standard game load has endured. Thus, the 6½ or 6¾ lbs 20-bore and the 30g or 32g 20-bore cartridge in a 70mm case. As the table on page 161 shows, the Victorian hammer 20-bore is a very different creature. It performs best with a lighter load and the chamber is likely to be 2½". A typical load would be 23g. I like my small bores choked a bit tighter than my 12-bores, to compensate for the smaller number of pellets in the shell. There is no doubt that they can be very effective game guns.

There is also no doubt that small bore guns delight the collector. They are harder to find and they are undoubtedly pretty and beguiling. As part of the pleasure of collecting involves the hunt for the elusive ideal, the added challenge of finding a rare object enhances the experience of the seeker. This is all part of the fun. I would urge readers to retain a sense of perspective, however. Holding out for something that is unlikely ever to emerge and turning down scores of guns that are potentially workable as solutions to your imagined problem is, ultimately, pointless.

A beautifully made miniature gun by William Ford with 22" barrels and weighing only 3lbs 1oz. It is a 32-bore and is opened by pulling back on the trigger guard. As it slides backwards, the bolts are withdrawn from the bites and it drops open conventionally.

Chamber Sleeving

Most readers will be familiar with conventional 'sleeving', where the entire barrel is cut, about 3" ahead of the chamber and a new tube fitted into the breech stubs to make a new barrel, when the old one is worn out. On double barrelled guns, the old ribs are generally re-laid and the barrels blacked, with joints TIG welded to disguise them. If done well, it is a very practical way of re-barrelling a gun at a fraction of the cost of new barrels.

Less familiar to most sportsmen is the concept of boring out the chambers from the breech end and inserting 'chamber sleeves', which are then welded into place. Chamber sleeving has two main applications. The first is to renovate a gun with pitted or misshapen chambers. By inserting chamber sleeves, the new inner surface is clean, regular and ideal for practical purposes. If done properly, the work will be invisible.

However, the process has been applied in the past, especially by some American dealers to convert guns from one bore size to another. A personal example of this concerned a nice quality Lang & Sons double hammer gun, which I bought as part of a small collection, in 59-bore. It appeared to be a special-order collector's gun. Unfortunately, the bore size killed any practical value, as ammunition is not available any more. Rather than condemn it to the status of curio, I had it chamber sleeved to take the standard 2½" .410 cartridge, thereby giving it a new lease of life. The process involved re-jointing, chamber sleeving and re-proofing for the new bore size and it was a considerable success, the gun proving to be delightful in use and being very much better made than many Victorian .410s, which are typically low-grade guns for dispatching vermin.

The use of chamber sleeving to which I alluded at the start of the previous paragraph is more controversial than the simple conversion of a useless calibre to a modern one or the restoration of a worn gun. It concerns the alteration of an unfashionable bore to a more widely sought one. In the case of the Americans, this was taking 16-bores, which were very much under-rated in the early 1990s, and chamber sleeving them to the very much in demand 20-bore. Less common, but certainly practised, was the conversion of 10-bore guns to 12-bore.

This '.360 gauge' shotgun will chamber sleeve into a nice 3" .410 and become more usable.

A 16-bore chamber-sleeved to 20-bore. This made them easier to sell in the 1990s, when 16-bore was unfashionable. Note the 16.7 bore and 20 chamber stamps.

The obvious benefit to the converter is that he is able to sell 20-bores but not 16-bores but he can buy 16-bores cheaply. So, the conversion by chamber sleeving makes a hard-to-sell gun into an easy-to-sell gun, as if by magic. It was especially acceptable in the USA, as American guns are all heavy for gauge, compared with English guns, so a 20-bore weighing 6lbs 2oz was not seen as overweight.

There are legitimate objections to this practice, I believe. The first, of bastardising an original gun, built carefully as a 16-bore and making it a 20-bore totally outside of the norms of the gauge as it was originally built is one that I can see being made by purists. It is a point of view with which I have some emotional sympathy. The second is that it is on the border of honesty, as you are selling the, perhaps unknowing, buyer a gun purporting to be what it is not. It may take 20-bore cartridges and bear 20-bore proof marks but it is not a 20-bore in its DNA. The third is practical; how can a 20-bore cartridge work in 16-bore barrels?

The truth is sometimes counter intuitive and delving into the merits of chamber sleeving is a good case in point. We do so to explore the practical effects of firing smaller cartridges with wider bores. The results are interesting; surprising even.

There are a number of questions to raise and areas to examine in assessing the effect of having a smaller chamber and wider bore:

1. The step between the chamber, the chamber cone and the true bore.
2. The relationship between the shot column and smaller wad, as it progresses down the wider bore.
3. The effect of choke on the shot as it exits the barrel.
4. The down-range pattern regularity.
5. The down-range penetration and retained energy of the pellets.

In short, does a chamber sleeved gun (16-bore to 20-bore) perform worse than, the same as, or better than a conventional gun of the same gauge?

When beginning this analysis, some knowledgeable colleagues raised a number of concerns. The main one was this: surely there would be gas contamination pushing past the 20-bore wad to interfere with the shot as it travelled down the bore – this would lead to more 'balled' shot and to loss of energy and penetration.

Reflections on current gun making practice were more supportive. Many modern makers are 'over-boring' their competition guns. Typically a 12-bore will have a bore size of .729" but Browning are making trap gun with bores of .750 or more, claiming it reduces recoil and improves patterns. Certainly, modern guns are generally wider bored than their early Victorian counterparts. I have 12-bores that were actually proofed at 14-bore in the tubes, with 12-bore chambers. So, a tight-for-bore Victorian 16-bore, for example, will make a nice, open bored 20-bore, or a tight 10-bore can usefully be chamber sleeved to 12-bore 'Superior' (the old magnum), making use of the more widely available heavy 12-bore ammunition in a gun with the added weight and wider bores desirable to make them comfortable to shoot.

It is a relatively common modern modification to 'ease' the forcing cones on Victorian guns in order to reduce recoil and relieve pressure at the breech. Whatever the reasons behind many of the old barrels being made tight for size, the modern trend is towards more open bores and modern ammunition appears to make this practicable, especially the use of one piece shot-cup/wad components.

In practice, there seems to be very little evidence that pattern and penetration are affected detrimentally by chamber sleeving. I provided a client in the US with a 10-bore Stephen Grant pigeon gun, chamber sleeved to 12-bore with 3" chambers. He reported that it was one of his most effective clay busters and gave him an edge in many competitions.

I prepared another gun for a client in the UK who wanted a 20-bore hammer gun to use on high pheasants. The 16-bore Alex Henry he now uses was chamber sleeved to take 20-bore 70mm shells and with the extra weight, of about 6lbs 2oz and 3" damascus barrels, it swings well and more dependably than a typical light Victorian 20-bore. He kills pheasants with it just as reliably as he would with a more conventional gun.

The advantage is that he has greater flexibility in choice of ammunition and 20-bore shells are easier to find the world over.

Pattern testing proves that chamber sleeved guns work very well indeed, often throwing very regular, dense patterns, possibly due to less pellet compression. The concern often expressed about the duration of fibre wads in a wide bore is not one borne out by experience. However, with plastic shot cup type wadding, there is no issue either theoretical or practical. Some companies are now making 'fibre wad' cartridges with wadding actually made from wool felt, just as our muzzle-loading forebears used. This, being softer, has greater expansion capability than vegetable fibre wads and suggests itself as the perfect combination with a chamber sleeved gun.

In order to test for penetration, an interesting experiment can be carried out with old telephone directories. First soak them in water for an hour to make the paper soft. Then set them in a holder and shoot from 30 or 40 yards. Use only one directory per shot. Try them with different cartridges and then see how the pellets penetrate. By opening the directory, you can see how the bulk of the pattern has penetrated in each case and compare by using the page numbers.

When viewing hammer guns, chamber sleeving, relatively uncommon as it is, is something to look for. Sometimes it will be stamped on the barrel flats, sometimes not. The weight of the gun in proportion to its bore will give an idea that investigation is worthwhile. However, when well done, chamber sleeving is not something to consider a detriment. A slightly heavier 20-bore will actually perform better in sporting clays and field situations than a light one. New chamber walls will ensure cartridges fit properly and do not stick in pitted chambers. As with all gun repairs and adjustments, the precision of the work is the key to its durability and functionality.

An interesting experiment that one of my gunsmiths is working on at present is the salvaging of clean chambers from damascus barrels which are otherwise pitted or dented and beyond use. He strips the tubes, turns down the outside of the barrels at the breech end and uses this (chamber plus forcing cone) as the chamber sleeve; dropping it into the machined-out chamber of the gun being repaired.

The new chamber is damascus steel, as are the original barrels and, when welded into place, the metals suit one another and the join is invisible. It is too early to be sure if this will prove to be a cost-effective and viable repair but it is a process worthy of investigation.

Beautiful old big bore guns like this 1871 Purdey 8-bore were designed to use lead shot, which is no longer legal to use on wildfowl in England & Wales. Bismuth is the best alternative but it is expensive and ammunition suppliers in the UK are reluctant to encourage the home-loading market. They fear the home loader will compete with their products, despite the fact that none now load 8-bore bismuth commercially. The American market caters better to home-loaders in general.

The Future of Lead Shot

In England the current lead shot regulations ban the use of lead shot over all foreshore, over specified SSSIs, and for the shooting of all ducks and geese, coot and moorhen; wherever they occur. The Welsh Assembly introduced similar regulations in September 2002. Scotland's regulations came into force at the end of March 2005 and Northern Ireland's came into force in September 2009.

Although no great believer in conspiracy theories, I think the shooting public in England and Wales were set up by the legislators for a sucker punch when the first lead shot ban was introduced in 1999.

The stated aim of the legislation was to protect wetland birds from ingesting spent lead shot, which was said to be present in the gravel at the bottom of rivers and streams. Fishermen had already been banned from using lead shot to weigh down their lines. Now, shooters found the authorities planning to restrict the use of lead as a projectile in shotgun ammunition.

In Scotland, the law makers showed a degree of common sense. Their restrictions targeted the actual problem, as perceived by the anti-lead agitators. The problem, as stated, was the presence of lead in wetland environments, where ducks dabble. So, shooters were told they may no longer use lead in designated wetlands.

In England and Wales, the issue of enforcement was evidently more of a concern than the fairness or effectiveness of the changes in law. In order to police the Scottish legislation, officers would need to do spot checks on shooters where they were shooting. That meant actually sending police officers out to find shooters in wet, cold, muddy places at dawn or dusk and ask to check their ammunition.

Far easier, the authorities in Westminster must have thought, to simply ban shooters from shooting any duck or goose in any location with lead shot. Now, shooting a commercially bred mallard that finds itself over the line during a driven pheasant day, perhaps from a pond adjacent to the woods being driven, is of no concern to the environmentalists claiming they need to protect wetlands and dabbling waterfowl. Their supposed concern is the wetlands. Here, the duck is being shot over dry farmland or woodland, just as if it were a pigeon or pheasant.

The motivation for the total ban in England and Wales on shooting waterfowl with lead was one of ease of enforcement. All the authorities have to do now is to take samples from game dealers of ducks shot on commercial shoots, test them for lead shot and extrapolate the percentage to gauge compliance nationally.

The modern wildfowler has to face ammunition restrictions that his grandfather did not.

So, set up a nonsensical and difficult to comply with law. Watch and test to see the poor level of compliance and then use it as an excuse to ban lead for all shooting on the evidence that shooters cannot be trusted to regulate themselves. This is exactly what has happened.

Of course, most wildfowl shot on the foreshore is shot by responsible, law-abiding wild-fowlers but they rarely sell their few ducks and cannot sell geese, as that is illegal. Therefore, I would venture, 100% of the ducks tested for lead come from commercial shoots and are not shot over wetlands anyway.

The reason for the stitch-up? It can only be explained by the over-riding will in certain circles to remove lead from the environment entirely, regardless of the evidence. The other influence is the anti-shooting pressure being applied by those who dislike shooting instinctively or politically and see a lead ban as another weapon against the shooting community. If you cannot get rid of shooting through moral or legal arguments, use money. If every shot fired cost five pounds, a lot of shooters would give up the sport.

The trap has been sprung, the legislators have done their data collection and the evidence is clear: the lead ban is not being complied with. The answer, say the anti-shooting lobby, is to ban lead from all sporting ammunition. This appears to be a real possibility. If it becomes reality, what future for the user of a 19th century hammer gun?

At present, the following alternatives to lead exist in the market as shotgun ammunition and the table (opposite) indicates their potential as alternatives to lead shot for users of guns with damascus or early steel barrels, proofed for standard British game ammunition.

Hevi-Shot is 10% heavier than lead and is, therefore, the best ballistic choice as a shot material, as it delivers more shock and penetration per pellet of any given size than any of the alternatives. When compared to steel, Hevi-Shot is 54% denser. It patterns very well and is used with success by shooters of modern guns. It is however, not yet loaded into ammunition suited to shorter chambered English guns and it is very hard, risking barrel damage.

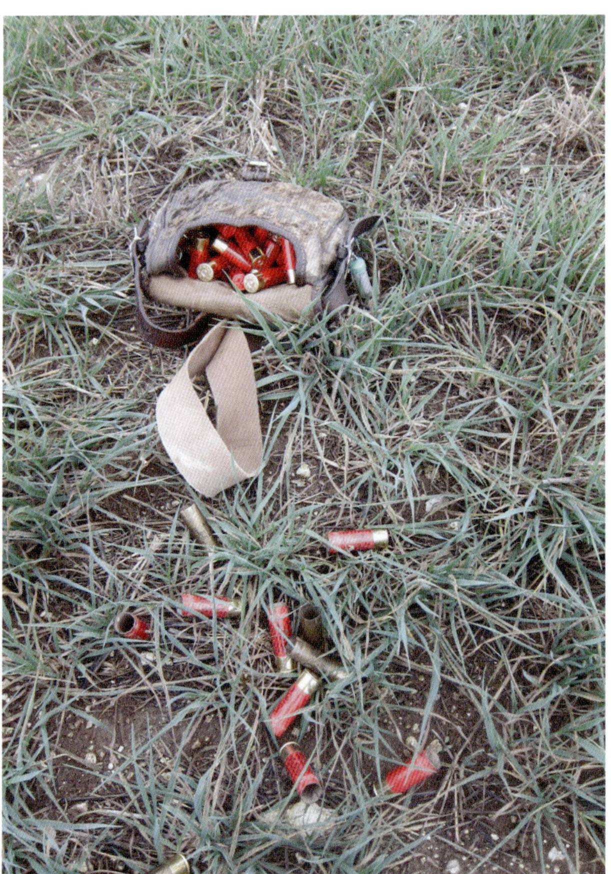

The picture has not changed for a hundred and fifty years but ammunition *has* gradually altered over the decades.

The major factor preventing Hevi-Shot from becoming a mass market lead alternative is the very high price. New versions of Hevi-Shot loads are now available. Express offer a 1oz (28g) load suited to 2½" chambers but its hardness remains a worry for guns not designed with harder projectiles in mind.

Tungsten is a much denser metal than lead at 19.6g/m3, and is also very hard. In order to prevent barrel damage, particles of the metal are suspended in a form of epoxy. Most tungsten shot can be fired through normally proofed guns. The cost of tungsten cartridges can be up to ten times that of lead.

There are also concerns that tungsten can be dangerous for human and animal health. The US army, after producing so called "green" training rounds made of tungsten in place of depleted uranium, removed them from use in 2007, after research by the University of Arizona suggested that tungsten may elevate the risk of cancer, placing troops at risk. In addition, *The Lancet* reported a case of a soldier developing seizures having consumed alcohol and trace amounts of tungsten metal.

Although evidence suggests that tungsten is not good for human health, we are not aware of any study which looks into the issue of tungsten in the environment, or indeed, in the toxicity in wild animals.

Bismuth, being less dense than lead, at 9.7g/m3, does not match lead's performance. Also, being less malleable, it does not deform in the target, but can fragment. This was particularly an issue with early versions of bismuth shot but recent improvements have largely removed this issue. Slightly larger shot is required to retain energy at the target, reducing the pattern of the shot. The cost of bismuth is around five times that of lead.

Despite the metal chemically resembling arsenic, bismuth has relatively low toxicity. Nevertheless, bismuth is a byproduct of the lead mining process, and its price is kept low by the extraction of lead. There would be a decrease in supply if lead mining was curtailed, which would also result in an increase in price.

Steel shot is actually made of iron and is comparable to lead in terms of price. However, being much less dense than lead, at 7.8 g/m3 (69% the density of lead), it shares very different ballistic capabilities. As such, larger shot is required to retain energy at the target, thus reducing the number of pellets in a given load. The reduced load density and hardness of steel increase the probability of wounding the target species, rather than killing outright.

Pat Murphy, gun room manager of Holland & Holland, was quoted by Mike Yardley in a recent *The Field* article: *'All our new guns are designed to be compatible with standard steel shot, but, as far as older English guns are concerned, we advise caution. We have modified a number of older guns to use steel at the request of customers. This would include lengthening the forcing cones – to ease the pressures and passage of the wad and shot into the main bore – and a reduction in choke constriction to a maximum of half. We do not routinely carry out these modifications, however. Nor do we sell steel shot cartridges because of their limited range and lethality. Our preference for classic guns is bismuth and suitable tungsten.'* This is a view shared by many other knowledgeable members of the gun trade. It is also significant that no steel loads are available for 2½" chambered guns; the chamber length of the vast majority of older English guns.

Patterns when using lighter steel shot, and the penetration of the pellets suffer. Ricochets are also common, and to prevent injuries or loss of sight, it is not recommended to use steel shot in wooded areas or other areas where ricochets could occur.

Although there is no known biological effect of ingesting steel shot, ferrous metal pellets inside the body have the potential to cause complications and internal damage during certain medical procedures, such as MRI scans. My thanks to the Countryside Alliance for providing much of the data on these lead alternatives.

The other complication with steel is that it cannot be shot through chokes tighter than ½ and it suffers by overly damaging game at ranges inside 20 yards and has insufficient penetration to kill well beyond 35 yards.

In summary, I would advise vintage gun users to choose Bismuth or Tungsten matrix loads. I would restrict this recommendation to ammunition guaranteed as suitable for English guns of traditional type by the manufacturers (Gamebore and Eley do so) and to completely avoid steel, cheap though it is.

Ammunition alternative to lead	Suitability for use in damascus or early steel barrels	Typical cost per shot
Hevi-Shot	No. Express offer a 1oz, 65mm load for traditional guns but insufficient trials with older guns remain a worry.	1.80p
Tungsten Matrix	Yes. Gamebore offer this shot as an option advertised as 'safe for your old side-by-side'.	£1.12
Bismuth	Yes. Eley VIP bismuth loads are available for 2½", 2¾" and 3" chambers.	£1.05p

(I) After crawling in this
fashion for over half an hour, Jones gets
a good chance and fires.
(II) He proceeds to searc
for the dead buck, whe
a native informs him, that the bulle
has just slain his grandmother!!
(III) After a lengthy palaver, Jones agrees to
console the afflicted relatives with the sum
of two hundred rupees, and decides to give
up blackbuck shooting.
(IV) Notwithstanding a gentle hint sent,
that he should shoot there again, as
old women were "plenty" and rupees scar

Where have all the Gunmakers Gone?

In the era in which our hammer guns were made, gun-making was a job for life. An apprentice would begin at his master's side at the age of fourteen and by twenty one he would be a gunmaker in his own right, with a trade that would serve him until he died or retired.

Gun-making was often a family affair, with the same surnames turning up in the pay rolls of the major firms and small associated businesses for generations.

The Great War was perhaps the first major stumbling block. Society at large was massively affected and gun-making was no different. The post-war world kindled aspirations to mobility and a more rebellious attitude towards institutions and authority was fostered.

The 1920s and '30s saw bicycle manufacture and the motor trade offering better wages for less skilled work. Many gunmakers were tempted away from their benches.

After World War II, the social order changed massively and industries involved in non-essential manufacture were sidelined as the country was hastily rebuilt and remodelled in a new image. The Empire began to disintegrate and the gun-making firms who supplied it fell on hard times. Birmingham's Gun Quarter was decimated by urban development and road building. Factories and workshops dwindled, emptied and were finally demolished.

Those firms which did weather the storm of the next half century were generally not expanding their businesses. They relied on old hands staying on, apprenticeships did continue but numbers were much reduced.

David Sinnerton, formerly with Purdey but now based in his own workshops. David is considered by many to be the finest finisher working in the trade today.

Ian Sweetman at the bench while apprenticed at Atkin, Grant and Lang. After a spell at Westley Richards, Ian is now at Purdey and doing very well.

Today, the apprentice gunmakers of the 1960s are approaching their seventies and retirement beckons. Prospects for the future of the best hand-built guns in the UK looked bleak. However, the past decade has seen something of a resurgence and the numbers of self-employed artisan gunmakers making a good living on their own terms is better than it has been for some time.

Apprenticeships are still a challenge and few, if any, one-man or two-man operations are able to take them on. The problem is that a gunmaker is paid for what he does with his hands during the working day. If he takes time to train an apprentice, he loses money. Once trained, the apprentice will probably leave and earn better money starting his own business – a business in direct competition with his master, for

Facing page: From 'Sketches of Indian Life'. Thousands of sporting guns found their way into the hands of colonialists. Many have been repatriated and pose a challenge to gunmakers restoring them after decades of serious neglect.

Stephan Dupille trained in Belgium before stints at Watson Bros and Holland & Holland. Steph stocks guns for all the top London makers. Here he is discussing a project with Denver Marchant.

whom the proposition looks like a lose–lose one.

Westley Richards, Holland & Holland and Purdey are still training gunmakers. Some are arriving in the UK from Italy, Belgium and Eastern and central Europe. When aided by home-grown gunmakers and familiarised with the particulars of British guns, many of them become expert in their fields.

One can only hope that gun-making continues to attract talented craftsmen and that they continue to find vintage British guns as fascinating and worthwhile as I do.

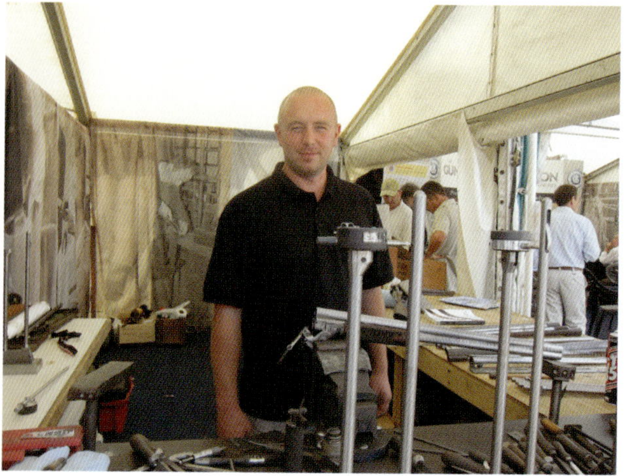

Jim Blacker, of Bill Blacker & Son, a firm generally considered at the top rank of British barrel makers.

THE GUNMAKERS' CHARITABLE TRUST

In acknowledgement of the challenges faced by small firms and individuals within the gun trade with regard to training apprentices, the Gunmaker's Charitable Trust exists to support the training of our would-be gunmakers of tomorrow.

The Trust offers bursaries, typically of £5,000 a year for three years. This off-sets the difficult early years, when an apprentice is least productive to his master gunmaker. Modern gun-making involves old-world craft skills like hand-inletting of metal to wood, barrel regulation and fine engraving as well as modern technical skills like the use of CNC and CAD machines to prepare close-to-form parts. Modern apprentices are encouraged to learn as many aspects of modern gun-making as possible.

Graham McKinley (in bow tie) with his American protégé Dan Morgan (in kilt), who has learned his skills unconventionally but is very capable.

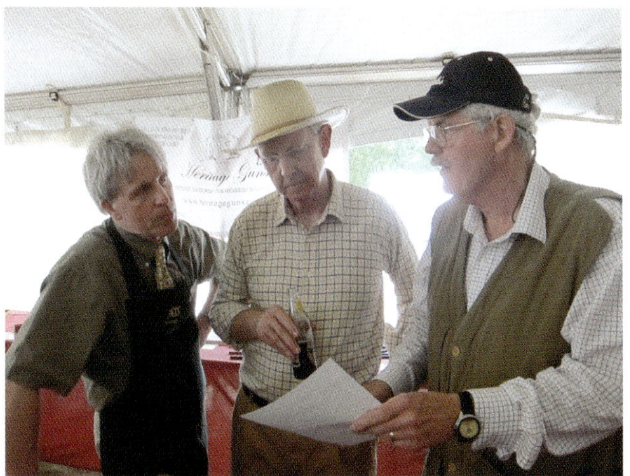

Toby Barclay of Heritage Guns. Toby is a talented, self-taught gunsmith who renovates his own stock and runs a successful business catering largely to US clients.

To date, some prestigious firms, including Westley Richards and Watson Bros have participated in providing apprenticeships under this scheme and others, like Holland & Holland have supported apprentices by providing expert examination and assessment of their work, ensuring that their credentials in the gun trade are recognised and worthwhile.

A relatively new organisation, the Charitable Trust seeks to expand its cash reserves in order to offer further apprenticeships and a solid foundation for the future. Readers who want to support the gun trade might consider making a donation or a bequest. It is certainly a worthwhile charity to support.

Midlands Gun Services, started by ex-Holland & Holland actioner Kristian Reilly (right). The firm is providing traditional best quality gunmaking to the trade and has seen business boom since setting up in Shropshire in 2015.

Travelling Overseas with Hammer Guns

I travel with old guns frequently. It started when I took my old 12-bore Thompson to Botswana, to accompany my friend Michael Joseph on an elephant hunt in the Okavango Delta.

Since then, I have travelled to Africa annually to hunt birds. We do this by walking-up the local game birds; francolin and guinea fowl, over pointers. We then shoot pigeons over the crops in the afternoons and finish with an evening flight for ducks and geese: including the biggest goose in the world, the spurwing.

Other overseas trips have included Romania, hunting quail; again over pointers, and Italy for rough shooting; mostly walked-up pheasants.

My hunting in the US with a shotgun has included wild turkey in Texas, live pigeon shooting in North Carolina and doves; again in Texas.

A key question to ask yourself when preparing an overseas trip with a vintage hammer gun is availability of suitable ammunition. This is where it pays to have a gun that has been re-proofed for nitro, as black powder shells are unlikely to be available in most places. If the chambers were lengthened to 70mm from the original 2½", then that removes another layer of complication, as the shorter, British standard cases are not universally available elsewhere.

When I travel with my hammer guns I take with me a nipple wrench, turn screws, oil, cloth, cleaning rods and jags. The beauty of the inert action, like the Jones, or the Dougall 'Lockfast' is the lack of complication.

I have watched my guns soak up days of high-volume shooting in alternately dusty, wet and muddy conditions without a hiccup while the modern guns of my friends suffered ejector or single trigger problems.

If the gun needs stripping and thoroughly cleaning, it is a simple job requiring few tools.

Rough Shooting over Dogs

Having lusted for ever more driven pheasant shooting in my twenties and thirties, in my late forties I find myself increasingly drawn back to my rough-shooting origins. It may not offer the glamour or the bonhomie and social networking opportunities of a good driven day but it is more of a workout for mind and body.

What it does offer is the chance to see my young vizsla bitch, Vesper, working for her supper. It provides healthy exercise of a type that my rugby-ruined right knee can handle and it hardly costs anything.

The other, not inconsequential, benefit is that loading and firing quickly is much less of an issue. That

The author rough shooting in Shropshire with Vesper.

means taking out a slightly more eccentric contraption is a viable option.

Open chokes and a beautifully balanced 12-bore of 7lbs or less is perfect. A Lancaster slide and drop action is too slow for driven birds really, but when walking the hedges it is as good as anything.

Non-rebounding locks do not frustrate on an armed ramble like they can when birds are pouring overhead. The experience is slower and each success a bonus rather than an expectation. I find a couple of friends, some interesting old guns and a Land Rover full of dogs on a late November day makes a perfect antidote to the winter blues. If the woodcock are in, so much the better.

High Pheasants

My opinion of the kind of high pheasant shooting now fashionable to those with the pockets and the inclination is that it is a specialist sport. Modern solutions are being sought and guns like the HPX are being created to enable ever greater ranges to be tackled. It looks spectacular when done by an expert and pointless when attempted by the occasional participant using his normal kit.

The most important factor is the shooter. Whatever kit is supplied, unless the type of shot encountered is known, expected and practised, there can be little expectation of success.

I am a better than average grouse shot, because I am quick and agile. I am a better than average pigeon shot, partly for the same reasons but also because I have spent many hours in the pigeon hide or on a flight-line paying attention and honing my skills.

I'm an average driven pheasant shot and when it comes to the super-high, curling down off a mountain kind of birds that I get to shoot perhaps once or twice a season, I am worse than average. It is not that I could not learn to shoot these birds, it is just that I do so infrequently and therefore worse than someone like Dave Carrie, who seems to do it every other day.

I also prefer to use my 1870s hammer guns and they don't have any choke, nor the weight to help the long, steady swing and maintained lead shooting style than is generally favoured in these circumstances.

If one were to approach the task of building a high pheasant gun on a hammer action, it could be done. I would begin with a pigeon gun of best quality. It would ideally want to be re-stocked and re-barrelled with weight and balance characteristics befitting the shooting required.

The over and under guns the specialists are using weigh over 8 lbs and have 32" barrels and tight chokes. They also need to be chambered for 2¾" or 3" shells and capable of firing up to 40g loads repeatedly.

The benefits of the pigeon gun action are the likely third grip, side clips and heavier than normal bar and fences.

This is a project I have not yet undertaken but would find interesting. If only I had the time and finances to build such a gun and spend the summer with Peter Croft learning the correct technique!

Pheasant shooting in the woods. Traditionally shown birds, skimming over the trees and often visible only for a second or two. Open choked guns are perfect.

Hammer Gun Disassembly

Basic stripping

This is a basic strip. Now the gun can be inspected, cleaned, dried, lubricated and reassembled. Make sure your turnscrews are hollow ground and a tight fit.

Remove the forend.

Remove the barrels.

Remove the lock pin.

Pull out the locks.

Release trigger plate pins.

Remove pins and place in tray.

Remove breech pin.

Take trigger plate and action off wood.

The parts safely placed in a box.

Stripping the locks

Complete stripping of the locks is not recommended unless you have fair gun-smithing experience, more harm than good can result in amateurs going further than their competence suggests wise.

Use a spring clamp to compress the mainspring – gently.

Carefully remove the spring from the lock plate, unhook from the swivel.

Once removed, gently release the pressure on the spring.

Put all parts once removed into a stripping box.

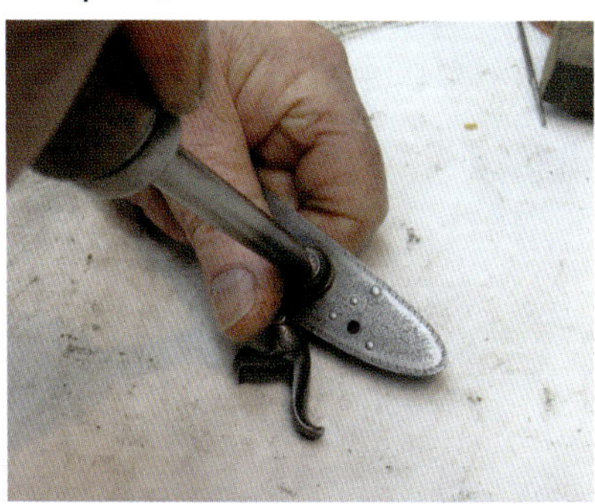

Turn the lock over and remove the hammer stop pin.

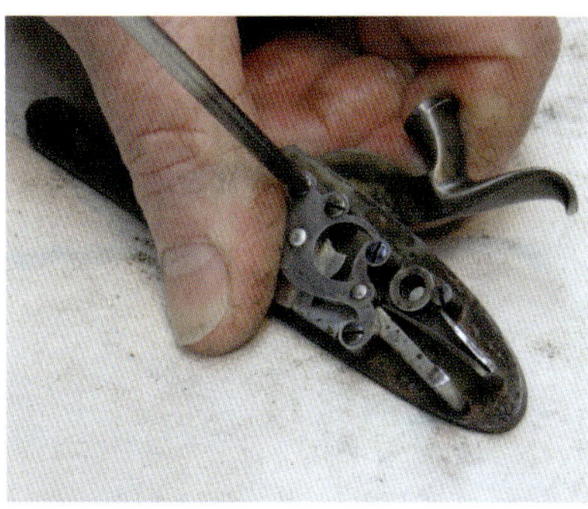

Loosen each bridle pin half a turn, then remove the pins.

Lift off the bridle, keep each pin in the original hole for reassembly.

Remove the hammer.

Remove the tumble and control the sear and sear spring tension.

Remove the sear.

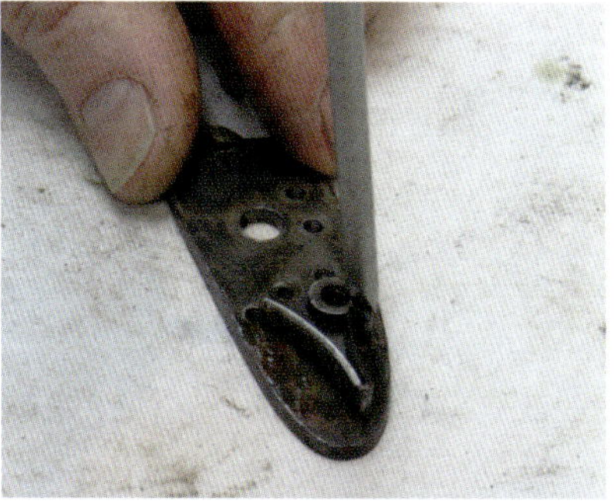

Finally remove the sear spring.

Reassembling the locks

Secure the sear spring with its retaining pin.

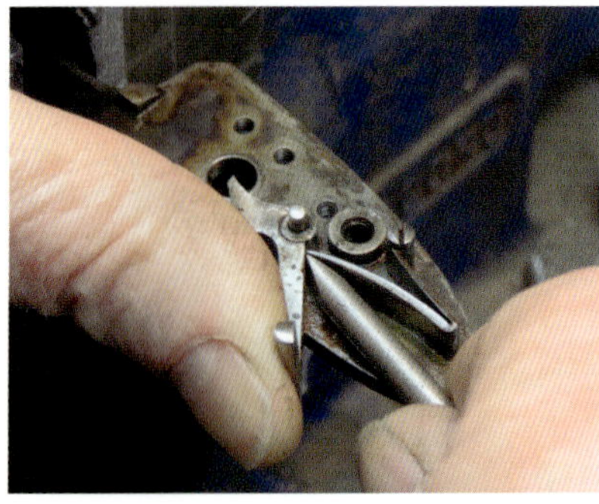
Seat the sear and compress the sear spring to locate it fully.

Holding the sear in place, replace the tumbler.

Place the bridle in position and locate the pins.

Tighten the bridle pins evenly.

Fit the mainspring into the locating hole.

Using the spring clamp, compress the mainspring.

Reattach the hammer and loosely secure the stop-pin.

Fit the mainspring into the front locator hole and hook onto swivel.

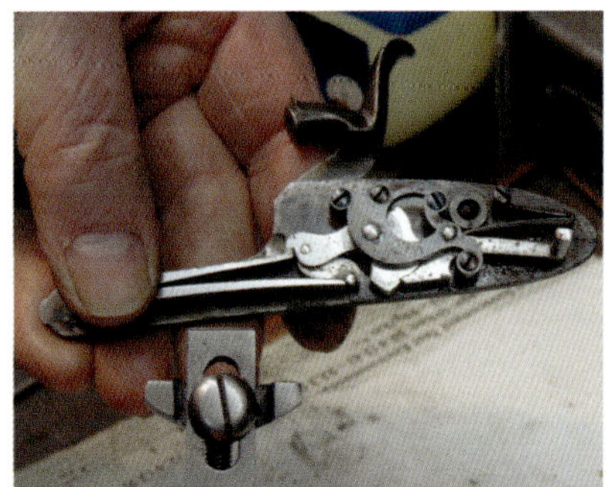
Gently loosen the clamp and remove it from the spring.

Tighten the hammer stop pin.

The lock should now be complete and functional.

Reassembling the gun

Fit the action back onto the stock.

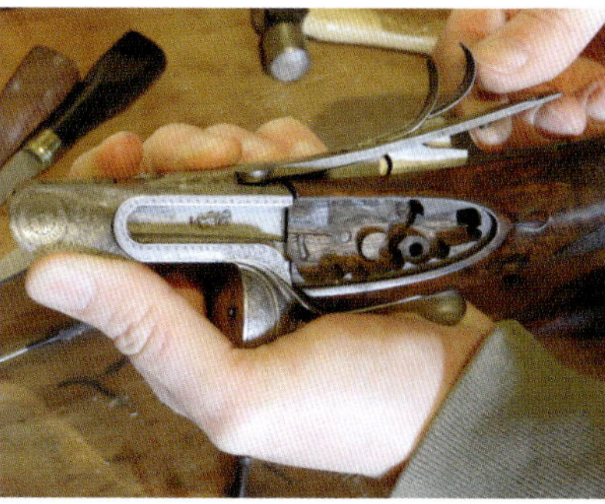
Fit trigger plate back in place.

Secure the breech pin.

Keep trigger clear of sears as you replace the locks.

Reattach the trigger guard.

Replace the guard screws.

Check everything works.

Reassembly is basically a reversal of the disassembly process. Just be careful that all parts are free and properly aligned as you go. Don't force things, they should have an engineering fit. If it feels wrong, it is. Stop and reassess rather than get frustrated.

Butt plates

Butt plates on hammer guns follow their development from muzzle-loader to breech-loader and from walked-up shooting to driven-bird shooting. Early breech-loaders follow the muzzle-loader style of a full metal butt plate covering the entire butt sole. They are generally plain and blued.

As breech-loaders progressed, the butt plate became less important, as the butt was no longer placed on the ground when loading the gun. Consequently, the butt plate began to shrink; first by a cut-away process, which became known as a 'skeleton butt plate', as it retained the outer edges but was cut-away and the wood chequered in the central sections.

The skeleton became increasingly smaller until, on many guns, the only parts remaining were the tip of the toe and the tip of the heel. Guns exclusively for driven game in the 20th century generally have no metal at the butt, they are simply finished with a chequered panel on the butt sole.

Protective metal butt plates date back to the flintlock era. 1860s breech-loaders inherited the feature but they gradually gave way to skeleton plates, then heel and toe plates and, finally, horn butt plates. Modern restoration options include a rubber pad, a leather-covered pad or a new horn plate.

To Restore or to Preserve?

When one is fortunate enough to find what we call a 'sleeper', that is, a gun which has been in private hands, safely locked away and barely used for decades, we are faced with a decision about whether to keep the gun as original as possible or to restore it to the finest working and cosmetic order. Guns like this will have seen little or no gun-smithing, so they may be dirty inside and dull outside but they will have clean screw heads and plenty of original finish under the tarnish.

There are two schools of thought. Some people want condition made as close to new as possible. Ideally, this involves applying new finishes, using traditional methods and skilled gunmakers, to replicate the original appearance the gun may have had over a century ago.

This typically includes re-browning barrels, re-cutting chequer, raising dents, removing scratches, blacking furniture. It may go as far as picking out worn engraving, welding small external pits, re-striking barrels. It may even mean re-stocking, re-barreling and re-case-colour hardening. Whatever work is carried out, the desire is to make the gun look new.

2½" chambered and black powder guns will be re-proofed to modern nitro, often for the, now common, 70mm case.

The other school of thought it to accept the patina, the knocks, the scratches and the wear of age and do the minimum work necessary in order to keep the gun in sound mechanical condition. The result desired here is an old gun, resplendent with its battle scars, yet capable of regular use. In this case, original chambers will usually be retained.

Of course, these are two extremes. Most running repairs and simple restorations on vintage guns fall somewhere in between. A full, no-holds-barred 'do-up', on a gun in need of a lot of work, might cost £2,000 or more but most owners do what they feel necessary as the need arises. The most common scenario I encounter, for a full restoration, is when

A Thomas Horsley 12-bore wood-bar gun as it arrived and so far uncleaned or restored. It is worn but will respond to sympathetic work.

purchasing a gun for a client as the basis for one; either at auction or privately. In such cases, we normally begin with a rather grubby piece to start the project but we try to avoid guns that have seen much earlier gun smithing, as it is easier to start our work without having to clear-up past mistakes.

Beauty is in the eye of the beholder and, to some, any residue of wear is ugly. They want their gun spotless when they take ownership. To others, originality and character are thought more pleasing. They want no sign of any restoration work visible. From my motorcycling days, I remember the riders of 'rat bikes' proudly blatting around on dirty, ugly bits of battered kit, however, they were mechanically sound and often invisibly improved. They contrasted with the owners of super-shiny, all original concours-type riders. Gun owners can be a bit like this.

Of course, we are discussing guns intended for use. The collector will always hanker after guns as original as possible and shun any cleaning or restoration. They want good 'sleepers' and will leave them as they find them. As a shooter, one can imitate this approach with a few practical modifications. At the very least, the gun will need to be stripped, cleaned and probably tightened, re-gripped or re-jointed to make sure it is fit for work and is safe. Barrels may need cleaning internally by lapping out pits and proof status will have to be established and remedied if it proves unsatisfactory. Having done that, the exterior can be given a rubbing of Renaissance Wax, which will keep it water resistant but preserve the patina on metal and wood. The gun may then be used, looking like the old girl she is but undeniably fit for service.

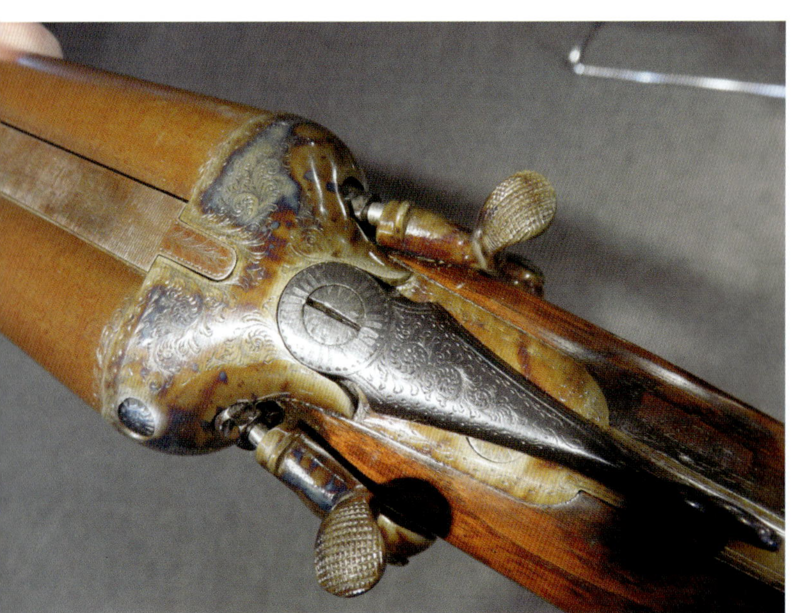

A badly over-restored Greener. The gun has lost all its old charm and looks terrible.

My personal approach is to restore with sensitivity. To do this you have to have access to artisans who understand what you want and can deliver it to order. Barrel browning has to be in-keeping with the overall condition of the gun: clean, correct but blending-in. One does not want people to say "look at that old gun with beautifully re-browned barrels". They should struggle to know. Woodwork too must not jump out at the viewer. I want to lift off the dirt and allow the figure and colour of the wood to show its beauty once more. However, re-finishing must be addressed with sensitivity to the degree of wear the stock may have suffered. Super-shiny finish with super-sharp chequer will not do. I like my guns to look like they have been cared for but they need to look 'lived in'. Achieving the balance is not easy and one unfortunately encounters legions of guns in auction houses or gun shops that have been ruined by an over-zealous restorer, or one with that very dangerous possession: a modicum of knowledge and a cavalier attitude about applying it.

It is difficult to explain an over-done gun but if your eye is acute, you can spot one from thirty yards. I have learned it is best to keep one's opinion to oneself on these occasions, as the owner will invariably be defensive of his, doubtless expensive purchase or proud of his restoration. A critical evaluation is rarely welcome, however well meant.

A number of American dealers and gunsmiths have taken to the trade in, and restoration of, British guns. Some of these have developed quite a following. However, few appear to have a real understanding of the aesthetics of British guns and they are in a hurry to add new and shiny to the outcome rather than subtle and appropriate. This is not a uniquely American problem, but it is an identifiable one. I must also mention that some of Britain's very finest gunmakers have made the trip across the Atlantic to provide services to the American enthusiast: Kirk Merrington, in Texas is an excellent man to send all types of general gunmaking jobs and repairs on British guns and Paul Hodgins is as good a stocker as any working today.

When restoring, one should be careful to refer to the original finishes on the gun. A good example of where many get this wrong is in the treatment of the lever work and hammers. Stephen Grist, formerly of John Wilkes, recounted his approach to the issue when he was involved in restorations: "*When I was with Wilkes the approach was to black only parts that were steel – which would have been charcoal blued originally – everything else was hardened iron and was left coloured or patinated or, if very tarnished, was lightly brushed. The parts were tested with a file on an under surface – if it left a mark it was steel. In the 1800s very few parts were steel, even the guards were often hardened iron – as they are on most Grant hammer guns. Steel only started to be widely used on fore ends when ejectors started to appear requiring a tougher structure around the knuckle to support the workings. I have a collection of wooden forging patterns from Woodward's factory dating from between 1870 and 1910, only a very few of these, like bolts, levers and springs have labels attached indicating to the smith that the forging is to be made of steel – all the rest were expected to be made of iron and would have been colour hardened on the finished gun.*" Modern restorers would do well to pay heed to these observations.

American collectors are more prone than any others to want their guns case colour hardened again. The exponents of the art in the USA are adept at re-finishing Colt revolvers and lever-action Winchesters but these colours are not appropriate on an 1879 Purdey hammer gun or a Manton muzzle-loader. Any inspection of an un-worn hammer gun of the 19th century will show the colours to be subtle, dark and soft. Newly 'restored' colours will usually be waxy, bold, and dominant. In my opinion, they kill the gun.

The other issue with re-case colour hardening is that the metal will often move under heat. It needs re-fitting by a good finisher. This is rarely done well outside the UK, as suitably qualified and experienced finishers are as rare as Alaskan Democrats. There is also the issue of the strength of the steel being compromised by the heating process.

Re-colour hardening is popular in the US. I have no time for it, especially when the gun shows some wear.

There are perhaps three men in Britain to whom I would entrust the job, and I would be very specific about the required finish. In 98% of the restorations I negotiate with a client, I dissuade them from renewing the colours. Where it is successful, falls generally on the otherwise very plain action, which needs 'lifting' or on a very sharp 1930s side lock which can be brought up to 'as new' because the entirety of the gun can be made to match it for crispness. However, when the gun is very clean and crisp, it rarely has all the case colours worn off.

The blacked hammers on the Cashmore (top) hint at inexpert work. The Purdey (above) looks rather better.

One also needs to be aware of the need for a full restoration to prepare a gun for actual use. Done correctly, a restored gun will function beautifully, bed-in as it is used (which is why the action may seem stiff when delivered after re-jointing) and age gracefully over time. Traditional oil finishes will become a satin sheen, rather than a deep gloss, as they get wet and dried off and buffed repeatedly. Ultra-glossy, hard oil-finishes will scratch and chip and generally look tatty after a bit of proper work in normal field conditions.

To summarise my approach to restoration, I would say that I try to make a gun look its best, with a realistic eye on what age and use have done to it. For a gun to look its best, I believe it should not try to pretend to be what it is not. I want the restoration work to complement the gunmaker's original efforts, not overwhelm them. I want observers to think 'What a lovely gun', not, 'What an amazing re-colouring job' or, 'What nice barrel browning' etc. If one element shouts much louder than all the others, I think I have failed.

Restoration

PROCURING THE RIGHT GUN

It takes a mere ten or twenty seconds per gun for me to dismiss most of the guns in a sale room. That is how it is possible to see hundreds in a single day at a London auction and reduce the list of what you want to bid on to a sensible number.

This E.M. Reilly is a real 'sleeper' and is probably best left alone bar a strip, clean and basic service.

Adsett 14-bore back-lock. Sound wood and metal here and no external issues, however barrels are badly pitted.

Closer inspection is required, once your short-list has been made. This is where the real work begins, as the viewer has to observe the gun in its entirety, identify any problems, calculate which can be corrected and what the likely cost would be, then plan a bid, plus costs, to establish a final figure and see if the venture is commercially viable.

Let's step back a paragraph. How is it so easy to dismiss so many guns with such an apparently cursory glance? One word sums it up: 'crispness'. Maybe not an especially elegant or technical term but it does capture the essence of the issue at hand. Upon opening a case or picking a gun from the stand, eyes first go to the action.

Turn it around and inspect the furniture, lock plates and other metal parts. While doing this, wood-to-metal wear and fit will also become apparent. If the view coming back to you shouts of polishing, buffing, excessive cleaning and re-finishing, the gun is of absolutely no interest. This visual information speaks of a tired gun that has been subjected to an over-aggressive 'do-up'. There is nowhere to go with it.

In most auctions, this quick and simple first inspection removes 80% of the guns on view from my list. For these I have no time, no interest and will warn clients away from them. The only exception might be if a gun were at the less extreme end of this spectrum and otherwise very sound and shootable; and very cheap. In that case, the occasional enthusiast on a budget may find such a gun provides an accessible route to owning a class of gun he could not afford if he were seeking a really good example. Sometimes one has to fit expectations to budget. A view must be taken.

However, what the experienced eyes in the viewing room are looking for are guns of quality and novelty. Not those which have been to market several times in the last fifteen years, nor those that have been renovated to showroom condition, all shiny and resplendent with new chequer, blacked barrels and glowing stock finish. What they are seeking are the three or four guns in most sales which fall into a category known in the trade as a 'sleeper'.

A 'sleeper' has been in a case under a bed for thirty years, or it may have adorned a magnificent gun room in a minor stately home, having been put on the

This single barrel Reilly was found in a house being restored by developers. It had been in a cupboard under the stairs for decades. It can be made functional but barrels and action have extensive rust damage.

Fully restored Grant .500 BPE. This came in as a true 'sleeper' with plenty of original finish and responded well to renovation.

rack when the family changed to more modern guns, perhaps in the 1920s or after the last war. It might have languished at the back of a retired gamekeeper's gun safe, an old gift from his employer that he neglected, in favour of his trusty AYA 'Yeoman' and BSA 'Sportsman'. Sleepers can be hammer guns, or rifles, sidelocks, boxlocks or many of the transitional guns that bridged the hammer/hamerless period of the 1870s and 1880s. Of course, since our particular interest here is in hammer guns, that is where our focus will be.

What 'sleepers' have in common is that they are new to market. They will not have been seen by anyone in the trade for sixty years or more. They will not have been renovated and they will not have been badly neglected. They may be dirty and they may look dull but these are the fabled 'diamonds-in-the-rough'.

Many retail 'punters' frequenting London auctions will walk past these because they look old, dirty and in need of a lot of work. They often want a gun they can take out and shoot without too much extra effort or expenditure.

What serious collectors and trade buyers want is a blank canvas. With the grime cleaned gently off, the original finish shows through, blackened wood starts to glow, congealed oil and dirt lifts off the lock plates to reveal crisp engraving and sharp beads on the fences. Original chequer cleans out to reveal that it is clogged with 'palm grease' rather than worn smooth. Removal of the forend reveals original case hardening colours on the iron, the pin slots are not enlarged or burred from multiple ham-fisted strip-and-clean operations over the years.

When measured, the bores will be true and the walls thick, there may be some light pitting and the exterior may be dry and tarnished, perhaps with light rusting on the outside of the barrels but overall sound and unmolested. Proof marks may well be original, either early nitro or black powder. Whatever we need to do to 'lift' the gun, we will be the first to attempt the job, which means we can preserve originality and we do not have to rectify earlier, badly-executed efforts.

The problem with the 'sleeper' at auction is that every keen-eyed professional in the viewing room has seen it. If there are only three or four in the sale, a number of these people will be keen to secure what they want, in order to make the two or three days in London worthwhile. This can push the prices up. For this reason, auctioneers are very keen to get 'sleepers' into the catalogue.

Whenever I make one of my frequent calls to the head of one auction house for a preview of a sale, perhaps two or three months hence, I detect a note of excitement when one has uncovered a really new-to-market gem. It might not be a Purdey, it might not be an obvious highlight to the untrained eye but to the men who spend all their days looking at old guns in a professional capacity, these are the stand-outs that make the job exciting.

If fortunate enough to buy one or two of the 'sleepers' in a sale, or if you manage to find one privately, the restoration process has to begin. Here one can get it very wrong. I have seen beautifully original guns turn up at Game Fair dealer stands, ruined by over-restoration. Original acid-etched damascus barrels, polished and re-browned rather than left in their black and silver, mottled glory; a finish very hard to replicate.

Guns with nice, crisp actions and good hints of original case colours and charcoal blacking speaking through the years of their original quality and telling their story, brutally re-colour hardened with deep, thick, enamel-like modernity; ruined in the eyes of the connoisseur, forever lost in pursuit of a commercial edge to entice a part-educated but wealthy, enthusiastic buyer to whose eye 'as new' is the desired aesthetic and to whom many dealer will pander. Some cannot see, others will not see.

'Sleepers' lie in an ever-diminishing seam of richness. There are fewer every year, but still they do seem to emerge, often from the most surprising sources and most unexpectedly. Whether you are an auctioneer, a dealer or the 'friend of a friend', when the phone rings and a voice on the other end tells you "I've got this old gun that belonged to my grandpa and nobody in the family shoots any more..." the hairs on the back of the neck start to prickle and the juices start to flow – could this be a sleeper?

The questions start to formulate, the tinder box of the imagination ignites and another adventure begins.

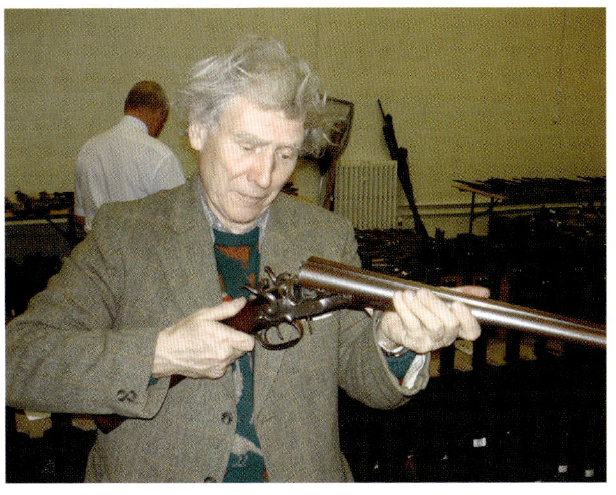

Right: Robin Knowles checking out potential at Holt's. The Enos James (below) is too worn and of insufficient quality to restore economically.

Restoration Case Study

The phone rang one day and the middle-aged caller told me he had found a gun under his recently deceased father's bed. It was not known to the family and there was no shotgun certificate.

Was it worth anything, he wondered, and would I come and sort out the legalities? A couple of hours later and I was driving through the Essex countryside to rendezvous with the unwitting inheritor of the 'old hammer gun' described down the line.

There on the coffee table lay a rater dirty but dry looking pigeon gun by Charles Boswell. Fairly typical of its type but a good example. 30" damascus barrels, side clip, flat, filed rib and semi pistol grip stock.

We agreed a fair price and I took the gun away. In accordance with the law, I asked the owner his name but he declined to give it, I therefore informed the police that it had been handed to me anonymously.

This gives the authorities a chance to consider whether the gun was reported as stolen, otherwise missing, belonging to someone else, or suspected of use in a crime. Since it raised no questions, I was free to enter it into my book, as a Registered Firearms Dealer, and consider it my property.

The locks had not been removed in a generation.

The gun had been dry stored for many years and was covered with encrusted oil and dirt. Some minor rust pitting was evident and the wood to metal seams showed the characteristic expansion of rust affecting the metal where it is in contact with wood – around the trigger strap, the lock plates, forend iron etc.

The action was full of dried oil and dust.

Once on the bench, I stripped the metal work from the woodwork to uncover the decades of accumulated rust, sludge and congealed oil covering all the internal parts.

An alcohol bath removed the worst of the grime and revealed the inner workings. Wood remained sound, though blackened with the ingress of mineral oils over the years. Again, alcohol softened the exterior shell and a flat edge scraped the old finish off to reveal the colour and figure in the wood. A soft brass brush gently cleaned out the chequer on the forend and hand.

The damascus barrels retained their original finish and I decided to leave it as it was, though re-oiling the surface brought it somewhat back to life.

Fate dictated that the phone rang as I worked and it was a friend from the USA. He was asking if anything interesting was available. He also just happened to be a live pigeon shooter and mention of the Boswell piqued his interest. After a brief chat and a few e-mailed photos, a deal was struck.

The decision was a soft restoration. The gun would be cleaned and put mechanically right but as much originality as possible would be retained.

Typically, a full refurbishment would involve re-cutting the chequer, re-finishing the woodwork, re-jointing the barrels to the action, stripping, cleaning

and lubricating the mechanisms, including the locks.

With the Boswell, I did re-joint the gun to make sure it was tight, we did the full strip, clean and service and papered, coloured and re-oiled the stock and forend wood.

It cleaned up nicely and looked like an honourable old gun in good mechanical condition, despite retaining some of the scars and patina that life had worn onto it. The effect was pleasing and I took the gun to Texas on a trip to meet Cyril Adams. While there, Cyril took me to shoot ZZ with his regular group of friends. I took the Boswell and shot well with it. The gun was fast enough to get onto the targets gun-down. The balance was such that it swung nicely and predictably and the weight and construction just right, so the trap shells we fired at the ZZ targets were comfortable on the shoulder.

I despatched the Boswell to its new owner confident that I was sending him a gun that I liked, could shoot and was proud of.

To American tastes, the Boswell restoration was perhaps rather 'shabby chic' and not as comprehensively re-finished as most would have ordered. Many people stateside want their restorations to be shiny and new-looking. I'm working on bringing them around to my way of thinking.

Above: All the woodwork was black and oil-stained, the chequering filled with grease.

The locks after degreasing.

The locks as they came out of the wood.

The furniture had rusted where it came into contact with wood. This is typical damage from storage in houses where the air can be damp and cold. The wood holds moisture from the air and the metal in contact with the wood rusts.

Much of the rust is held in the grease that once covered the metal. It had lifted the guard strap slightly proud of the wood.

All metal parts were coated with a mixture of dried oil and dust. However, the surfaces of the metal remained relatively free from serious rust or pitting.

It will never look 'new' but it will respond to a sympathetic restoration and become fully functional and attractive.

Externally, the Boswell appeared to have been stored badly, too much mineral oil had got onto the stock, while the metal parts had dried out and minor surface pitting had become apparent.

Above: After cleaning off the mineral oil and re-finishing, the stock began to show its colour and figure once again. A leather-covered Silver's pad added an extra 3/4" and finished the butt nicely. The original flat-top chequer was cleaned out and retained.

For finishing, we used a traditional recipe 'slacum' oil that has a soft, resilient sheen without the gloss shine of many modern guns. A very glossy finish on an old gun showing some wear makes it look wrong. The objective is to make the gun look honest and genuine, accepting some of its historical scars while making it attractive and mechanically perfect.

The action after cleaning. Pins have been blued..

The finished restoration sought to retain as much originality as possible, while returning the Boswell to attractive functionality.

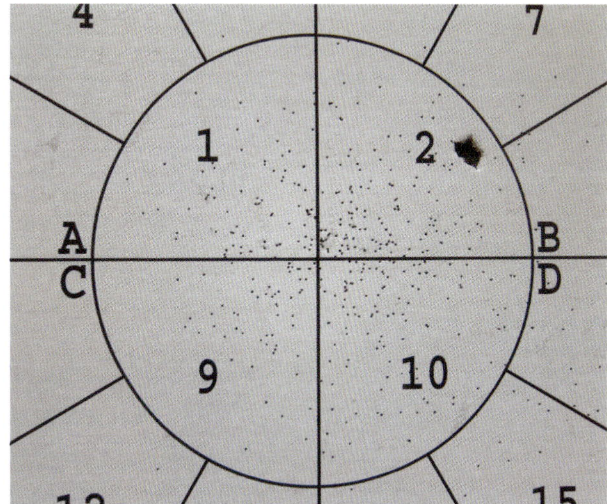

Above: At the pattern plate, the Boswell showed the old barrels still throw nice tight patterns. I tested it on Helice targets in Houston and it performed very well.

Barrel Browning - Getting it Right

FIFTY SHADES OF BROWN

Sympathetic restoration is the key to so much of the challenge we face when tackling old guns that need some help to get back to good health but will not benefit from some parts looking brand new and others tired and tarted-up. To be successful, a restoration must blend all the parts together again, so they look as if they belong together. Colour, finish and texture are very important.

The browning of damascus barrels is a very good example of this. Get it wrong and the barrels look as if they do not belong with the gun. Get it right and the new finish blends in beautifully with the old features of the gun; protective, attractive and appropriate.

Getting the colour to look in-keeping with the style and age of the gun is tricky, especially if the original finish is very worn or has been replaced once or twice in the past. The chemical rusting process involved in re-browning a pair of barrels is rather like cooking – a good cook with the right ingredients will often produce a cake like no other – it comes down to a feel for the baking process, experience and expertise. My best barrel browners experiment tirelessly, curious as to how slight variations in the process or the mix will affect the finish.

Browning is a rusting process, albeit controlled. It is sensitive to temperature, humidity and time. Different chemicals will affect the iron and steel parts of a damascus barrel in different ways and a skilled browner will be able to offer a wide variety of colours and degrees of contrast. No two barrels are the same and no two browning processes can be exactly replicated on every barrel type.

There is, of course, room for variation. For new guns, some gunmakers choose silver and black as the finish, others chocolate brown and yet others a very dark or very light finish without much contrast. However, when restoring a gun, I think subtle but classy is the way to go, as with every other aspect of the job.

I like to see contrast and colour but I don't want the barrels to shout at me – they need to complement the overall aesthetic. I want my 'Brown' to be a team player, not a dominating superstar. Fortunately, the craftsmen who provide my browning solutions know exactly what I want and they manage to deliver every time.

When starting a restoration, one of the key decisions is the browning of the barrels. Should one leave a faded original finish or re-brown? If so, replicating the original colour and figure needs to be carefully handled.

These acid-etched Rigby barrels are beautiful and distinctive. The style is evocative of Dublin gunmakers in the 1870s, though they occasionally occur elsewhere. Examples by William Ford of Birmingham have been seen and continental makers like Springer also used them.

Early twist barrels can be beautiful if correctly browned. Stub twist and single iron skelp indicate earlier guns, even of very high quality. Damascus became more intricate as the 19th century progressed.

A skilled browner will be able to adjust his process to make the best of whatever barrel material has been used.

The fine damascus barrels on this Reilly 12-bore retain their original brown. It has tarnished somewhat from dry storage without regular oiling. Some collectors would keep the finish as it is for the sake of originality, others would polish and re-brown them to enhance the figure.

I'm fortunate to have barrel browners who can replicate any colour and figure in order that a newly-browned pair of barrels can be put into best order without looking out of place on an un-restored gun.

The browning on this William Powell has worn off and these barrels need re-browning. In this case, the wear is beyond what one could consider an attractive patina. They really need polishing and re-browning to restore their beauty and extend their life.

THE PHOTOGRAPHS BELOW SHOW SOME OF OUR CONSIDERATIONS WHEN BROWNING OLD GUN BARRELS

Consider originality. This damascus has been blacked.

Lettering may need re-cutting if faded like this Dougall.

External light pitting can be struck off before browning.

These damascus barrels have been sleeved to steel and blacked.

Check the gutters for leakage before re-browning.

Note original colours and contrast on faded barrels.

The correct finish on a gun barrel will depend on a number of factors. They include the maker, the period and the type of barrel. For example, John Rigby produced beautifully acid etched damascus finishes in Dublin but appears to have discontinued the practice when he set up business in London. Other Dublin makers, like Trulock & Harriss made use of the same barrel type and finish, so it was a Dublin fashion for a time in the 1860s and 1870s.

The latter firm may well have been buying their barrels from Rigby. The finish on these is not meant to be smooth, the acid etching produces a silver figure with a mottled surface, which is stunning when seen in its original form. I have seen gun dealers polish and brown them; consequently, utterly spoiling them, during restoration of the gun.

THE RISE & FALL OF BARREL LINING

Back in the 1950s, the method of restoring shotgun barrels which became known as 'sleeving', was developed. It was recognised as a safe and legitimate procedure by the proof authorities and guns subjected to this process were duly stamped 'SLEEVED' by the London or Birmingham proof house, once the work and re-proof tests were complete.

Sleeving involves cutting the old barrels off about 4" in front of the breech. New tubes are then machined, as are the old breech ends, and the two fitted together and welded into place. Tubes are then struck-up and polished before being blacked. The old ribs are re-laid and the effect is workmanlike if done the 'budget' way and just like new barrels if done properly, with the seam TIG welded so as to become invisible. The former costs under £1,000 and the latter around £3,000.

For over half a century, sleeving was recognised as the budget way to rescue a good gun with scrap barrels. Re-barreling is much more costly and

These barrels have been nicely polished and browned, showing the gold inlay to good effect.

in all but the most expensive side-locks it is generally not economic.

Then along came Nigel Teague with something different. His new method was to line the barrels with hard steel, after boring them out from inside. The new barrel was inserted into the enlarged bore, complete with new chamber, and restored the barrels internally. This ingenious system enabled the outer dimensions to remain unadulterated. It was especially good for damascus barrels, as they retained their beautiful patterns.

The fixative for the 'Teague Liners' is an adhesive, sandwiched between the two metal skins. For the past half decade, 'Teague Lining' became something of a buzz-word in restoration circles. It cost around £1,500 and it seemed for a while that it would replace sleeving as the preferred method of budget re-barreling. The proof houses even provided a new proof stamp: 'LINED', to mark barrels submitted after having the new process applied. Many in the gun trade mused on the long-term performance of lined barrels and now we have sufficient evidence to appraise them objectively.

The blunt answer is that the experiment failed. Lined barrels always felt to me as if they were dead weights in the hands. Beautifully balanced hammer guns became dull and barrel heavy. But they looked great! The seams were invisible. Externally the guns appeared to have been restored to their former glory. So, perhaps the negative effect on balance was an acceptable compromise? Many though so and modern shooters used to barrel heavy guns sometimes liked the forward weight.

A Purdey sleeved during the early months of the announcement of the lining process by Teague.

Unfortunately, there were more fundamental flaws in the process with commensurate effects on longevity. Once lined, the barrels cannot be heated because it would melt the adhesive. Therefore, loose ribs or loops cannot be repaired. Sometimes, the liners twist in the barrels. Other complaints included a rivveling effect developing in the outer skin. This has been attributed to the cooling and heating of the barrels during use and the different rates of expansion and contraction at molecular level of the three sandwiched components – the liner, the original barrel steel and the thin gap filled with adhesive.

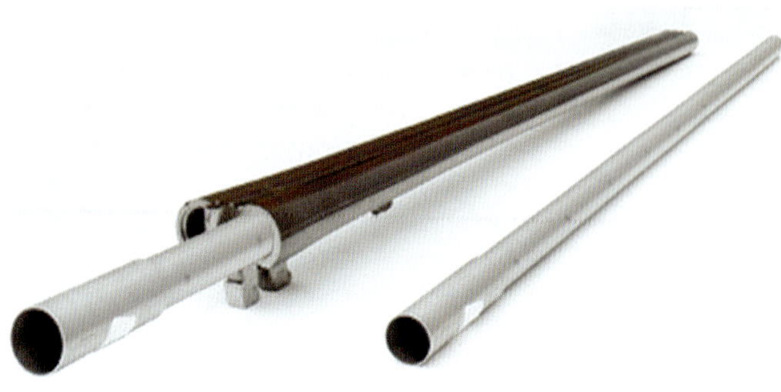

Teague's barrel liners were the great hope for damascus restoration.

Barrel makers started reporting that dented barrels which had been lined were impossible to repair. The hard lining and the soft outer skin reacted differently to dent raising techniques and dents could not be raised acceptably. The result was often scrapped barrels.

Perhaps the signal which sounded the beginning of the end was when Nigel Teague stopped offering the process he had devel-

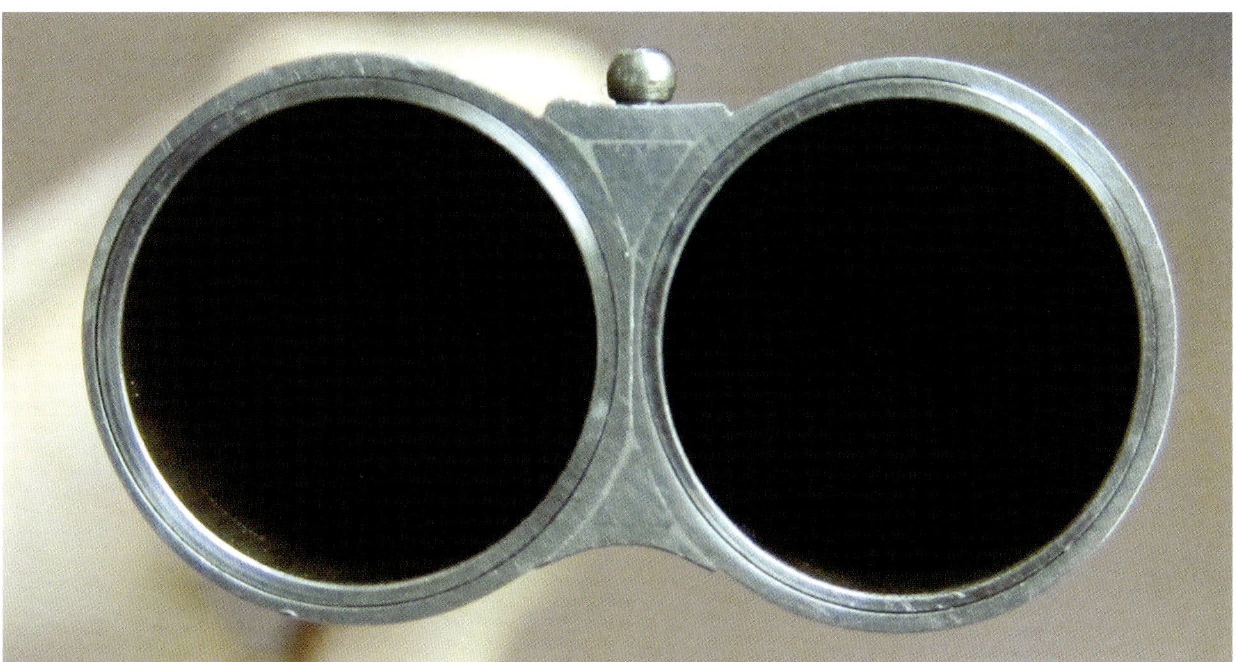

Lined barrels viewed from the muzzle.

oped. It was licenced to a colleague in Britain and again licenced to an American representative. The trajectory is downwards and I predict the process will ultimately fall out of favour entirely. As a restorative process, we are again turning to traditional sleeving methods to revive guns with worn-out barrels.

With regard to damascus barrels, we are back to square one. Sleeving destroys the very qualities of the barrels that make these guns appeal to so many enthusiasts. Occasionally, one does encounter damascus tubes re-used and sleeved to Damascus guns. Such supplies are very hit and miss so it will never be more than an occasional option for the local gunsmith.

One of my barrel makers is experimenting at present with stripping damascus tubes from old guns with thick barrels but suffering from other terminal defects, in order to turn the tubes, clean the bores and re-use them for damascus-to-damascus sleeving purposes. Doubtless, I shall report on the success or otherwise of this venture at a later date.

Perhaps another method of barrel restoration will emerge in the future but the thought and technology required to approach the problem and exploit what is only a small market is considerable and I very much doubt we shall see any further advances in this regard. Lining was a great idea, the people involved in developing it and the quality of the engineering involved in delivering the finished work were impressive.

It looked like a solution but time has shown that its limitations largely outweigh its benefits. British gunmakers are constantly inventive and I wonder if some other clever individual will revisit the lining idea and come up with a more resilient means of achieving the desired result?

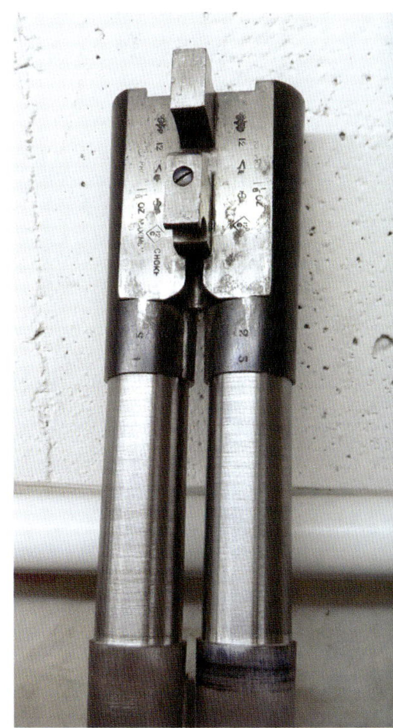

With the demise of lining, traditional sleeving has come back into demand.

This Purdey is having new tubes, which will be filed and balanced to the highest standards before re-fitting to the gun.

HOW TO MEASURE THE BORES

Proof law requires that the bores on gun with imperial proof marks be within ten thousandths of an inch of the size stamped by the proof house. If the gun has metric proof or re-proof marks, the measurement is the millimetre equivalent of eight thou'. The place to measure is 9" from the breech. One simply inserts the bore gauge and expands the end in size by twisting the protruding end. When it stops due to being tight against the bore, a reading can be taken. Record the measurement (for example .733") and compare the with the proof size (for example '12', which is .729"). In a barrel showing these measurements, the result is that the gun is safely 'in-proof', being only four thou' larger than original.

Using a bore gauge to measure internal diameter and check proof status.

HOW TO MEASURE THE WALL THICKNESS

There is no legal minimum wall thickness for a shotgun. However, twenty thou' is the notional trade-preferred 'recommended minimum' and guns with thicker walls generally command better prices than guns with thin walls. To determine thickness, a wall measuring tool is a necessity. The most common type in use has upward standing poles on a cast metal base. Each has a dial and a sliding spring-loaded gap measure with a ball bearing tip. The barrel is pushed down onto the rod, with the measure on the outside, the wall acts as a barrier between the measuring tip and the receiver, which

Measuring the barrel walls is perhaps the most critical part of the evaluation.

is now inside the barrel. The muzzles sit on a brass sliding end cap. This is moved up and down, allowing the ball bearing ended measuring tip to get closer or further from its receiver, depending how much metal divides them. This thickness is indicated by the dial, in thousandths of an inch.

LISTENING FOR LOOSE PACKING PIECES OR RUST

Tap the barrels with your knuckle and turn them up, then down, listening for a sound inside the rib. Any falling noises will be rust or loose packing pieces between the ribs. This indicates corrosion or loose ribs.

LOOKING FOR DENTS AND BULGES

Hold the gun barrels to the window or light source. Move them around and watch the light and shadow thrown along their length. Distortions or movement in the shadow will show up dents, rivvels and bulges.

LOOKING FOR PITS

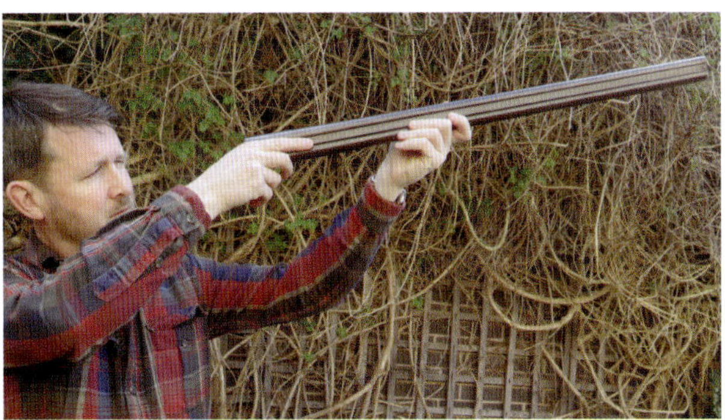

Hold the barrels to a light source and look into the bores, first from the breech end, then the muzzle end. Look in at an angle so light is thrown onto the internal walls, don't look straight down, or the shine will disguise the flaws. Pits will show as black shadows and mottled patches, either deep or shallow. Dents can also be seen from inside in this manner. If a dent shows on the outside but not the inside, some lazy individual has simply lapped the bores and not bothered to raise the dent.

RINGING THE BARREL TO CHECK INTEGRITY OF RIB, LUMPS AND LOOP

Hold the barrels by suspending the hook on your index finger. Make sure the extractors are seated tightly. Tap the barrels sharply with the back of your other index finger. It should ring like a bell. If not, it may have loose rib or lump or loop. So, investigate further. If the barrels have 'dead spots', where your tap just makes a flat sound, that may indicate where your rib is starting to lift.

CHECKING FOR 'HEADACHE'

If the gun is loose, it is easiest to check by removing the forend, then holding the stock by the hand and locking the butt under your arm and into your body. Give it a quick shake from side to side. You will feel or hear any movement. If it is loose, the problem is the jointing and it will need to be attended to either by repairing the hook, the hinge pin, the bites, or a combination of one or two of the three.

CHECKING FOR BITE/GRIP

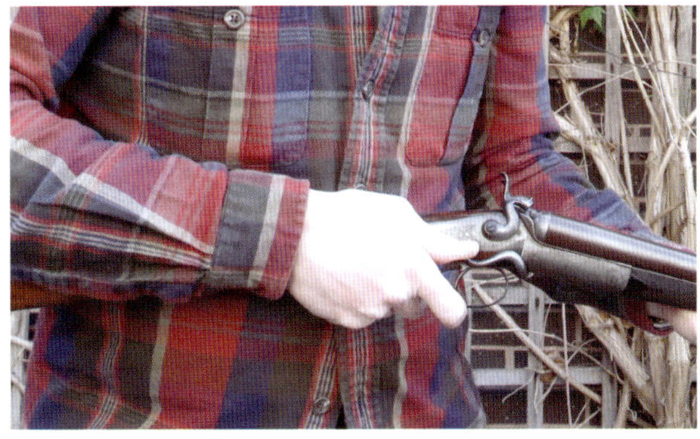

Hold the gun closed and move the lever. It should not be sudden or have an uneven catch, nor should it feel sloppy and loose when it slides the bolt in and out of the bites. The grip of the bolts on the bites should be progressive and finish tight but should not 'click' in and out, nor feel like it is slotting into a big void.

Trouble Shooting: What to look for when buying hammer guns

In our enthusiasm for keeping and using old guns we must not lose sight of the fact that many are approaching the end of their life. Barrels especially need to be carefully health checked.

By their very nature, the hammer guns we seek are old, they have been through many hands and they may not have been looked after very well. If little used, they may well have been left in a safe or a cupboard for decades, perhaps in dusty or damp conditions. They may have been kept too dry or too wet, they may have been repaired or restored in the past by those without the finest skills or to a painfully tight budget.

Life has often been hard on the guns and, as buyers, we must be careful to ensure that we pay close attention to these matters when deliberating over a prospective purchase.

Of the types of gun to seek out, I like to find a 'sleeper', but that is largely because I have a team of gunmakers who can take a gun of this type and restore it sympathetically, exactly the way I want the work done. Many less fortunate than I would do better to seek a well cared for gun or a well restored one. This requires less post-purchase work and expense and should remove a good degree of uncertainty from the process. I would generally advise buyers to avoid guns that have been badly restored. It is harder to reverse bad work than it is to restore a dirty but un-abused gun.

However, when one has a particular gun in mind that would be perfect for a particular task but a good example is unavailable, taking a gun that needs considerable replacement of major parts, like stock or barrels, can be a good alternative to compromising on these issues or having to contemplate the cost of a new-build. This is what we shall consider over the next few pages.

AREAS OF COMMON DAMAGE FOUND IN HAMMER GUNS

1. A careful inspection of every area of the gun is imperative. The gun will very likely be over a hundred years old and there will have been ample opportunities for neglect, damage, alterations or major repairs to take a toll. Here we can see either side of the trigger plate pin there is a crack. This goes right through the trigger plate and is of structural importance.

2. Wood work is potentially the weakest area of the gun and the hand takes a lot of strain when the gun is opened and closed as well as channeling recoil when fired. The hand pin is an obvious area to check for damage. Loose hand-pins allow movement, which promotes stress and can create cracks. This back-lock gun has a repaired crack, which is clearly visible. Many repairs are well disguised, so look carefully.

3. The ribs are attached to the tubes by soft solder in most British hammer guns. In time, these can lift if the solder breaks or if rust gets into the valley and lifts the ribs. Here we can see clear gaps between barrel tube and rib at the breech end.

4. Check the forend fittings carefully. They can provide indications that the gun has had new forend wood, or if the forend fittings have been replaced, or become badly rusted and repaired. Here we can see a badly fitting finial around an Anson pushrod button, indicating the historical removal of rust and the gapping that results between wood and metal.

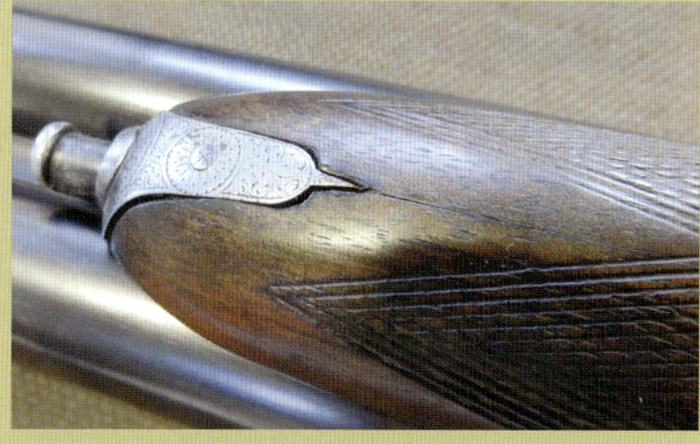

5. The standing breech (or breech face) of this bar action gun show pitting around the striker holes. These are the result of blow-back from pierced primers. Early centre-fire ammunition with black powder and corrosive primers was prone to causing rust if guns were not properly cleaned. Breech face rust can be exacerbated from long-term storage in baize or felt lined cases. The material holds moisture and promotes rusting on any metal touching it.

6. Hammers stick out and are an obvious area to check for damage. Common problems will include a repaired or replaced spur, a replaced hammer (or hammers) or some deviation of form. Check the two hammers for shape and alignment. Look at the size, quality and style of the chequer on the spurs for signs of variation, which would indicate repairs.

7. Some damage is not clear without some dismantling. The broken swivel on this Boss back-lock gun was evident when the gun was stripped but the owner thought the spring had broken. Care must be exercised when dealing with lock problems, as the spring can damage the delicate woodwork when it jumps free of its housing. If the hammer won't cock, leave the stripping to a professional unless you are confident you know what you are doing.

8. Pay close attention to attempts at repair, if they have been done badly or have failed to correct the issue, it suggests a deeper problem than may be obviously apparent. This gun shows an attempt to weld-repair the pitted face, around the striker holes. It has not worked.

9. Chequer should be carefully inspected. It will either be worn to a greater or lesser degree or re-cut. If it is worn, it can be re-cut but pay attention to the width of the remaining wood. Every re-cut weakens the hand by removing wood. If badly re-cut, it can be impossible to make a satisfactory repair.

10. Wood-bar guns need special attention in this area under the bar. The veneer of wood here is thin and cracks often appear along the grain. Also pay attention to the condition of the wood around the trigger plate and the metal around the knuckle or forend iron. Oil or rust will often have caused damage in these sensitive areas.

11. Take the forend iron off and have a good look at the wood-to-metal fit, any evidence of mineral oil impregnation, replaced screws. Ideally, the metal will retain some case colours, the pins and screws will be unmolested and the wood in good condition with sharp, tight seams abutting the metal work.

12. Another area to check is the muzzle. Here can be seen a gap between the tubes and the rib. This can indicate shortened barrels or repaired ribs. The muzzles should not be dented or thin. Feeling into the bores will indicate the choke profile and the wall thicknesses at the muzzles can be an early indicator that bores have been lapped to the point that the tubes are no longer concentric.

13. One of the key areas of wear in a neglected gun is the fit of wood and metal around the locks. Avoid guns with pronounced gaps as they have been resurrected from a poor state and the wood is unlikely to prove robust.

14. Be careful of guns with very blackened woodwork. Mineral oils will break down the structure of the wood and cause it to crumble over time. It may be necessary to strip the gun to assess damage fully. If it looks badly oil impregnated on the outside, it will very likely be worse inside, especially around wood and metal joints and where screws penetrate the wood. This Pape is dirty but restorable.

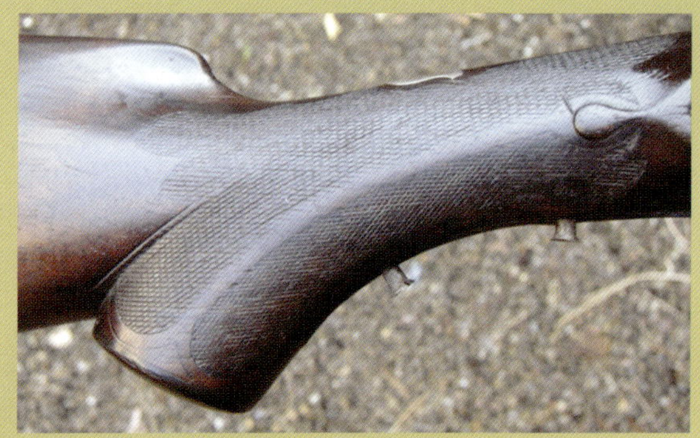

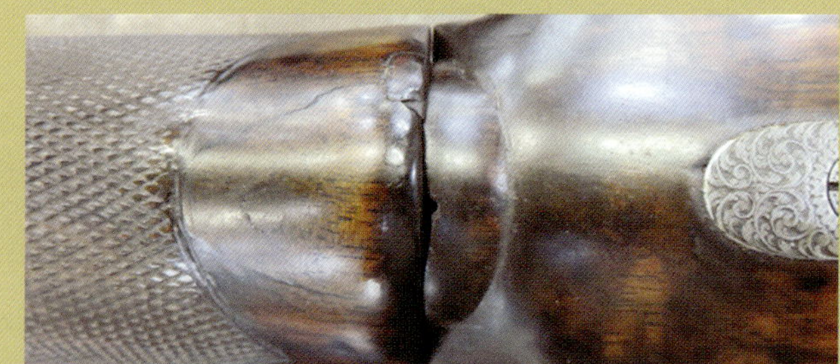

15. The 'crab joint' on this 1860s Westley Richards shows old damage. These sections of wood, where they are relatively thin, in areas prone to damage and fitted close to metal parts are necessary to inspect closely.

16. The pistol grip of this Lancaster 10-bore double rifle has a serious and unrepaired crack. At this stage, a good stock maker could make a working repair but left unattended, the stock will break into two pieces.

17. The edges of woodwork are vulnerable to damage, check areas around lock plates and trigger guards for missing splinters. A good gunsmith can repair damage like this almost invisibly.

18. Many horn butt plates are nearing the end of their useful lives. Damage like this is common. Replacing the original with new horn, or lengthening it with a rubber pad is straightforward.

Customisation: possibilities and limitations

A CASE STUDY:
W&C SCOTT PIGEON GUN
(W&C SCOTT S.N 73371)

The subject of this restoration was bought on my advice in the USA by a client called Bob. He was looking for a donor action on which to base his ideal sporting clays gun. It is a bar-action hammer gun of pigeon weight, by W&C Scott.

Bob came along to see me at SCI in Vegas, with the gun he had found and was then considering as a purchase. He wanted, he said, to construct a competition gun, primarily for Sporting Clays. He really wanted it to be based on a hammer pigeon gun and was looking for a good starting point. He told me he had very non-standard fit requirements and always struggled to get guns altered to suit him.

Bob un-slipped the gun and there, in the aisle of the busy show, we discussed it as a prospect. The first thing of note was the condition of the action. It was a long-bar W&C Scott hammer gun with bar-locks, side-clips, Scott patent, square section 'Improved Bolt' and very best scroll engraving on all the metal surfaces. The engraving was sharp, the action and locks still had traces of original colour, the edges were clean; no visible softening, polishing or pitting to spoil the aesthetic. Here was a turn-of-the-century pigeon gun action of the very highest quality, showing almost no wear and tear.

I took a breath and had a closer look. Evaluating a gun is a process by which realisation comes to you in layers; first impressions, closer inspection, individual checking of function and careful examination of potential areas of weakness or fault. It was apparent that the stock was much altered, cracked through the hand and too short. The barrels were shorter than Bob really wanted and not perfect but they could be restored.

Capt. Brewer at the pigeon traps. He was well-known in his day and his exploits widely recorded in the newspapers.

I noticed an interesting inscription below the forend, on the underside of the left tube: 'Jack Brewer 100 straight, Dexter Park 1897'. The gold escutcheon on the stock also carried 'JB' intertwined. Now, I recognised Jack Brewer from the research I put into my 2007 book *Vintage Guns for the Modern Shot*. On page 33 I included a photograph of a stuffed pigeon under a dome with the following words painted onto the glass: *'Championship of the World. Winning blue rock shot by W.B. Bingham Esq. at the Welsh Harp, Hendon, who killed 22 out of 25 Rocks, shot at 30 yards rise, beating the American crack shot Capt. Brewer, April 30th 1888.'* This was not just a very nice pigeon gun, it appeared to be one with some history. Brewer was a noted American competition shooter, whose exploits are extensively recorded in the newspapers of his day.

Bob and his father, Cecil, visited the Birmingham Proof House while in the UK.

The record books suggest the serial number of the Scott approximates to the year 1904, which is at odds with the 1897 inscription on the barrel. We can look to the proof marks for further help with dating. The London Proofs on the flats bear the NP with arm holding scimitar above, denoting 1904 rules of proof, as well as indicating CHOKE in both barrels and a load marking of 1⅛oz, which was actually the standard game gun load at the time.

This information backs up the serial number dating and throws some question on the 1897 inscription. The 30" barrels are further marked W&C Scott & Son 'The Premier' with the London address of 78 Shaftsbury Avenue, at which Scott resided from 1900-1921. All this evidence suggests a date of manufacture later than that suggested by the inscription on the underside of the barrels. How could Brewer have shot 100 straight at Dexter Park in 1897 with a gun made seven years after the event? It is all most interesting and a mystery I am unlikely to solve conclusively. Perhaps he, or another, engraved the information of a previous match on a later Brewer gun.

A bit of historical digging is all part of the process involved in reviving an old gun. The price list of W&C Scott guns lists the Premier model, in 1897, at £68 (wholesale) as a hammer gun; significantly less than the Premier hammerless gun at £82. These prices were maintained until the 1920s. The Premier was sold as a hammer gun from 1873 to 1921. It features Scott's 'Improved Bolt' of 1892 in addition to the Purdey double under-bolt of 1863. The three bolts are all operated by Scott's patent spindle and top-lever of 1865. Mechanical function, materials and finish are all impeccable and the mechanism feels as solid and perfectly aligned today as it would have over a century ago.

Engraving is very fine quality full-coverage scroll. This grade of gun could be further embellished with carved relief engraving and some game scenes or pigeons, as an option. The Whitworth steel barrels are of dovetail lump construction, with a stippled, concave rib. The Premier was certainly a 'best' gun, just one step down in finish from what we would consider 'exhibition grade', or 'presentation grade', as some gunmakers preferred to call it.

So, having assessed the gun's provenance, quality and condition, we had a job on; it needed proper restoration.

We contemplated simply re-stocking, retaining the original (bent) barrels and renovating the rest of the gun. Bob went off to find the seller, with a price in mind. He did the deal at a figure agreeable to him

The original 30" barrels are Whitworth steel, as evidenced by the Whitworth stamp and wheatsheaf trade mark.

Engraving on the barrels attesting to Capt. Brewer's '100 straight'. Whether he did it with the Scott or won the Scott for doing it, I have not been able to verify.

and I collected the gun at the Southern Side-by-Side Championship at Deep River a couple of months later. After a chat, Bob decided he would take the plunge and go all out to make this exactly the gun he had always dreamed of. Instead of holding on to Brewer's bent, old barrels, Bob would invest in best new chopper-lumps at 32" with a full set of Teague chokes (ten in all) to cover all eventualities. I brought the Scott back to London to begin the project.

There were a number of considerations to grapple with. First the specification of the job, the allocation of the work and some historical research. The project involved a sequence of work and a different gunmaker taking the gun through each stage. I had to project manage barrel making, choke cutting, actioning, re-proofing, fitting, re-stocking, finishing, blacking, engraving, casing and delivery. It would prove quite demanding but very interesting. The first port of call was Scott Wood, the ex-Purdey barrel maker.

The original stock had been much abused and altered.

BARREL MAKING

Some people imagine it is simply a matter of making a call, ordering tubes of whatever length you desire and having a chap make you the barrels. Think again. I was not going to use Spanish tubes as the quality is horrible. Italian tubes are a bit better but they rust too easily and also lack the quality of the best English tubes. However, English tubes are hard to get, they are made in small quantities, the bigger firms tend to monopolise orders and getting non-standard sizes is really quite hard. The tubes I wanted for the Scott had to accommodate the long bar (3" barrel flats with lumps measuring ¾" rear and 1⅜" front) and they had to be 32" long. Additionally, we had to make 32" ribs, as finding them from stock anywhere proved impossible.

With tubes supplied, Scott machined the barrels and lumps to fit, brazed them together, made

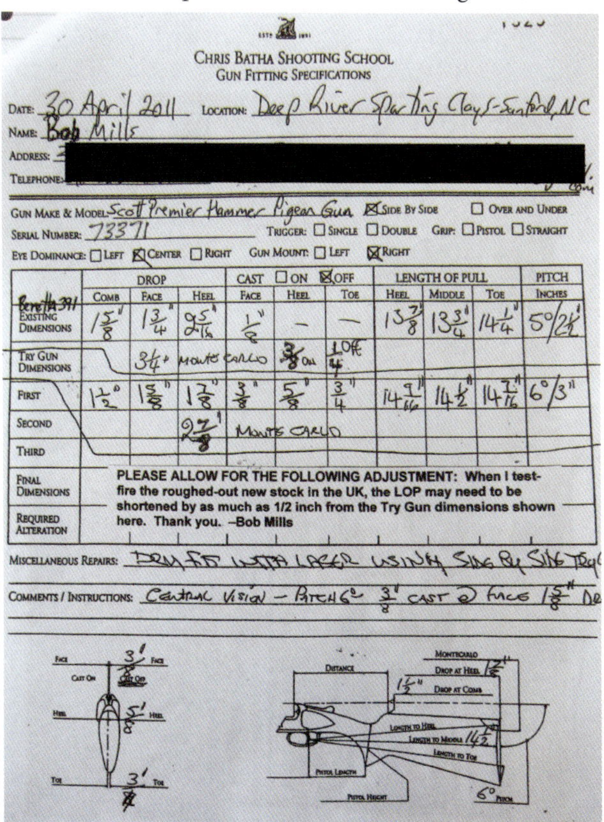

CHRIS BATHA SHOOTING SCHOOL
GUN FITTING SPECIFICATIONS

DATE: 30 April 2011 LOCATION: Deep River Sporting Clays - Sanford, NC
NAME: Bob Mills
ADDRESS:
TELEPHONE:

GUN MAKE & MODEL: Scott Premier Hammer Pigeon Gun ☒ SIDE BY SIDE ☐ OVER AND UNDER
SERIAL NUMBER: 73371 TRIGGER: ☐ SINGLE ☐ DOUBLE GRIP: ☐ PISTOL ☐ STRAIGHT
EYE DOMINANCE: ☐ LEFT ☒ CENTER ☐ RIGHT GUN MOUNT: ☐ LEFT ☒ RIGHT

	DROP			CAST ☐ ON ☒ OFF			LENGTH OF PULL			PITCH
	COMB	FACE	HEEL	FACE	HEEL	TOE	HEEL	MIDDLE	TOE	INCHES
Beretta 391 EXISTING DIMENSIONS	1 5/8"	1 3/4"	2 5/16"	1/8"	–	–	13 7/8"	13 3/4"	14 1/4"	5°/2 1/2"
TRY GUN DIMENSIONS		3 1/4 + Monte Carlo			3/8 on	1/4 off				
FIRST	1 1/2"	1 5/8"	1 7/8"	3/8"	5/8"	3/4"	14 9/16"	14 1/2"	14 7/16"	6°/3"
SECOND			2 7/8"	Monte Carlo						
THIRD										
FINAL DIMENSIONS	PLEASE ALLOW FOR THE FOLLOWING ADJUSTMENT: When I test-fire the roughed-out new stock in the UK, the LOP may need to be shortened by as much as 1/2 inch from the Try Gun dimensions shown here. Thank you. –Bob Mills									
REQUIRED ALTERATION										

MISCELLANEOUS REPAIRS: Dry fit with laser using Side By Side Try
COMMENTS / INSTRUCTIONS: Central vision – Pitch 6° 3/8" cast @ face 1 5/8" Dr

Chris Batha provided the gun fit while we were at the Southern Side-by-Side event in North Carolina.

and fitted the loop, rough chambered them, fitted the ribs and struck them up, leaving excess metal where the actioner would need margins to work with. When making fitter-in barrels, the barrel maker has to be keenly aware of the dimensions of the old barrels. They will have to fit the existing action and forend.

ACTIONING

From the barrel maker, I took the gun to the actioner, along with the old barrels, which will be interchangeable. He has to work out the angles for striking, get the flats filed to the right thickness, file the loop, line up the chambers, machine the correct angle to the flats, the lumps and the loop, making sure all are centred.

He then cuts the cross pin hole and cuts the lumps to fit, cuts the bites in the lumps and the loop. He makes off the barrels around the breech, shaping into the side-clips and extractors. From here, the gun went back to the barrel maker for rims and chambers to be cut. Nigel Teague then fitted the ten chokes Bob had asked for and sent the gun back to Dave Mitchell, the finisher.

Dave then machined out the first lift cam slot for the extractors, fit the forend iron, cut under the loop and fitted the forend wood to the new barrels, using smoke black. He then made the forend push-rod fit and function in the new loop.

Barrels and action then went back to barrel-maker Scott for final striking up, fine finish and smoothing.

PROOF

Dave jointed it, ready for proof. It then went to the London Proof House and was subjected to London standard nitro proof for 2¾" (70mm) chambers. It passed and was returned to Dave for freeing off and blacking down onto the action. When submitted for proof, a gun should always be very tightly gripped; far more tightly than you would want to use it.

The stock blank I selected was pretty without being fussy.

FITTING AND STOCKING

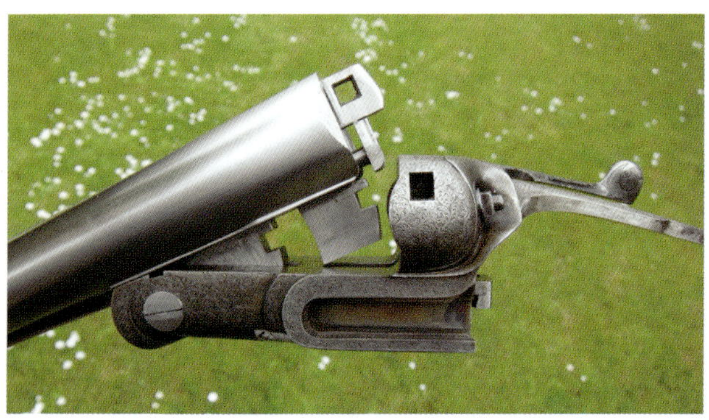

The Scott fresh from the barrel maker, new chopper-lumps fitted.

Bob had specific stocking requirements. He has a deceptively large frame, with thick neck, developed upper arm and chest muscles and a broad head. He likes a recoil pad and decided on a straight-hand stock, being careful to remark that he did not want a Monte Carlo type profile to it.

In the UK, I would normally send the client to Mike Yardley for a fitting. Bob, however, was in the US, so I arranged for Chris Batha to do the honours. This he did and provided a very detailed fitting instruction, which I discussed with Bob, and with the stocker, Stephane Dupile, before making a final plan of action. Bob needed a swept face and a profile that was close to central vision. Chris noted that Bob likes to float his target and likes a pattern delivery of 60% high, 40% low.

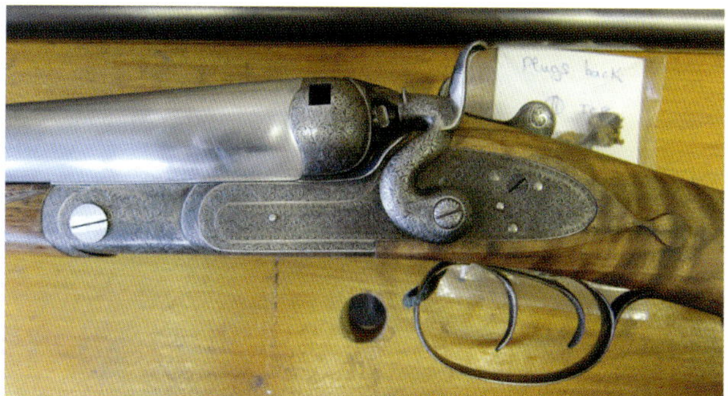

The Scott with new barrels and stock fitted, now the finisher needs to get to work.

The final dimensions we settled on were:

Drop at Comb 1½"
Drop at Face 1¾"
Drop at Heel 2⅛"+
Cast off at Face ⅜"
Cast off at Heel ½"
Cast off at Toe ⅝"+
Length to Heel 15⅜"
Length to Middle 15⅜"
Length to Toe 15¼"
Pitch 7 deg. / 3½"

Once we were clear on the dimensions and characteristics of the stock, we had to choose a piece of wood. I suggested one or two candidates but was personally keen to push Bob towards a classic piece of well-figured walnut, which I felt would complement the style of the Scott. It was expensive, at £1,200 but good wood is expensive and selecting it is harder than most people think. Cheap wood is available and people often think they can buy a bargain and save some money. All too many of these 'bargains' crack after a couple of years or are horrible to work, or just lack the quality necessary to justify the cost of the stocker.

Finished: with barrels blacked, stock chequered and oil finish still soft.

Bob went with my suggestion and Steph stocked the gun, fitted the leather pad and cut the drop-points. He retained the original pins and screws, except the guard screws, which he made new but left as 'slaves' for the finisher.

FINISHING

After Stephane had done his work, the entire gun went back to Dave Sinnerton for finishing. He used the original stock to match the chequer borders, size and shape. He chequered the hand, coloured and oil-finished the stock, made off the screws and hinge-pin, finely bedded the bolts and lever-work and ensured all mechanical operation was functioning perfectly.

New parts and old blended into a beautiful gun for a fraction of the cost of a new one.

ENGRAVING & BLACKING

The hinge pin was engraved to match the action, guard pins likewise. The breech ends of the barrels were engraved to match the originals. Pins were blacked and the barrels then sent to the blacker. New barrels cost more to black than old ones, as the process takes longer. Once back from the blacker, they were polished and oiled.

CASING

The ideal case for the Scott would be a period example in good condition, which could be fitted internally to accept the stock and action, along with both sets of barrels, the forend and the choke key, choke tubes, oil bottle and turnscrews. Unfortunately, 32" cases are very scarce and I struggled to find anything in good condition of the required length. I did manage to find one and had it re-lined and fitted for both sets of barrels, the Teague chokes and a set of turn-screws and rods.

Bob wanted a soft, leather-covered pad to finish the butt. A practical option for competition shooting.

Multi-chokes are flush-fitted Teagues, shown here without choke tubes in place. The original 30" barrels were kept as interchangeable options but the new 32" chopperlumps will be the ones in regular use.

RESULTS

The challenge of this project was to keep the heart and soul of the old gun but make it into a no-compromise, modern clay shooter's competition tool. The quality of the work carried out at every stage was to be the best available. There is always more than one way to get a job done but these, in my estimation, can be boiled down into two categories; the cheap way and the right way.

Could I have found a cheaper piece of wood with pretty figure? Could I have got the blacking done for half the price? Could I have used Italian barrel tubes? Could I have got the stock work started on a pantograph? The answer is 'yes' and there are numerous more ways of shaving pounds or dollars off the restoration budget but I believe they are false economies.

It is true that, were I to have compromised and sought cheaper solutions, very few people have the eye or the knowledge to know the difference. My curse is that I do and I can. When faced with an exciting project like Bob's Scott, I believe the difference between viewing the result with quiet satisfaction, or with simmering disappointment is a fine one. Having project managed a renovation costing several thousands of pounds, I am not prepared to finish on the wrong side of that line.

Gun restoration, indeed gun ownership, when considering the objects readers concern themselves with, is a balancing act on so many levels. Knowing when not to compromise and when not to be pointlessly obsessive over something which does not matter, or over which you cannot achieve an unrealistic outcome, is a hard perspective to keep.

On balance, I'm pleased with the completed Scott. We took Brewer's battered old gun with the drooping barrels and put some mojo back into it. I doubt anybody could come closer to getting the bespoke gun of their dreams in the time it took and at the monetary cost of this project. For those curious about figures, the total restoration, including purchase of the gun, re-barreling, re-stocking, casing and delivery cost in the region of £18,500. Go shopping for a best quality new side-by-side by any manufacturer you care to name and see what kind of price they quote you for this quality and finish of gun, built to order. Your starting point will be in excess of £60,000.

Keeping pin-fires alive

Owning and using centre-fire hammer guns is a straightforward business. As long as suitable ammunition is selected and the gun in good condition, it can be as easy to live with as a modern hammerless gun. Pin-fires are another matter.

Keeping a vintage pin-fire shotgun 'alive' and in use can be extremely challenging but pin-fire enthusiast Paul Robinson gave me this insight into preparing the cartridges:

'The art of making your pin-fire reliable centres around making a reliable pin-fire cartridge. Unlike a centre-fire shotgun where new factory loaded black powder cartridges are available (for a price!), you may only be lucky enough to find old stock pin-fire cases available for reloading. These tend to be relatively short supply, often of French origin with paper cases, quite old, with unreliable primers. New primers of the correct size are in equally short supply.

Faced with these problems, the members of the local vintage gun club have been developing their own versions of the pin-fire cartridge. Many of the latest designs revolve around adapting a fired centre-fire case. The centre-fire case has a larger base flange. This needs to be reduced or removed. The preferred method is to remove the 'brass' from a compression-formed case such as a Winchester AA.

Next is to deal with the existing fired centre-fire primer, as this is in the way of the pin or the new primer. The original pin-fire cartridge design had a very small primer on its side in a pocket in the base wad. Boothroyd in his book *The Shotgun History and Development* suggested making up a small, brass, machined cylinder to replace the centre-fire primer and hold a smaller pin-fire primer: a reasonable solution if you have access to a lathe.

An alternative method is to cast a primer pocket in hot glue that is squeezed into the centre-fire cap void before it sets. Number 10 percussion caps are preferred for this technique and, surprisingly, the hot glue makes a gas-tight seal that does not burst out of the back of the cartridge when fired.

Other options are to fill-in the centre-fire cap void with either epoxy or a glued-in wad, and then place the new primer on the wall of the case. With this method, a hole is drilled (at the correct angle with the aid of some rudimentary tooling) right through the case for the pin. Then a larger hole the right size for the new primer is drilled part-way back along the pin hole. A longer than standard pin is used and the gun's chamber wall effectively becomes the anvil for the primer. Either number 10 percussion caps or child's toy gun caps can be used.

Pin-fires tend to leak gas anyway, so the extra hole only moderately adds to the extensive cleaning that is required with black powder.

A completely different approach is to have the pin-fire cartridge case machined from brass. It is quite a time consuming machining operation to create a full box of 25, but the cases would be reusable. The plastic cases in the methods described above tend to last only a few firings.

The rest of the pin-fire load is no different to a typical black powder cartridge. For a 12-bore around 2¾ drams of medium grain powder, over powder card, felt wad, 1oz (28g) of number 7 shot, thin over shot card and a roll turnover is sufficient for clays.

Our local vintage gun club is primarily for muzzle-loaders, but there has been so much interest in pin-fires there is now a dedicated clay shooting competition once a year. Everyone tries to rack up a big score, but the cheers and banter that follow the dreaded click of a misfire makes the occasion all the more enjoyable.'

Paul's efforts illustrate how a few friends with a shared interest and a bit of dedication can keep even pin-fire guns usable. The pin-fire lags behind the centre-fire hammer gun in value because of the lack of commercially loaded ammunition. For collectors, pin-fires in the UK do not require a licence. However, if you decide to try and make ammunition and put them to use, they will be classified as a Section 2 shotgun and be entered onto a Shotgun Certificate.

Hammer guns and small, informal driven shooting days make for great fun with a group of friends.

Back to Basics: Hammer Gun Syndicates

The majority of game shooters in the UK fall into either the 'Driven Shooter', the 'Rough Shooter' or the 'Wildfowler' category. Driven bird shooting, be the birds grouse, pheasants or partridges, is the formal and social summit of the sport.

It is a fact that many who aspire to formal driven shooting cannot afford it. A full, good-sized day at a top quality shoot will cost in excess of £1,000 per Gun. On a 250-bird day, with eight Guns in the line, each Gun should average 32 birds, with a cartridge to kill ratio of 3-to-1, they should each fire an average of 96 shots, perhaps a few more if the birds are very challenging, at 4-to-1, the figure would be 128 shots. On a day with six drives, that means each Gun can expect to shoot five or six birds per drive, for around 20 shots.

It does not require a huge bout of complicated arithmetic to see that on days that cost less than £1,000 per gun, the action could prove very sparse indeed. On a 100 bird day, over six drives, each gun might expect to shoot only 2 birds per drive. Because averages hardly ever happen, many a Gun can come home from a 100-bird day having shot only one or two birds.

Many readers will now be muttering 'it is not about numbers, it is about sport', and right they are but if our sport is called shooting, we do generally expect to pull the trigger one or twice in return for our cash – otherwise we may as well go and join the beating line and end the day with twenty pounds and a free lunch instead of a hole in our wallet.

So, how can we make pheasant shooting more fun and less expensive? The old raison d'être of sporting gun development can on this occasion pass us by. We are no longer on huge Edwardian pheasant slaughtering tests, where the object, indeed the social necessity, is to get as many shots off as possible and kill as many birds as possible in order to beat the last team or next estate in the numbers game.

Suddenly, ejectors, rebounding locks, snap actions and the like seem redundant. We want quality birds, we want to select the most sporting and we want to shoot them with old guns. I ran successful hammer gun syndicate for a few years, where fellow enthusiasts would gather to play with their favourite old guns or newly acquired curios. Sometimes we used black powder for the fun of it.

Eventually, some asked if they could bring muzzle-loaders. We came upon a system where each peg would contain two Guns, each with a muzzle-loader. Both guns would be loaded, the first to shoot would occupy the peg and stand ready with nipples capped and hammers cocked. His companion would stand back with nipples capless awaiting his turn. Once the first Gun fired, he would step back to re-load (taking about 30 seconds) and the next would step forward to engage any bird that flew over. Not only is this enormous fun, it also reduces the cost of each peg by half. It also works well with a breech-loader and a muzzle-loader on each peg.

These ruses actually add to the banter, the fun and the sociability of the days and the focus slips easily away from the desire to kill as much as possible to the joy of using an old gun to shoot memorable birds in good company and friendly rivalry. I recommend it!

Obsolete Calibres and Section 58

There is good general knowledge within the British shooting community of the two most relevant areas of firearms legislation; those governing our ownership and use of shotguns and rifles. Section 1 covers 'firearms', essentially the type of shotgun we cannot have on a Shotgun Certificate (5-shot magazine pump-actions for example) and arms with rifled barrels, from the humble, bunny-bagging .22 rimfire to the mighty .577 nitro for elephant hunting overseas. Section 2 regulates the ownership of the shotguns we use for our sporting activities.

Rather more obscure and off the radar of many shooting people is Section 58. This explains what legislators refer to as 'obsolete calibre' weapeons and mechanisms of various types. If a gun meets the criteria, it can be held without any kind of licence. Furthermore, it does not need to be kept in a safe, but can be hung on the wall and openly displayed.

This Greener howdah pistol is considerd an antique in the USA. In Britain it is a prohibited firearm because it is a smooth bored 20-bore.

Most people are vaguely aware that muzzle-loaders can be displayed and don't need a licence. Nor do you need one for rimfire rifles above .22 calibre or pin-fire guns of any type. Just be careful that all your muzzle-loaders pre-date 1939, or Section 58 does not apply. Newly made guns in obsolete calibres also miss the criteria, they must be obsolete calibre and pre-date the Second World War. This includes sleeved and chamber sleeved guns.

Collectors, interested in amassing an array of revolvers or rifles, can work within the guidelines of Section 58 to do exactly that, the wider ban on handguns in the UK does not affect them. You could, for example, go and buy a Smith & Wesson .44 Russian six shot single action revolver or a military rifle, like a straight-pull Model 1889 Swiss service rifle in 7.5x53.5mm. Both these chamberings are on the official 'obsolete calibre' list and are free to own as curios.

If classic double rifles are more your thing, you can build and display a fantastic collection of black powder express rifles, in calibres like .577 BPE or .450 (3¼") BPE because they too are exempt from licence requirements.

Section 58 can be a bit counter intuitive. For example, many wild-fowlers still take their old big-bore hammer guns to the marsh and hold them on a SGC. This is where 'intent' and 'application' muddy the legal waters. If you bought an 1890 10-bore with 2⅝" chambers, took it home, hung it on the wall in the dining room and looked at it as an ornament, you would be perfectly free to do just that. If the police came knocking, they would have to lump it that you had a big gun on the wall! Section 58 allows for this.

If you want to fire your Section 58 rifles, you will need to put them 'on ticket' if you live in the UK.

Above: Kiri Kythreotis of Athina Sporting getting stuck into the grouse with his Holland & Holland 16-bore.

Below: John Hargreaves and the chaps from Pantiles Vintage Guns helping to keep the best of British in service.

However, if you wanted to take the same gun out and shoot the occasional duck, you would have to put it on your shotgun certificate and lock it in a safe. I guess it made sense to someone when they were drafting the law but I'm not sure it makes much sense to me!

So, how can the police know what you intend to do with the gun on your wall? The common test is whether you have any ammunition. If you want it for display, better that you don't have any shells or they may decide you want to use it. A funny case of it being perfectly legal to display a box of 10-bore ammo on the shelf and also to have a working 10-bore hammer gun on the wall, just not both at the same time!

I'm not a lawyer, so don't take my musings as a legal opinion; you would be much better advised to read Laura Saunsbury's *The British Firearms Law Handbook*. She *is* a lawyer and knows this subject intimately. You can see the Home Office 'obsolete calibre' list on line at www.vintageguns.co.uk/articles/obsolete-calibre-list

The beauty of Section 58 is that you can buy some very handsome firearms and display them in full view, a prospect that would be impossible with your modern guns. This has helped raise the prices of big bore guns in recent years, as ownership comes without the hassle of certification and security.

Collecting for Investment

COMPARING THE PRICES OF SIDELOCK, HAMMER & BOXLOCK MODELS

It is interesting to compare the data being used today to evaluate aspects of desirability in any gun for sale, with the place in the market that gun may have occupied when new. The conventional wisdom in vintage gun buying circles would make the assumption that a sidelock will cost more than a boxlock of similar age and configuration. Hammer guns can make a strong sale price in view of the rarity of particular models and features. The maker's name can also affect the attitude of the buyer today, as assumptions are erroneously made regarding name and quality.

I have compared some available data from catalogues dating back to the mid 19th century, to see what place each model and type of gun took in the pricing and quality structures of some major manufacturers and retailers of sporting guns.

The table (below) indicate prices for 12-bore guns. Where marked * the price is in guineas. Firms marked^ are trade suppliers; therefore wholesale prices are indicated.

Maker (date)	Lowest Price Boxlock	Highest Price Boxlock	Lowest Price Sidelock	Highest Price Sidelock	Lowest price Hammer Gun	Highest Price Hammer Gun
W.W. Greener (1879)	£27*	£42*	£20*	£35*	£10*	£40*
J.V. Needham (1891)	£8.10s	£48	£8	£8	£3	£42
William Evans (1893)	£21	£47.5s	£21	£47.5s	£7.10s	£42
Robert Hughes (1894)^	£19	£46	£14.14s	£28	£4.10s	£34
Webley & Scott (1914)^	£13.5s	£50	£12 12s	£112	£5. 5s	£76
Charles Osborne (1900)^	£13	£70	£11.10s	£60	£11	£17
WW Greener (1903)	£13.13s	£73.10s	£73.10s	£73.10s	£9.9s	£42
Bentley & Playfair (1911)^	£11	£53	£13	£72	£5 15s	£33.6s
William Powell (1912)	£25	£70	£80	£100	x	x

Hammer guns continued to be made alongside hammerless models of various types, as hammerless patents were filed and started to make inroads into the production models various gunmakers offered.

There was no sudden drop-off from hammer to hammerless gun production, it was a timid process spanning a number of years, until hammer guns gradually decreased in general popularity and hammerless guns took over. They continued to be made in lower price ranges well into the 1920s and all the major gunmakers continued to take occasional orders for best quality hammer guns from wealthy clients, often pigeon shooters until the First World War and beyond.

Buying today, sportsmen or collectors (in my experience most buyers are both) should be mindful of the original quality of the gun and then equally mindful of the current condition in which he finds it. Brand value is always a factor in these matters and a Purdey will always attract more interest and, potentially, a higher price than a W&C Scott of equal quality and condition.

My advice to clients over the years has been consistent. Buy a gun you like, preferably one that fits fairly well and that you can shoot. Buy the best quality you can afford in the best condition you can find it. When a market goes soft, the bottom goes softest, quickest. The rare, high quality, best brand value gun, in very original condition will ride most economic downturns confidently.

One can never predict the future with reliability but hammer guns, like all English guns of

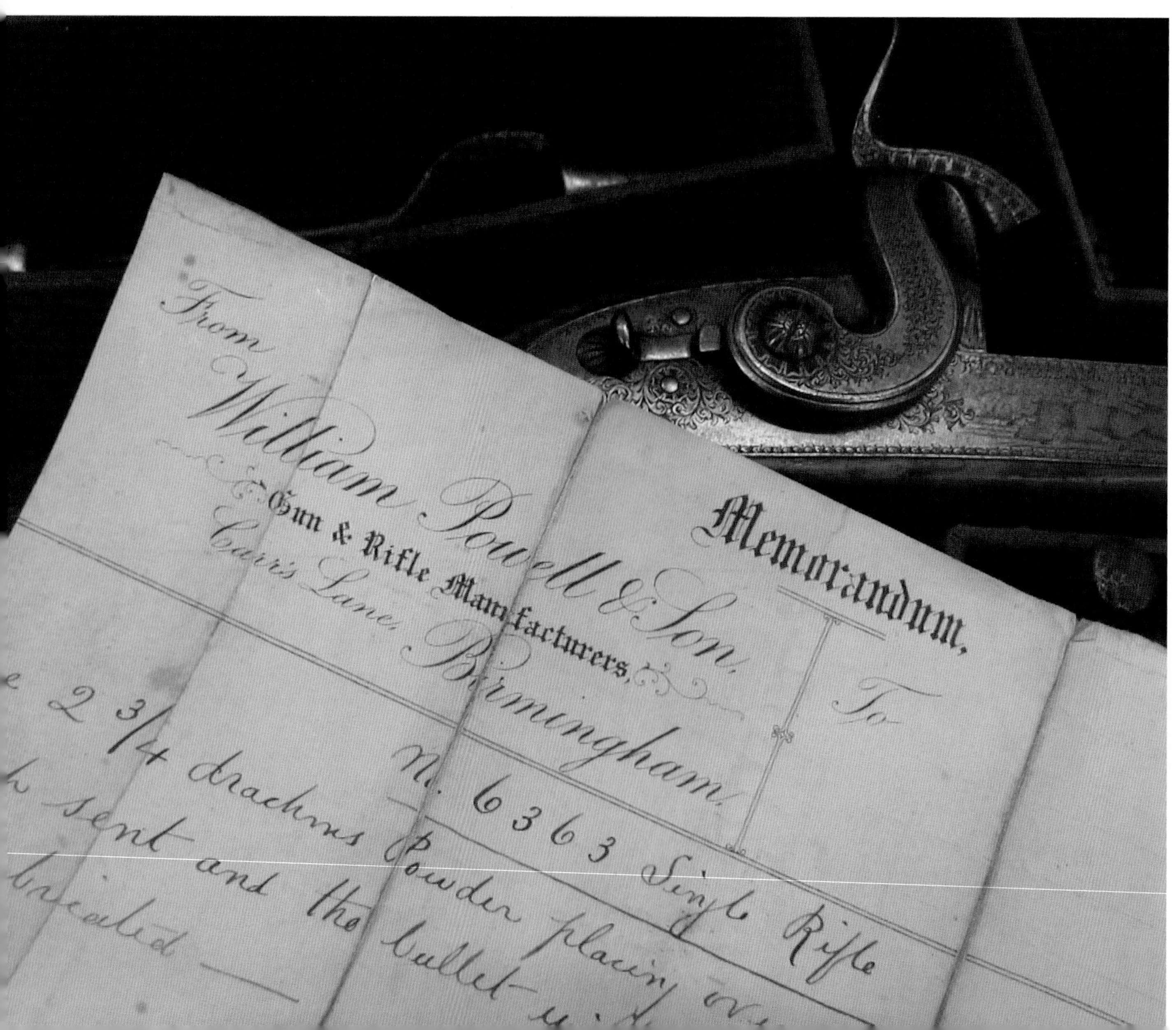

If you are fortunate, you may find historical paperwork with your gun.

What clues can you find on your gun about the maker or owner? Why did J.D. Dougall put P.O.W. feathers on many of his guns?

quality, have been good investments for the last 25 years. If you are a shooting man, even if the market has a temporary period of trouble, you still have in your possession a collection of beautiful, functional and rare guns, which are not easily replaceable and which should continue to give you the pleasure of ownership and the benefit of use.

If you are fortunate enough to have the disposable income to buy anything you want, when you see a best gun in very original condition, for a fair price; buy it. It is hard to lose. Get the best of everything and widen your collection to cover all the early and late hammer guns.

Some collectors cannot afford expensive best examples of the best makers. They can, however, buy interesting patent examples in poor condition, or with scrap barrels. Many a fascinating time-line of patents have been compiled this way and they give a great deal of pleasure to the collectors concerned.

RESEARCHING YOUR HAMMER GUN'S HISTORY

The pleasure of ownership afforded by an historic piece of gun-making is enhanced for many enthusiasts by discovering as much of the history of the gun as possible. One friend from the United States owns, amongst other fine guns, an early Boss shotgun, converted from muzzle-loader to centre-fire breech-loader.

By his own research he established the original owner was a wealthy clergyman, who lived not far from my home in Shropshire. I was able to visit the house one summer's afternoon and found a portrait of the father of the gentleman concerned, as well as his rectory and the church in which he took care of business back in the mid-Victorian period. We even found his grave in the grounds. My friends were delighted, a little later, to find themselves in the middle of the British countryside, kneeling by the last resting place of the man who once took delivery of their treasured Boss, walking around the edges of the fields and coverts of the estate where the gun was once used, before cars or telephones

Graham Greener has the records for his family firm's gunmaking over the years.

or aeroplanes transformed the world. With little perseverance, it is surprising what one can deduce about a particular sporting gun.

First, look at the clues the fabric of the gun itself provides. As hammer breech-loaders were made at a time during which new mechanisms were being invented every few months, the patents applied to them help establish earliest possible dates for manufacture. If the gun has a Jones rotary undercover, for example, it must be made after 1859. If it has Purdey's second variant thumb-lever it was made after 1868. If the Purdey thumb-lever is of the first pattern, the gun probably dates between 1864 and 1868. If the gun has a number of patent mechanisms, the deductions can be noted and compared and a date approximated with a fair degree of precision. Further help can be found in patent use numbers – these were applied to early guns, while the patent was still in force, and a low number will suggest it was made early in the life of the patent. So, a gun stamped with 'Purdey's Patent' for the underbolt of 1863 with use number '15' would indicate the gun dates from the first year of the patent. Be careful to check the number; sometimes it refers to the patent number, sometimes the use number and it is not always clear, unless you have memorised the patent number. Don't feel bad if you haven't!

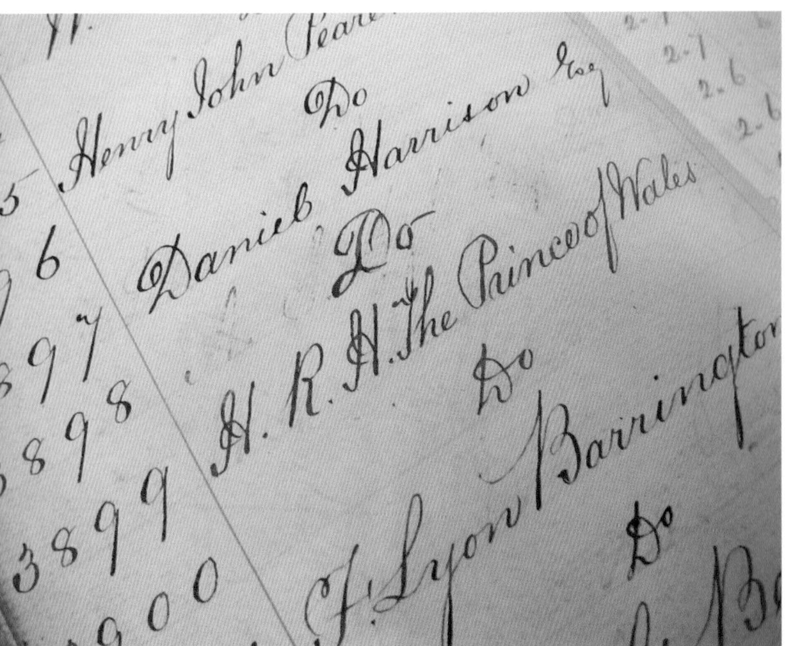

Gunmakers' records can help you find out when your gun was made and who it was made for. If it was the Prince of Wales, you might have struck gold!

While many gunmakers' records were destroyed for various reasons during the 20th century, others survive. Many closing businesses were bought by a rival or friend in the trade, and records were passed on. If these businesses survive, the record for your gun may well be there to take a look at. Did you know, for example that many long defunct names are under the ownership of well-known firms still trading? Theophilus Murcott and Joseph Needham, for example are now part of W.W. Greener, while Joseph Harkom, James MacNaughton and Alex Henry belong to John Dickson.

Some records were well kept and detailed (like James Purdey and Stephen Grant) but others may be more patchy, reflecting the times and the people involved. The fist step would be simple search in Nigel Brown's standard work on the subject *British Gunmakers*. This will probably have a reference to the date your gun was made, if the data is available.

Another useful indication, again using Brown's books as source material, is the address on the rib of your gun. Firms often moved address every few years and if these dates are recorded, you can establish the possible years of manufacture. For example, if you have a Purdey with the address 14½ Oxford Street, you can be sure the gun was made between 1826 and 1882 because they moved in that year to Audley House.

Then, one might look at making contact with the firm concerned, if they still exist. Many will be happy to look in the record for you and tell you what it says. If you want a photocopy of the page or a written reply, you may have to pay a small fee. This is fair enough, don't expect people trying to run a business to do your research for you free of charge. It takes time.

If the serial number and records cannot determine the age, have a close look at the proof marks. By isolating the earliest proof marks, one can narrow down the possible dates between which the gun was originally submitted for proof, and whether this was in London or Birmingham.

Another clue is the oval on the stock, which often features initials but may have a family crest or a peerage rank. An on-line search of the symbol will often help identify a family, a location, or both.

Once you have identified the person who ordered your gun, research into that person becomes straightforward. If there is anything notable about him or his family, it will be on public record. I recall a Purdey 20-bore hammer gun I once owned. It was made for Lord Lilford, who introduced the little owl to Britain. Another I had, an 1863 converted pin-fire, by Joseph Lang, was made for Capt. James Dundas of the Royal Engineers, who was awarded the Victoria Cross in the Second Afghan war of 1878 and was later killed in action in the same country. Finding out this kind of information is fun but can also be helpful in identifying provenance that may add value or interest to the gun, which is useful to pass on, should you decide to sell it.

Appendices

HOW TO GET A VISITOR'S SHOTGUN PERMIT FOR THE UK

A visitor to the UK may obtain a Visitor's Shotgun Permit. This enables him to arrive in the country with his shotguns and act with the same authority to possess, use and buy shotguns as a British subject, who is the holder of a Shotgun Certificate. The fee is nominal and the application process straightforward, though it must be completed by a local sponsor and applied for by him. The application forms are available on-line from any police service website.

European citizens will need to send copies of their European Firearms Pass and hunting licence from home. Non Europeans don't need any supporting papers.

A party of my American friends on the grouse moor at Fasque. Travelling with your guns is easy if you do a little basic paperwork. For the UK, a local sponsor is required but the process takes just a week and is straightforward.

Select Bibliography

THE VICTORIANS

The following books are especially interesting in providing contemporary commentaries from the years in which the hammer guns we use were made. Evaluation by more modern writers is useful but understanding the minds of some of the gunmakers and testers working in the mid 19th century has been invaluable. If one reads repeatedly and carefully, the personalities of the writers begin to emerge, as do rivalries and attitudes. Three of the most important commentators are Henry Sharp, John Henry Walsh and W.W. Greener. They all knew one another professionally and obliquely refer to the others' opinions or errors on occasion. I have drawn on the writings of Greener quite extensively in this book, when seeking comments or insights into processes, like barrel making, issues of the time, like selling guns to overseas customers, or contemporary critiques of what were, at his time of writing, emerging or recently-available mechanisms. Greener was a great gunmaker but his forthright opinions on some matters are certainly rather partisan.

Henry Sharp: *The Modern Sportsman's Gun & Rifle.*
W.W. Greener: *Modern Breech Loaders, Modern Shot Guns, The Gun & its Development.*
The Field (old issues)

Gough Thomas wrote some of the best books on the subject of guns and shooting.

David Baker has catalogued and narrated the finest books yet written on British gun making. His attention to detail and quality of research are second to none.

Cyril Adams (right) with the author, at Holt's in London. Cyril's success in the pigeon ring with English guns and his writing on the subject sparked a revival of interest in the 1990s.

THE ANALYSTS

Not gunmakers, but leading men of their time, who emerged as the premier evaluators of all things sporting gun. These men led and shaped public opinion in the early to mid 20th century and had a perspective when writing about hammer guns and their writing is reflective of the attitudes of their day. Some were trained in engineering or ballistics and others were natural historians. They covered many of the technical issues determining the fitness of Victorian guns transitioning into the modern nitro age.

Gough Thomas: *'Shotguns & Cartridges for Game & Clays', 'Gough Thomas's Gun Book'.*
Sir Gerald Burrard: *'In the Gun Room', 'The Modern Shotgun' Vol 1, Vol 2, Vol 3.*
Geoffrey Boothroyd: *'Boxlocks & Sidelocks', 'Shotguns & Gunsmiths', 'Boothroyd on British Shotguns'*
MacDonald Hastings: *'The Shotgun'*
Richard Akehurst: *'Game Guns & Rifles'.*
Adams & Braden: *'Lock Stock & Barrel'.*
Graeme Wright: *'Shooting the British Double Rifle'.*
Richard Arnold: *'Shooters Handbook'.*

THE HISTORIANS

We have been spoiled over the last two decades. From there being a dearth of available material for the interested amateur to buy in order to avail himself of historical knowledge about the maker of his favourite gun, there now exists a great deal of well compiled data. Following on from the articles Geoffrey Boothroyd first wrote for *Shooting Times*, then condensed into three volumes, others (Donald Dallas being the most prolific) have picked up the baton and taken it further.

Most major, currently active, gunmakers now have an official or unofficial history book, many of these are very well-researched and methodically constructed to provide a readable and accurate story of the firm from inception to the present day. They contain lists of workers, models and prices of guns, address changes, patents attributed to the firm and plenty more besides.

Crudgington & Baker set the standard with their *British Shotgun* series, which has recently been re-issued as a three volume set. There is no better examination of the development of the shotgun; one patent at a time.

We all owe a debt of gratitude to the wonderful Nigel Brown for his huge work attempting to catalogue as much information about British gunmakers as can be found in the papers, records and anecdotes available. Without his magnificent effort, much of what is now chronicled would have been lost. Here is a short list of essential reference and reading:

Donald Dallas: *'Purdey', 'Boss', 'Holland & Holland', 'John Dickson', 'The British Sporting Gun & Rifle' 'Magnificent Madness'.*
David Baker & Ian Crudgington: *'The British Shotgun'* Vol 1, Vol 2, Vol 3.
David Baker: *'Heyday of the Shotgun', 'Thomas Horsley'.*
Douglas Tate: *'Birmingham Gunmakers'*
Don Masters: *'Atkin, Grant & Lang', 'The House of Churchill'.*
Nigel Brown: *'British Gunmakers Vol 1 (London), Vol 2 (Birmingham, & Scotland) Vol 3 (Index, Appendices and Additional London, Birmingham, Regional and Scottish Records)'.*
Patrick Unsworth: *'The Early Purdeys'*
Graham Greener: *'The Greener Story'*

Donald Dallas, historian to the finest gunmakers, and the author swapping stories at Holt's in London.

ELEY
HAWK

Index